V - G0 BYD 082

ᵛATH

ITS USE

AND MEANING

᾽ΑΤΗ

ITS USE AND MEANING

A STUDY IN THE GREEK POETIC TRADITION
FROM HOMER TO EURIPIDES

RICHARD E. DOYLE, S.J.

New York
FORDHAM UNIVERSITY PRESS
1984

PJC LEARNING RESOURCES CENTER

© Copyright 1984 by FORDHAM UNIVERSITY PRESS
All rights reserved
LC 83–80059
ISBN 0–8232–1062–6
First edition 1984
Second printing 1985

Printed in the United States of America

87-860

For

MY MOTHER

The passages and quotations from the Greek authors are taken from the following editions.

Aeschylus	*Septem quae supersunt tragoediae.* Ed. Denys L. Page. Oxford: Clarendon, 1972. *Agamemnon,* Ed. Eduard Fraenkel. 3 vols. Oxford: Clarendon, 1950. Repr. 1962. *The Persae of Aeschylus.* Ed. H. D. Broadhead. Cambridge: Cambridge University Press, 1960.
Alcaeus	*Poetarum Lesbiorum fragmenta.* Edd. Edgar Lobel and Denys Page. Oxford: Clarendon, 1955.
Euripides	*Fabulae.* Ed. Gilbert Murray. 3 vols. Oxford: Clarendon, 1901–1913.
Hesiod	*Carmina.* Ed. Alois Rzach. Leipzig: Teubner, 1902.
Homer	*Iliad.* Edd. D. B. Munro and T. W. Allen. 3rd ed. 2 vols. Oxford: Clarendon, 1920. *Odyssey.* Ed. T. W. Allen. 2nd ed. 2 vols. Oxford: 1917, 1919.
Ibycus	*Poetae melici Graeci.* Ed. Denys L. Page. Oxford: Clarendon, 1962.
Pindar	*Carmina cum fragmentis.* I. *Epinicia.* Edd. Bruno Snell and Herwig Moehler. Leipzig: Teubner, 1971.
Solon	*Iambi et elegi Graeci.* Ed. M. L. West. 2 vols. Oxford: Clarendon, 1971.
Sophocles	*Fabulae.* Ed. A. C. Pearson. Oxford: Clarendon, 1923.
Theognis	*Iambi et elegi Graeci.* Ed. M. L. West. 2 vols. Oxford: Clarendon, 1971.

Throughout this book, ἄτη will appear consistently in lower case, even though some editors may have used an upper-case α. Personification of abstract Greek terms is an area of great complexity. Since most editors do not explain why they capitalize, it has seemed best simply to refrain from doing so.

CONTENTS

SIGLA

AAL	*Annals of Archaeology and Anthropology*
AJP	*American Journal of Philology*
CJ	*The Classical Journal*
CPh	*Classical Philology*
CQ	*The Classical Quarterly*
CR	*The Classical Review*
HSPh	*Harvard Studies in Classical Philology*
JHS	*Journal of Hellenic Studies*
LEC	*Les études classiques*
LSJ	*A Greek–English Lexicon.* Edd. H. G. Liddell and Robert Scott. Rev. ed. H. S. Jones and Roderick McKenzie. 9th ed. Oxford: Clarendon, 1940.
OCD	*The Oxford Classical Dictionary.* Edd. N. G. L. Hammond and H. H. Scullard. 2nd ed. Oxford: Clarendon, 1970.
REG	*Revue des études grecques*
RFIC	*Rivista di filologia e di istruzione classica*
RhM	*Rheinisches Museum für Philologie*
RPh	*Revue de philologie*
SFIC	*Studi italiani di filologia classica*
TAPA	*Transactions of the American Philological Association*
YClS	*Yale Classical Studies*

ACKNOWLEDGMENTS

The idea for this book began a number of years ago and has been helped through the kindness of many. I am grateful to the National Endowment for the Humanities for a summer grant which permitted me to embark on my research, and to the Jesuits of Fordham Inc. for their generous support. Fordham University granted me a faculty fellowship in the spring of 1974 and again in 1978–1979 which enabled me to devote full time to writing, and successive years of Fordham graduate students have aided me by discussing many of the ideas developed in these pages.

Earlier versions of portions of Chapters 3, 5, and 6 appeared in *Traditio*, and of sections of Chapter 7 in Παράδοσις: *Studies in Memory of Edwin A. Quain* (New York: Fordham University Press, 1976), and I wish to thank the editors of both publications for their kindness in allowing me to re-use the material here. My friends Gerry and Colleen Ryan, and Jack and Pat Clark, have been very patient and helpful while this manuscript has been in preparation. Dr. Mary Beatrice Schulte of Fordham University Press deserves special thanks for the care and attention to detail with which she edited my work.

Lastly, I wish to thank my various teachers through the years who always encouraged my interest in Greek literature and did so much to help shape my ideas. I remember in particular the late John Creaghan, s.j., whose ideals of scholarship were extremely formative in my work, and Professor Gordon Kirkwood who read the manuscript and offered many valuable suggestions. Of course, any defects which remain are mine alone. Most especially I should like to thank my greatest teacher, to whom this book is affectionately dedicated.

Fordham University   RICHARD E. DOYLE, S.J.

INTRODUCTION

ANY STUDY OF ἄτη must have Greek tragedy at its center. ἄτη initially meant "blindness," and in one Homeric passage seems almost to be used in its original meaning of *physical* blindness.[1] At any rate, the evidence for a metaphorical "blindness" is overwhelmingly manifest in Greek epic and archaic lyric poetry, and the meaning does not disappear with the development of tragic poetry in the fifth century. What does occur in tragedy is the emergence, and in Aeschylus and Euripides the emergence to the point of preponderance, of another meaning: namely, not the subjective state of mental "blindness," "infatuation," or "folly," but the objective state of "ruin," "calamity," or "disaster."[2]

Once these two notions are juxtaposed in the same word, one of the major themes of Greek tragedy can begin to appear: that is, the problem of human freedom and responsibility, or, if you will, the tension between fate and free will, between the divine plan and human choice, between determinism and freedom. This problem, still very much with us, was central to the concerns of Aeschylus, Sophocles, and Euripides, and for this reason a study of ἄτη must have Greek tragedy at its center.

Indeed, that is how this book came to be written. In investigating the extant tragedies of Aeschylus, I was struck by the number of times the poet employed ἄτη and how often the word appeared in connection with such overriding Aeschylean themes as freedom and responsibility. This observation naturally led me to examine the extant works of Sophocles and Euripides to see if a similar careful study of the development of the concept of ἄτη would help to provide fresh insights into their outlook on man and his condition, as it had with Aeschylus. Ultimately, of course, this research led me back to Homer and the lyric predecessors of the tragedians in order to discover the use and meaning of ἄτη which had evolved in Greek prior to the fifth century and had been inherited by Aeschylus, Sophocles, and Euripides.

This process accounts for the subtitle of this book. My study is an investigation of the "tradition" of Greek poetry in two senses. First, words have meaning, and they are much better understood if this fact is firmly recognized and a given concept is seen in its historical development. Sophistry is a recurrent human temptation. Secondly, the body of poetry from Homer to Euripides forms an organic whole, not only because a Greek poet, in spite of the emergence of new poetic genres, always felt the impact of his predecessors,[3] but also because, with the death of tragedy, something entirely new arose in Greek letters: philosophy and oratory. My decision to limit my investigation of ἄτη to a study of the poetry from Homer to Euripides was prompted as much by the realization that such an organic whole provided an adequate body of literature to delineate the boundaries of a serious investigation as by the fact that, with a rare exception (Herodotus 1.32), ἄτη is a word not used in Greek prose.

The importance of the concept of ἄτη has been recognized by a number of scholars and in recent years a series of partial treatments of ἄτη has appeared, focusing at various times on the concept as it surfaced in Greek thought concerning the irrational or, more specifically with regard to tragedy, as it is linked with another key tragic concept, ἁμαρτία.[4] Yet to date there has been no comprehensive investigation of ἄτη in the extant Greek poetry from Homer until the end of the fifth century. This book undertakes such a study.

Several remarks concerning the methodology employed in the writing of this book are in order. First, I have excluded all consideration of such cognate words as ἀπάτα or ἀάω. My work is already long enough, and, I fear, such further considerations would only discourage already dedicated readers. Secondly, with rare exceptions, I have not felt it necessary to try to resolve textual problems. Aware of many difficulties which arise in given passages, I refer the reader to the best critical editions for a presentation of the textual evidence. When ἄτη itself is involved, some textual discussion is, of course, unavoidable. Three passages, therefore — *Persians* 107–114, *Suppliants* 443–445, and *Libation-Bearers* 829–837 — seemed best left to appendices in order not to burden the pages of my book with detailed discussion of textual problems.

The mention of appendices brings me to the third and perhaps most critical methodological consideration. Appendix A contains a chronological list of all the ἄτη passages in extant Greek poetry from Homer to Euripides. As this list began to take shape, early in my investigations, I began to notice that two clusters of characteristic concomitants regularly appear with ἄτη. One such cluster includes the following three points of usage: (*a*) ἄτη is frequently said to affect man's φρήν or his θυμός; (*b*) when it does, the context is generally erotic; and (*c*) when both these conditions are present, ἄτη is used in the plural. On the other hand, a second group of concomitants tends to cluster in the following three characteristic points of usage: (*a*) ἄτη is predicated of a group rather than of an individual; (*b*) the immediate context contains the word κακά or some synonymous expression; and (*c*) as adumbrated in the lyric poets, from Aeschylus through Euripides this type of ἄτη, and only this type, is attributed to the activity of a δαίμων.[5] The question naturally arose whether the clustering of these two different sets of concomitants used with ἄτη might also indicate the meaning of the word. It came as no surprise that such an interrelationship between usage and meaning proved to be present. Thus, when ἄτη affects man's φρήν or his θυμός, appears in an erotic context, and is used in the plural, it means "blindness," "infatuation," or "folly." But when ἄτη is predicated of a group, is synonymous with κακά or a similar expression, and is attributed to the activity of a δαίμων, its meaning is "ruin," "calamity," or "disaster."

Once the question of meaning is raised, the problem of translation soon follows. In stating that one possible meaning of ἄτη is "blindness," "infatuation," or "folly," and that another is "ruin," "calamity," or "disaster," I do not assume that all occurrences of the ancient Greek word may be translated with total accuracy by one or another of these modern English words. Languages seldom offer such neat correspondences in semantics in non-technical words. Rather, the translations offered are meant to indicate the emphasis and general conceptual content of ἄτη in any occurrence, while fully admitting the possibility that other English equivalents might be found for a given context. In one meaning of ἄτη, the working of human mental faculties is impaired; in the other, the phenomenon involved is disastrous. To be capable of translating accurately, to everyone's complete satisfaction, each instance in which ἄτη occurs in Greek poetry, is impossible.

For the two meanings for ἄτη, then, I have adopted the terms "subjective" and "objective" to show the emphasis attaching to each meaning. By "subjective" I mean a state of personal, interior, mental "blindness," "infatuation," or "folly," something which affects a human being from within his own faculties and being. By "objective" I mean something which comes on a human being from the outside, some "ruin," "calamity," or "disaster" which is inflicted on him independently of himself.

Though much importance is made of the opposition between "sub-jective" and "objective," the antithesis, albeit certainly necessary (because, I would argue, it is present in the evidence for two different meanings for ἄτη), is sometimes difficult to render more precise, par-ticularly on the subjective side. For although we, as twentieth-century individuals, are accustomed to distinguishing between voluntary and involuntary mental and psychological phenomena, ancient Greeks, even in the fifth century, were not. That they became progressively aware of the differences involved and of the necessity of distinguishing be-tween these differences is clear; what is not so clear is the precise moment at which this type of distinction dawned in the mind of a given author. Moreover, at times there is a definitive ambiguity in our English usage. So, for example, folly can be "subjective" either as something which is quite private to the subject (such as hallucination) or as something which visibly affects him (such as irrational behavior). The early Greeks do not distinguish between these two senses and are com-fortable in speaking both ways at the same time. Finally, such ter-minology as "psychological compulsion," "unconscious impulse," or "psychological catharsis" is clearly modern and would have bewildered an ancient Greek. These limitations notwithstanding, I trust that the general notions "subjective" and "objective" remain valid and useful categories of analysis.

My research was all but complete when I came upon the following remarks by Professor Barrett in his commentary on the *Hippolytus*. I quote them at length because they precisely focus my own ideas and help to indicate some of the major areas of confusion which have arisen concerning ἄτη. Commenting on line 241 of the play, Barrett writes:

> For its [ἄτη's] nature, cf. Dodds, *The Greeks and the irrational*, 2ff.; it is "a tempo-rary clouding or bewildering of the normal consciousness" which results in unwise or unaccountable behaviour of any kind (*pace* L.S., the word of itself describes this condition quite neutrally, without any suggestion that it is a pun-ishment for guilt: Homeric evidence in Dodds, and an evidently neutral instance 276 below). — ἄτη is also common in the sense "calamity, ruin"; so 1149, 1289. This use is usually regarded as derivative from the other (L.S. Dodds, op. cit. 38): the mental ἄτη sent as a punishment causes a man to involve himself in ruin, and the word is then applied first to this punitive self-furthered ruin and then to ruin generally. But I do not find this process very likely (esp. the back-and-forth development: mental ἄτη *from* non-punitive, ἄτη as ruin *to* non-

punitive), and prefer to regard the two uses as parallel: in each case ἄτη is a humanly unaccountable and disastrous deterioration, in the one case of one's wits and in the other case of one's fortunes; in each case the deterioration is ascribed to the direct and harmful intervention of a supernatural power. The notion that this ἄτη is a punishment for guilt is in each case secondary: when it arose the interplay between the two uses of the word became strong (as it is strong, notably, in Aeschylus), but it was an interplay, I think, between two uses that were already there.[6]

As the following several score of pages will show, there is extraordinary insight in these remarks. My own investigations of Greek poetry from Homer to Euripides corroborate, and bring together in one place all the evidence to substantiate, such a view of ἄτη.

Thus, it will be seen not only that from Homer through Euripides there were, and remained, two fundamental meanings for ἄτη, but also that between the "subjective" and "objective" concepts of ἄτη there remained throughout the course of fifth-century tragedy a great and profound ambivalence. But such ambivalence should not be surprising. In our current concern with the problem of human freedom and responsibility, we are the beneficiaries of some two thousand years of thought, but Aeschylus, Sophocles, and Euripides were by no means in a position to offer sophisticated and nuanced solutions. Indeed, they were poets, not philosophers. Yet in their work there is a compelling awareness of the fact of man's freedom and the degree of his responsibility, and the implications of the two for his destiny. Yet such an awareness on the part of the tragedians is in no sense incompatible with their ambivalent attitude toward the possible avenues of solution for the problem. One of the concepts which they saw as pertinent to the problem was ἄτη.

But just as ἄτη is not the only term employed in the great fifth-century intellectual struggle to understand man, his condition as a human being, and his human freedom and responsibility, so ἄτη does not appear suddenly or for the first time in Greek literature in the works of the tragic poets. It reached them, as far as we can trace it, from the mid-eighth-century epics of Homer through the seventh- and sixth-century developments of the lyric poets. Aeschylus, Sophocles, and Euripides stand at the end of a long, distinguished tradition of Greek poetry. The following pages will trace the use and meaning of ἄτη in that poetic tradition. I hope that they will prove useful to my fellow-scholars and -students of Greek literature in our ever-deepening quest for an understanding of Greek culture.

¹ Etymologically ἄτη is usually derived from the root aṷa or ṷa, as in the Sanskrit á-vā-tah, which means "not injured" or "not hurt." See Otto Hoffmann, *Geschichte der griechischen Sprache* (Leipzig: Göschen, 1911); Emile Boisacq, *Dictionnaire étymologique de la langue grecque*, 4th ed. (Heidelberg: Winter, 1950); and his references to the works of Fick, Hirt, Havers, and Solmsen; Hjalmar Frisk, *Griechisches etymologisches Wörterbuch*, 2 vols. (Heidelberg: Winter, 1960, 1970); Pierre Chantraine, *Dictionnaire étymologique de la langue grecque*, 4 vols. (Paris: Klincksieck, 1968–1980). See also the recent, detailed work of William F. Wyatt, Jr.: "Homeric ἄτη," AJP, 103 (1982), 247–76, esp. 268–73.

² See below chaps. 5, 6, and 7.

³ Aristophanes is not included in this study since ἄτη does not appear in the extant comedies.

⁴ The best recent discussions of ἄτη are E. R. Dodds, *The Greeks and the Irrational*, Sather Classical Lectures 25 (Berkeley: University of California Press, 1951; repr. 1963), chap. 2; R. D. Dawe, "Some Reflections on Ate and Hamartia," HSPh, 72 (1967), 89–123; and J. M. Bremer, *Hamartia: Tragic Error in the Poetics of Aristotle and in Greek Tragedy* (Amsterdam: Hakkert, 1969), pp. 99–134.

⁵ The fact that this represents a shift from *Homeric* usage is quite significant and will be treated at length on pp. 147–51 of the Conclusion.

⁶ *Euripides: Hippolytos*, ed. W. S. Barrett (Oxford: Clarendon, 1964), ad loc.

HOMER AND *ATH

In *The Greeks and the Irrational*, E. R. Dodds states that ἄτη never,

at any rate in the *Iliad*, mean[s] objective disaster, as it so commonly does in tragedy. Always, or practically always [in Homer], ate is a state of mind — a temporary clouding or bewildering of the normal consciousness. It is, in fact, a partial and temporary insanity; and, like all insanity, it is ascribed, not to physiological or psychological causes, but to an external "daemonic" agency.[1]

With respect to Homer, it would be difficult to find fault with this general statement, except perhaps to distinguish some nuances of the generic idea of "a temporary clouding or bewildering of the normal consciousness."

ἄτη appears twenty-six times in the *Iliad* and the *Odyssey*.[2] For twenty-five of these occurrences, it seems possible to distinguish three slightly different connotations within the generic denotation mentioned above: "blindness," "infatuation," and "folly." For the twenty-sixth, there is a completely different use of ἄτη: at *Odyssey* 12.372, it means "ruin."[3]

BLINDNESS

The most frequent use is in the sense of "blindness," and consequently this seems the most convenient use with which to initiate an inquiry.[4]

In *Iliad* 16, Patroclus is struck from behind by Apollo, just before his death at the hands of Hector. Patroclus' eyes are whirling; he is without a helmet; his spear is broken; his shield is gone; and his corselet, loosened:

τὸν δ' ἄτη φρένας εἷλε, λύθεν δ' ὑπὸ φαίδιμα γυῖα,   805
στῆ δὲ ταφών·

Walter Leaf, who would translate ἄτη here as "stupor," remarks: "this purely physical sense is hardly found again (cf. Ω 480), but it must have existed before the moral connotation had been developed."[5] There are two other facts to be noticed: (*a*) even in this sense, ἄτη comes as a result of the direct action of a god; and (b) ἄτη affects Patroclus' φρήν, the seat of emotional or mental activity.[6]

Though Leaf sees a parallel to this "physical" sense in *Iliad* 24.480, *Odyssey* 21.302, in Antinous' account to the disguised Odysseus of the fate of the centaur Eurytion, offers a far better parallel:

ὁ δ' ἐπεὶ φρένας ἄασεν οἴνῳ,
μαινόμενος κάκ' ἔρεξε δόμον κάτα Πειριθόοιο·
ἥρωας δ' ἄχος εἷλε, διὲκ προθύρου δὲ θύραζε
ἕλκον ἀναΐξαντες, ἀπ' οὔατα νηλέϊ χαλκῷ   300
ῥῖνάς τ' ἀμήσαντες· ὁ δὲ φρεσὶν ᾗσιν ἀασθεὶς
ἤϊεν ἣν ἄτην ὀχέων ἀεσίφρονι θυμῷ.

Not only is the physical mistreatment of Eurytion as violent as that suffered by Patroclus, but the ἄτη affects Eurytion's θυμός as Patroclus was affected in his φρήν. It may well be possible even to see a "dae-monic agent" responsible for the ἄτη, as Dodds does, who, in speaking about this passage, remarks: "the implication, however, is probably not that *ate* can be produced 'naturally,' but rather that wine has some-thing supernatural or daemonic about it."[7]

The association with φρήν occurs again in the *Iliad* (19.88), in a passage which affords a good insight into the extension of the meaning of ἄτη to a metaphorical sense of "blindness." In Book 19, after Achilles has renounced his wrath, Agamemnon says:

πολλάκι δή μοι τοῦτον Ἀχαιοὶ μῦθον ἔειπον,   85
καί τέ με νεικείεσκον· ἐγὼ δ' οὐκ αἴτιός εἰμι,
ἀλλὰ Ζεὺς καὶ Μοῖρα καὶ ἠεροφοῖτις Ἐρινύς,
οἵ τέ μοι εἰν ἀγορῇ φρεσὶν ἔμβαλον ἄγριον ἄτην,
ἤματι τῷ ὅτ' Ἀχιλλῆος γέρας αὐτὸς ἀπηύρων.

Here there is no question that the daemonic agents associated with ἄτη are very much present.[8]

Agamemnon continues:

ἀλλὰ τί κεν ῥέξαιμι; θεὸς διὰ πάντα τελευτᾷ.   90
πρέσβα Διὸς θυγάτηρ ἄτη, ἣ πάντας ἀᾶται,
οὐλομένη·

After recounting how Hera tricked Zeus at the time of the birth of Eurystheus and Heracles, Agamemnon proceeds:

ὣς φάτο, τὸν δ' ἄχος ὀξὺ κατὰ φρένα τύψε βαθεῖαν·   125
αὐτίκα δ' εἷλ' ἄτην κεφαλῆς λιπαροπλοκάμοιο
χωόμενος φρεσὶν ᾗσι, καὶ ὤμοσε καρτερὸν ὅρκον
μή ποτ' ἐς Οὔλυμπόν τε καὶ οὐρανὸν ἀστερόεντα
αὖτις ἐλεύσεσθαι ἄτην, ἣ πάντας ἀᾶται.

ὡς εἰπὼν ἔρριψεν ἀπ' οὐρανοῦ ἀστερόεντος   130
χειρὶ περιστρέψας· τάχα δ' ἵκετο ἔργ' ἀνθρώπων.
τὴν αἰεὶ στενάχεσχ', ὅθ' ἑὸν φίλον υἱὸν ὁρῷτο
ἔργον ἀεικὲς ἔχοντα ὑπ' Εὐρυσθῆος ἀέθλων.
ὡς καὶ ἐγών, ὅτε δὴ αὖτε μέγας κορυθαίολος Ἕκτωρ
Ἀργείους ὀλέκεσκεν ἐπὶ πρύμνῃσι νέεσσιν,   135
οὐ δυνάμην λελαθέσθ' ἄτης, ἣ πρῶτον ἀάσθην.
ἀλλ' ἐπεὶ ἀασάμην καί μευ φρένας ἐξέλετο Ζεύς,
ἂψ ἐθέλω ἀρέσαι, δόμεναί τ' ἀπερείσι' ἄποινα·

That ἄτη in line 91 means "blindness" is guaranteed by the relative
clause in the same line, and by the content of the myth.

It is equally certain that ἄτη also means "blindness" in lines 126, 129,
and 136. First, φρήν, which has already been connected with ἄτη in
the sense of "blindness," appears twice in the passage (lines 125, 127);
and, secondly, the function of ἄτη in line 129 is described by the same
relative clause used in line 91. But most telling of all perhaps is the
explicit analogy which Agamemnon himself draws in lines 134ff.
He has already stated in lines 86–88 that he is not to blame as far as
Achilles is concerned, that daemonic agents have cast fierce blindness
on him; now, after introducing ἄτη, Zeus, and Hera, Agamemnon in
line 134 applies the allegory to his own situation: ὡς καὶ ἐγών. His
"blindness" is again made explicit in lines 136 and 137: ἣ πρῶτον ἀάσθην. ἀλλ' ἐπεὶ ἀασάμην.

Once such an allegorical use of ἄτη has been encountered, the use
and meaning of the word in lines 9.504, 505, and 512 must also be considered.[9] But to appreciate them fully, the speech of Phoenix in lines
496–523 must be examined. This is a very carefully constructed passage, with a neat balance and contrast in ideas and phrases — as the
following diagram will illustrate:

A. ἀλλ', Ἀχιλεῦ,
    δάμασον θυμὸν μέγαν   496
    νηλεὲς ἦτορ ἔχειν   497
    στρεπτοὶ ... θεοὶ ...,... ἀρετὴ τιμή τε βίη τε   497–498
    θυέεσσι καὶ εὐχωλῆς ... λοιβῇ τε κνίσῃ τε   499–500
    λισσόμενοι, ὅτε ... τις ὑπερβήῃ καὶ ἁμάρτῃ   501
 καὶ γάρ
    Λιταί εἰσι Διὸς κοῦραι   502
    χωλαί ... ῥυσαί ... παραβλῶπές ... ὀφθαλμώ   503
    αἵ ... μετόπισθ' ἄτης ἀλέγουσι κιοῦσαι   504

ἣ δ' ἄτη σθεναρή ... ἀρτίπος 505
οὕνεκα ... ὑπεκπροθέει, φθάνει ... βλάπτουσ' ἀνθρώπους 505–507
αἱ δ' ἐξακέονται ὀπίσσω 507
ὃς μέν
αἰδέσεται κούρας ... ἆσσον ἰούσας 508
τὸν ... μέγ' ὤνησαν καί ... ἔκλυον εὐχομένοιο 509
ὃς δέ
ἀνήνηται καί ... στερεῶς ἀποείπῃ, 510
λίσσονται ... Δία ... κιοῦσαι / τῷ ἄτην ἅμ' ἕπεσθαι,
ἵνα βλαφθεὶς ἀποτείσῃ 511–512
B. ἀλλ', Ἀχιλεῦ,
πόρε καὶ σὺ Διὸς κούρῃσιν ἕπεσθαι / τιμήν, ἥ ... ἐπιγνάμπτει νόον 513–514
εἰ μὲν
μὴ δῶρα φέροι, τὰ δ' ὄπισθ' ὀνομάζοι 515
ἀλλ' αἰὲν ἐπιζαφελῶς χαλεπαίνοι 516
οὐκ ἂν ἔγωγέ σε μῆνιν ἀπορρίψαντα κελοίμην 517
νῦν δ'
πολλὰ διδοῖ, τὰ δ' ὄπισθεν ὑπέστη 519
ἄνδρας ... λίσσεσθαι 520
ἀρίστους / κρινάμενος κατὰ λαόν 520–521
μὴ ... μῦθον ἐλέγξῃς / μηδὲ πόδας 522–523
πρὶν ... οὔ τι νεμεσσητὸν κεχολῶσθαι 523

It is obvious that the main point of Phoenix' remark is contained in the generic and specific "frame" ideas: θυμὸν μέγαν (496), οὐδέ τί σε χρὴ νηλεὲς ἦτορ ἔχειν (496–497), τῶν μὴ σύ γε μῦθον ἐλέγξῃς μηδὲ πόδας (522–523), and πρὶν δ' οὔ τι νεμεσσητὸν κεχολῶσθαι (523). Indeed, Phoenix goes on to illustrate this point in his narrative of Meleager's conflict with the Curetes (524–599), much as in Book 19 Agamemnon illustrates his main point with the Heracles myth.

Now, several interesting features combine to suggest the meaning of ἄτη here. First of all, Phoenix expresses his appeal in terms of θυμός, which is frequently connected with ἄτη in Homer. Secondly, though the point is not expressly made in lines 496–497, it is clear that the lines refer to Achilles' μῆνις. And surely his μῆνις is just as blind, just as instinctive, just as visceral, a reaction as the ἄτη, the "blindness," which seized Agamemnon and which is frequently alluded to as

instinctive, visceral "blindness."[10]   The point is that Phoenix recognizes
the same type of phenomenon in Achilles as there is in Agamemnon.
Finally, Phoenix introduces the idea that Achilles is totally blameless
(523), a notion which accords with the concept of ἄτη as "blindness"
and one which is frequently operative in Homer.[11]   Taken together,
these factors do not prove that the meaning of ἄτη is "blindness" in this
passage, but they do indicate that "blindness" is in keeping with certain
general characteristics of the use of ἄτη in this sense which are also
present here.

   With these general observations as background, a specific analysis of
the use and meaning of ἄτη in lines 504, 505 and 512 may now be undertaken.   Though the basic question of personification or allegory is
posed not by ἄτη but by Λιταί,[12] there are two positive indications
from the use of ἄτη in lines 504 and 505 that the word is employed
allegorically: (a) the descriptive epithets σθεναρή and ἀρτίπος in line
505 (which, incidentally, neatly balance the description of the Λιταί
in 503, just as the *effects* of both Λιταί and ἄτη are neatly balanced;
cf. the diagram on pp. 9–10) resemble the epithets οὐλομένη and ἁπαλοὶ
πόδες of the allegorical passage at 19.92; and (b) the effect attributed to
ἄτη in line 507 — namely, βλάπτουσ᾽ ἀνθρώπους — is identical with
the effect attributed to the allegorical use of ἄτη in 19.94.   These two
parallelisms — the one of description, the other of effect — cannot be
ignored, and they are decisive for ascertaining an allegorical use of ἄτη
in lines 504 and 505.

   Yet the *use* of ἄτη (the context and circumstances of the word's occurrence) is one thing; its *meaning*, another.   But the meaning can
perhaps best be appreciated from line 512.   (It is evident that the
meaning, as well as the use, of ἄτη are consistent throughout the passage, and that whatever meaning is established for it in 512 will also be
applicable in 504 and 505.)   The first thing of note is that it is *Zeus*
whom the Λιταί implore to see to it that ἄτη follow the recalcitrant.
Since, in Homer, Zeus is frequently said to produce ἄτη in the sense
of "blindness,"[13] this is a good indication that ἄτη may mean "blindness" here.   Next in importance is the purpose for which the Λιταί
want ἄτη to pursue the recalcitrant.   That purpose is ἵνα βλαφθεὶς ἀποτείσῃ (512).   The important word is βλαφθείς, which has already been
mentioned as the effect of ἄτη in 504 and in 19.94, and which, when
applied to the mind, means to "distract," "pervert," "mislead."[14]   The
Λιταί pray, therefore, that such an individual may have ἄτη pursuing him

and, consequently, be "blinded" in his mind. This prayer is in strong contrast to Phoenix' plea to Achilles in lines 513–514 (see the diagram on p. 10), for Phoenix wants Achilles to have τιμήν follow (ἔπεσθαι again!) the daughters of Zeus — τιμήν rather than ἄτην. And to ensure that the contrast is not missed, he specifies the type of τιμή which he has in mind: ἥ . . . ἐπιγνάμπτει νόον. Zeus, then, is the origin of ἄτη; the effect of ἄτη is to mislead the mind; and ἄτη is contrasted with τιμή ἥ ἐπιγνάμπτει νόον. The meaning of the word in 512 is clearly mental "blindness."

In view of all these considerations, then, the use and meaning of ἄτη in 9.504, 505, and 512 are clear. The word is used allegorically here as it is in 19.91ff., and it means "blindness," as it so often does in the *Iliad*.[15]

In the far different atmosphere of the *Odyssey*, the same two associations — the connection with φρήν and the agency of a δαίμων — which were noticed in *Iliad* 19.88 are present when ἄτη is employed at 15.233. Hence, it is likely that the same meaning, "blindness," is also to be found here. During an allusion to the myth of Melampus, the text states:

> ὁ δὲ τῆος ἐνὶ μεγάροις Φυλάκοιο
> δεσμῷ ἐν ἀργαλέῳ δέδετο, κρατέρ' ἄλγεα πάσχων
> εἵνεκα Νηλῆος κούρης ἄτης τε βαρείης,   233
> τήν οἱ ἐπὶ φρεσὶ θῆκε θεὰ δασπλῆτις Ἐρινύς.

In *Iliad* 19.88ff., in what constitutes an instance of one of the many formulaic repetitions in the *Iliad*, Agamemnon refers to the same blind obtuseness as Achilles and Patroclus alluded to earlier in two separate passages. At 1.412, Achilles asks Thetis to have Zeus pen the Achaeans in among their ships as they are slain:

> ἵνα πάντες ἐπαύρωνται βασιλῆος,
> γνῷ δὲ καὶ Ἀτρεΐδης εὐρὺ κρείων Ἀγαμέμνων
> ἣν ἄτην, ὅ τ' ἄριστον Ἀχαιῶν οὐδὲν ἔτεισεν.   412

At 16.274 Patroclus repeats the formula as he exhorts the Myrmidons to fight valorously.

> ὡς ἂν Πηλεΐδην τιμήσομεν, ὃς μέγ' ἄριστος
> Ἀργείων παρὰ νηυσὶ καὶ ἀγχέμαχοι θεράποντες,
> γνῷ δὲ καὶ Ἀτρεΐδης εὐρὺ κρείων Ἀγαμέμνων
> ἣν ἄτην, ὅ τ' ἄριστον Ἀχαιῶν οὐδὲν ἔτεισεν.   274

What seems particularly noteworthy in these two passages is the singular failure of both Achilles and Patroclus to accuse Agamemnon of any guilt. Their preoccupation is totally otherwise: they are concerned with the lack of τιμή, and with the consequent shame, which Agamemnon's ἄτη brings on Achilles.[16] The question of guilt and moral responsibility is never raised in the context of the Homeric poems' use of ἄτη. That entire range of problems will, of course, be central to the concerns of the tragedians several centuries later.

This use of ἄτη, meaning "blindness," in a context which also mentions a lack of glory occurs in another formulaic repetition, *Iliad* 2.111 and 9.18. In the first passage Agamemnon, deceived by the false dream, tests the Argives:

> ὦ φίλοι ἥρωες Δαναοί, θεράποντες Ἄρηος,   110
> Ζεύς με μέγα Κρονίδης ἄτῃ ἐνέδησε βαρείῃ,
> σχέτλιος, ὃς πρὶν μέν μοι ὑπέσχετο καὶ κατένευσεν
> Ἴλιον ἐκπέρσαντ' εὐτείχεον ἀπονέεσθαι,
> νῦν δὲ κακὴν ἀπάτην βουλεύσατο, καί με κελεύει
> δυσκλέα Ἄργος ἱκέσθαι, ἐπεὶ πολὺν ὤλεσα λαόν.   115

The second passage is in strong contrast to the first, and the contrast is ironic. In Book 9, with the Trojans bivouacked on the plain, Agamemnon, weeping, tells the Argives:

> ὦ φίλοι, Ἀργείων ἡγήτορες ἠδὲ μέδοντες,
> Ζεύς με μέγα Κρονίδης ἄτῃ ἐνέδησε βαρείῃ,
> σχέτλιος, ὃς τότε μέν μοι ὑπέσχετο καὶ κατένευσεν
> Ἴλιον ἐκπέρσαντ' εὐτείχεον ἀπονέεσθαι,   20
> νῦν δὲ κακὴν ἀπάτην βουλεύσατο, καί με κελεύει
> δυσκλέα Ἄργος ἱκέσθαι, ἐπεὶ πολὺν ὤλεσα λαόν.

Once again, in these two passages, there is no attempt to assign guilt, merely the recognition that ἄτη, "blindness," has resulted in loss of glory.

That Homeric heroes were not concerned with assessing subjective guilt is further revealed in two other *Iliad* passages which employ ἄτη in this sense of "blindness." Both are apostrophes to Zeus: one by Agamemnon, the other by Achilles. At 8.236, chiding the Argives for their cowardice in the face of Hector, Agamemnon shouts:

> Ζεῦ πάτερ, ἦ ῥά τιν' ἤδη ὑπερμενέων βασιλήων
> τῇδ' ἄτῃ ἄασας καί μιν μέγα κῦδος ἀπηύρας;   237

And at 19.270, in the presence of the Argives, Achilles says:

> Ζεῦ πάτερ, ἦ μεγάλας ἄτας ἄνδρεσσι διδοῖσθα·   270
> οὐκ ἂν δή ποτε θυμὸν ἐνὶ στήθεσσιν ἐμοῖσιν
> Ἀτρεΐδης ὤρινε διαμπερές, οὐδέ κε κούρην

ἦγεν ἐμεῦ ἀέκοντος ἀμήχανος· ἀλλά ποθι Ζεὺς
ἤθελ' Ἀχαιοῖσιν θάνατον πολέεσσι γενέσθαι.

In the first passage, Agamemnon quite definitely has his own κῦδος in mind. And it was the ἄτη sent by Zeus which robbed him of it. In the second passage, Achilles recognizes that the ἄτη sent by Zeus is part of the god's plan to bring death on many Achaeans. There is no accusation here, merely the simple recognition of objective fact.

INFATUATION

There are five texts which employ ἄτη in reference to either Alexander or Helen,[17] and since their story provides the generic framework in which ἄτη is employed, it seems clear that there is a common type of "clouding or bewildering of the normal consciousness," a particular type of "blindness," alluded to. The connotation of "infatuation" applies in each instance, and this particular type of ἄτη is quite appropriate to the Alexander–Helen story.

The most clear-cut instance of ἄτη in this sense occurs at *Odyssey* 4.261. Helen is recounting to Menelaus the various reactions within Troy after Odysseus had wreaked havoc among the Trojans:

ἔνθ' ἄλλαι Τρῳαὶ λίγ' ἐκώκυον· αὐτὰρ ἐμὸν κῆρ
χαῖρ', ἐπεὶ ἤδη μοι κραδίη τέτραπτο νέεσθαι   260
ἂψ οἶκόνδ', ἄτην δὲ μετέστενον, ἣν Ἀφροδίτη
δῶχ', ὅτε μ' ἤγαγε κεῖσε φίλης ἀπὸ πατρίδος αἴης, ...

The daemonic agent responsible for the ἄτη in this instance is Aphrodite, and "infatuation" is precisely the type of ἄτη which Greek mythology would attribute to her.

Aphrodite is implicitly referred to in another passage in which ἄτη is possibly used.[18] It is the *Iliad*'s only allusion to the "Judgment of Paris," in Book 24, lines 25ff., and the immediate reference in the passage is to Argeiphontes' concealment of Hector's corpse from Achilles:

ἔνθ' ἄλλοις μὲν πᾶσιν ἑήνδανεν, οὐδέ ποθ' ῞Ηρῃ   25
οὐδὲ Ποσειδάων' οὐδὲ γλαυκώπιδι κούρῃ,
ἀλλ' ἔχον ὥς σφιν πρῶτον ἀπήχθετο ῎Ιλιος ἱρὴ
καὶ Πρίαμος καὶ λαὸς Ἀλεξάνδρου ἕνεκ' ἄτης,
ὃς νείκεσσε θεάς, ὅτε οἱ μέσσαυλον ἵκοντο,
τὴν δ' ᾔνησ' ἥ οἱ πόρε μαχλοσύνην ἀλεγεινήν.[19]   30

The erotic overtone of the entire incident suggests the connotation of "infatuation."

In the sixth Book of the *Iliad*, Helen, speaking confidentially with Hector, says:

> ἀλλ' ἄγε νῦν εἴσελθε καὶ ἕζεο τῷδ' ἐπὶ δίφρῳ,
> δᾶερ, ἐπεί σε μάλιστα πόνος φρένας ἀμφιβέβηκεν   355
> εἵνεχ' ἐμεῖο κυνὸς καὶ 'Αλεξάνδρου ἕνεχ' ἄτης,
> οἷσιν ἐπὶ Ζεὺς θῆκε κακὸν μόρον, ὡς καὶ ὀπίσσω
> ἀνθρώποισι πελώμεθ' ἀοίδιμοι ἐσσομένοισι. [20]

Several concepts already discussed are contained in this passage: the general association of ἄτη with φρένας and the agency of Zeus. But perhaps most noteworthy of all, by way of contrast with the later usage of the tragedians, is the total lack of any conscious feeling of guilt. Contributing to the connotation of "infatuation" here, in addition to line 356, are the final line and a half.[21] The "song for men still to be" is neither the μῆνις of Achilles nor the ἄτη of Agamemnon, with which the *Iliad* as a whole is concerned, but the tale of the fatal mutual infatuation of Helen and Alexander which triggered the other events.

If Zenodotus' reading is followed at *Iliad* 3.100, Menelaus, speaking to the Trojan and Achaean armies, says:

> κέκλυτε νῦν καὶ ἐμεῖο· μάλιστα γὰρ ἄλγος ἱκάνει
> θυμὸν ἐμόν, φρονέω δὲ διακρινθήμεναι ἤδη
> 'Αργείους καὶ Τρῶας, ἐπεὶ κακὰ πολλὰ πέπασθε
> εἵνεχ' ἐμῆς ἔριδος καὶ 'Αλεξάνδρου ἕνεχ' ἄτης· [22]   100

Though the circumstances are quite different from those in the preceding passage, Menelaus seems to be referring to the same phenomenon — Alexander's infatuation — as Helen did in her conversation with Hector. It was this infatuation which caused κακά for the two armies, just as it had caused πόνος for Hector.

ἄτη also occurs as a cause of suffering in the final passage to be mentioned in which its connotation is infatuation. At *Odyssey* 23.223 Penelope employs it in discussing Helen with Odysseus:

> οὐδέ κεν 'Αργείη 'Ελένη, Διὸς ἐκγεγαυῖα,
> ἀνδρὶ παρ' ἀλλοδαπῷ ἐμίγη φιλότητι καὶ εὐνῇ,
> εἰ ᾔδη ὅ μιν αὖτις ἀρήϊοι υἷες 'Αχαιῶν   220
> ἀξέμεναι οἰκόνδε φίλην ἐς πατρίδ' ἔμελλον.
> τὴν δ' ἦ τοι ῥέξαι θεὸς ὤρορεν ἔργον ἀεικές·
> τὴν δ' ἄτην οὐ πρόσθεν ἑῷ ἐγκάτθετο θυμῷ
> λυγρήν, ἐξ ἧς πρῶτα καὶ ἡμέας ἵκετο πένθος.[23]

In Penelope's view, therefore, the proximate cause of their suffering was Helen's initial, ill-considered infatuation. Penelope knew the power of such infatuation and, for this very reason, was on her guard not to be "beguiled by the words" of a suitor (line 216).

FOLLY

With one exception — *Iliad* 19.270 — the instances of ἄτη discussed thus far have all involved the singular. There are two other *Iliad* passages which employ ἄτη in the plural, a usage which may signal a possible additional extension of the basic meaning of "temporary clouding or bewildering of the normal consciousness." Once the possibility of such an extension is recognized, there is a third *Iliad* passage, once again in the singular, which validly reflects this usage. The three passages in question are 9.115, 10.391, and 24.480, and the extended meaning which they seem to reflect is "folly."

The best text with which to begin, because it is the most revealing, is *Iliad* 10.391. Dolon, overtaken by Diomede and Odysseus as he tries to spy on the Greek ships, answers Odysseus' question about the author of his mission:

πολλῇσίν μ' ἄτῃσι παρὲκ νόον ἤγαγεν ῞Εκτωρ,   391
ὅς μοι Πηλεΐωνος ἀγαυοῦ μώνυχας ἵππους
δωσέμεναι κατένευσε καὶ ἅρματα ποικίλα χαλκῷ,[24]

The preliminary suspicions, based on the use of the plural, about a different connotation for ἄτη in this passage are confirmed by two other striking departures from previous usage.

First, ἄτη in this instance affects νόον. In all the Homeric passages investigated thus far, whenever a specific human faculty is mentioned — though at times no faculty is explicitly mentioned[25] — ἄτη affects either φρήν[26] or θυμός.[27] Without anachronistically attributing to Homer the subsequent careful distinctions of the Greek philosophers, it seems valid to discern a rather definite difference between the visceral, instinctive faculties φρήν and θυμός and the rational νόος.[28] And in this passage, ἄτη affects νόος.

Secondly, the agent responsible for ἄτη in this case is not daemonic but human. It is Hector.[29] This is unique in Homer (indeed, in the whole of pre-Aeschylean literature), and serves as another strong indication that the meaning of ἄτη here is different.

Neither "blindness" nor "infatuation" will fit the context. But "follies" or "false hopes" will.[30] And such an extension of the meaning of ἄτη is not too far removed from those already established.

In Book 9, after Nestor (lines 106ff.) has chided Agamemnon for his seizure of Briseis, contrary to the mind (νόος) of the Greeks and against Nestor's counsel, and for his consequent dishonoring of Achilles and subsequent retention of Briseis, Agamemnon replies:

ὦ γέρον, οὔ τι ψεῦδος ἐμὰς ἄτας κατέλεξας·   115
ἀασάμην, οὐδ' αὐτὸς ἀναίνομαι.

The context makes it clear that ἄτη means "follies," with reference to the list which Nestor had given.[31]

The meaning of ἄτη at *Iliad* 24.480 is quite controversial. This is the encounter of Priam with Achilles, and the text reads as follows:

ὡς δ' ὅτ' ἂν ἄνδρ' ἄτη πυκινὴ λάβῃ, ὅς τ' ἐνὶ πάτρῃ   480
φῶτα κατακτείνας ἄλλων ἐξίκετο δῆμον,
ἀνδρὸς ἐς ἀφνειοῦ, θάμβος δ' ἔχει εἰσορόωντας,
ὣς Ἀχιλεὺς θάμβησεν ἰδὼν Πρίαμον θεοειδέα·

LSJ lists the meaning here as "bane," "ruin," "doom." But this interpretation has been sharply contested by Ebeling, Ameis–Hentze, Leaf, and Dodds. They argue for the meaning "folly," and quite correctly. As Leaf notes:

> The only difficulty is in the word ἄτη, for from the construction of the sentence the ἄτη seems to have come upon him *after* the homicide. Thus Nägelsbach takes it to mean the overwhelming effect of conscience, Göbel the mental disorder due to his position. . . . I believe that the word can mean one thing only, the force which impelled him to do the deed. Then the relative clause ὅς τε . . . κατακτείνας is explanatory of ἄτη, 'as when Ate has come on a man who has slain another' = *so that* he has slain another. But the relative clause has been altered in the course of statement — the original κατακτείνῃ is put in a subordinate participial form, and ἄλλων ἐξίκετο δῆμον as the main thought usurps the principal verb. In other words the essential thought is ὡς ἀνὴρ φῶτα κατακτείνας ἄλλων ἐξίκετο δῆμον. The poet begins, however, for the sake of adding moral weight, as though he were going to say ὡς ὅτ' ἂν ἄνδρ' ἄτη λάβηι ὅς τε φῶτα κατακτείνηι but in the course of saying this he allows the other form of the thought, as the dominant one, to mould the second clause. The difficulty arises from the peculiar construction of the simile in having the point of comparison added independently, θάμβος δ' ἔχει, instead of connected immediately with ὡς ὅτ' ἄν, as is done in every other simile of this form. The result of the difference is that the minor touches are put in the foremost place, and are continually in danger of overshadowing the essential elements.[32]

RUIN

There is, however, one Homeric passage in which ἄτη clearly does mean "ruin": *Odyssey* 12.372. Odysseus is narrating his initial reaction after discovering the slaughter of the cattle of Helios:

> Ζεῦ πάτερ ἠδ' ἄλλοι μάκαρες θεοὶ αἰὲν ἐόντες,   371
> ἦ με μάλ' εἰς ἄτην κοιμήσατε νηλέϊ ὕπνῳ,
> οἱ δ' ἕταροι μέγα ἔργον ἐμητίσαντο μένοντες.

This is the sole instance in which we may follow Dodds in interpreting ἄτη as "objective disaster."[33] It is conceptually synonymous with κακὸν (275) and κακὰ (295) about which Odysseus has already spoken. And this disaster, consistently with the other meanings of ἄτη, is the result of the direct intervention of the gods.

CONCLUSION

In summary, then, a survey of the pertinent Homeric passages leads to the following conclusions about the use and meaning of ἄτη. In Homer ἄτη most often means "blindness" in a metaphorical sense.[34] Five times in such passages it is used in connection with τιμή or κῦδος, but not with any notion of guilt.[35] The second most frequent Homeric use of the word is in the sense of "infatuation."[36] And in all these instances the infatuation is described as a cause of suffering. Three times ἄτη means "folly," and in two of those instances it is used in the plural.[37] Only once does Homer use ἄτη to signify "ruin."[38] The agent responsible for ἄτη in Homer is usually daemonic and, when such an agent is explicitly mentioned, most often it is Zeus.[39] Finally, according to Homer ἄτη affects either φρήν or θυμός or rarely νόος.[40]

If this analysis is correct, the description of Homeric ἄτη given in LSJ must be challenged, for it is misleading on several counts. The primary definition given is "bewilderment, infatuation caused by blindness or delusion sent by the gods." So far there is no difficulty. But the definition goes on to assert that such bewilderment is sent by the gods "mostly as the punishment of guilty rashness." This last phrase is not borne out by the texts cited (all canonical);[41] as Dodds has so ably shown, and as our examination of ἄτη confirms, Homeric culture was, not a "guilt culture," but a "shame culture."[42] And it is precisely this transition from shame to guilt which constituted one of the most

significant differences between Homeric and Aeschylean man, and
which imparted dynamism to tragedy and tragic problems. Similarly,
LSJ's citation of ἄτη at *Iliad* 6.356 as meaning "an active consequence
of such visitations, reckless guilt or sin" must also be rejected. Not
only is this interpretation anachronistic but it does not do justice to the
context in which ἄτη appears.[43]

NOTES

[1] P. 5.

[2] See *Lexicon Homericum*, ed. Heinrich Ebeling, 2 vols. (Leipzig: Teubner: 1885);
and *Index Homericus*, ed. August Gehring (Leipzig: Teubner, 1891).

[3] It is this passage which prompts Dodds to restrict his general definition to the
Iliad.

[4] There are 17 such passages: *Iliad* 1.412; 2.111; 8.237; 9.18, 504, 505, 512; 16.274,
805; 19.88, 91, 126, 129, 136, 270; *Odyssey* 15.233; 21.302.

[5] *The Iliad*, 2nd ed., 2 vols (London & New York: Macmillan, 1900, 1902), ad loc.
An echo of this use may be seen in Sophocles, *Ajax* 909. Dawe does not mention
Iliad 16.805 in "Some Reflections on *Ate* and *Hamartia*," though it might have been
expected in the discussion on p. 97.

[6] This is one of only three passages in Homer where ἄτη is not used in direct discourse. The other two are *Iliad* 24.28 and 24.480. For a good discussion of this passage, see Bremer, *Hamartia*, pp. 103–104.

[7] *The Greeks and the Irrational*, p. 5.

[8] Dodds's remarks, ibid., pp. 6–8, on this point are quite penetrating, as are his
thoughts on the passage as a whole. The same may be said for Bremer, *Hamartia*,
pp. 107–109. But, as the rest of this chapter will show, I cannot agree with Hugh
Lloyd-Jones' treatment of these questions in his *The Justice of Zeus*, Sather Classical
Lectures 41 (Berkeley: University of California Press, 1971), pp. 9–25. To claim
that Homeric man is "responsible" for moral actions is not only to dismiss the work
of Dodds, Adkins, and Snell (to name a few modern scholars), but also to contradict
the evidence of a passage like the present one. Nor can I fathom Lloyd-Jones' psy-
chology for Homeric man when he attributes to man the responsibility for his visceral
reactions in φρήν and θυμός. It seems to me that, based on the texts of the ancient authors, Dodds's distinction between "shame culture" and "guilt culture" is quite valid.

[9] The "Homeric" authorship of both the embassy to Achilles in Book 9 and the
apology of Agamemnon in Book 19 has, of course, been seriously challenged. The
most recent review of the arguments is contained in Denys L. Page, *History and the
Homeric Iliad*, Sather Classical Lectures 31 (Berkeley: University of California Press,
1959; repr. 1963), pp. 300–304 (for Book 9) and 310–15 (for Book 19). All the evidence
for revision and all the learned argumentation expended on these two passages not-

withstanding, the point that the passages must be considered *as we have them* is perhaps best put by Werner Jaeger: "There is unmistakable evidence that an earlier form
of the [Phoenix] scene must have existed, in which Odysseus and Ajax were the only
envoys sent to Achilles by the army. *But it is impossible to reconstruct this earlier form
merely by excising Phoenix's great admonitory speech — as impossible as are most such re-
constructions, even where the traces of revision are as obvious as they are here*" (*Paideia:
The Ideals of Greek Culture*, trans. Gilbert Highet, 2 vols. [New York: Oxford University Press, 1945], I 26; emphasis added).

[10] At 1.412, 8.237, 16.274, and 19.270.

[11] See 1.412, 2.111, 9.18, 16.274.

[12] Just as Dodds (*The Greeks and the Irrational*, p. 6) saw ἄτη in Book 19 as the eldest
daughter of Zeus in an allegorical sense because it is Zeus who causes ἄτη, so here it
seems legitimate to take Homer's descriptions of the Λιταί as Διὸς κοῦραι μεγάλοιο
(502) in the same sense: Zeus is the one who causes prayer in men and so the Λιταί are
allegorically his daughters. Corroboration for this is to be found in the description
παραβλῶπές τ' ὀφθαλμώ. This attitude of "eyes askance" is usually interpreted to
reflect the *human* wrongdoers' unwillingness to look their victims in the face. Cf.
Bremer, *Hamartia*, p. 107n23.

It is interesting to note in the diagram on pp. 9–10 that the six lines (502–507) introducing the Λιταί (*a*) structurally unbalance the generic and specific sections of the
speech, i.e., without these six lines each section would be eleven lines in length;
and (*b*) stylistically disrupt the otherwise balanced ὃς μέν, ὃς δέ of the first section
and the answering εἰ μὲν, νῦν δ' of the second section. This indicates that the speech,
as analyzed in the diagram, is "archaic" rather than "classical" both structurally and
stylistically.

[13] Cf. *Iliad* 2.111; 8.237; 9.18; 19.88, 136, 270.

[14] Cf. LSJ for examples.

[15] Though the use of ἄτη in both *Iliad* 9.504 and 19.88 is allegorical, there is no
question of personification in either passage. Thus, LSJ's citing of both passages as
examples of "*Ate* personified, the goddess of mischief, author of rash actions" must be
rejected.

[16] That Achilles was greatly concerned with his τιμή is clear from 1.352–356.
Dodds, *The Greeks and the Irrational*, pp. 17–18, has some pertinent remarks on the
difference between "shame" and "guilt." See also Bremer, *Hamartia*, pp. 105–106.

[17] They are *Iliad* 3.100, 6.356, 24.28 and *Odyssey* 4.261, 23.223. It is interesting
to note that the Alexander passages are all from the *Iliad*, and the Helen passages
from the *Odyssey*.

[18] Its relevance to Homeric usage is not certain; *Iliad* 24.23–30 was rejected by
Aristarchus.

[19] Leaf, *The Iliad*, remarks ad loc.: "We should be justified in adopting the variant
ἀρχῆς, were we sure of the antiquity of the line. . . ."

[20] Zenodotus read ἀρχῆς instead of ἄτης in line 356. See the discussion of this and
the other *Iliad* passages concerning Paris and Helen in Bremer, *Hamartia*, p. 104.

[21] This point seems to be overlooked by LSJ, who continue to list this passage under
the meaning "reckless guilt or sin," as an *active* consequence of some divine visitation.
Dodds, *The Greeks and the Irrational*, p. 20n31, has remarked acutely: "Homeric man

does not possess the concept of will (which developed curiously late in Greece), and therefore cannot possess the concept of 'free will.'"

22 Leaf, *The Iliad*, ad loc., notes: "Zenod[otus] ἄτης, to which Ar[istarchus] objected ἔσται ἀπολογούμενος Μενέλαος ὅτι ἄτηι περιέεσεν ὁ Ἀλεξάνδρος certainly Achilles is not 'apologising' for Agamemnon in *A* 412. In *Ω* 28 Ar[istarchus] himself read ἄτης (though there was a variant ἀρχῆς). . . . A more serious objection is that ἄτη is for ἀϝάτη, and that the contracted form is found only in late passages, the first syllable being usually in *thesis*."

23 This passage was rejected by Aristarchus.

24 The scholiast remarks: ἄτας ἔφη τὰς ἐπὶ κακῷ ὑποσχέσεις (*Scholia Graeca in Homeri Iliadem*, ed. Wilhelm Dindorf, 6 vols. [Oxford: Clarendon, 1875-1888], III 445).

25 *Iliad* 19.91; 1.412; 16.274; 2.111; 9.18, 504, 505, 512; 8.237; *Odyssey* 4.261; *Iliad* 24.28; 3.100.

26 *Iliad* 16.805; 19.88, 126, 129, 136; *Odyssey* 15.233; *Iliad* 6.356.

27 *Odyssey* 21.302; *Iliad* 19.270; *Odyssey* 23.223.

28 See LSJ for examples. See also the clear distinction in Theognis 631, p. 29 below.

29 Leaf, *The Iliad*, ad loc., says: "ἄτηισι is so far peculiar here that it is used of 'blinding,' deception, of a purely human origin. . . . In every other instance it conveys the idea of some divine or mysterious blindness." Dodds, *The Greeks and the Irrational*, p. 19n20, tries to minimize the human agency of Hector by saying: "The meaning, however, may be, not that Hector's unwise advice produced ἄτη in Dolon, but that it was a symptom of Hector's own condition of (divinely inspired) ἄτη." The difficulty with this view is that ἄτη is never ascribed to Hector.

30 This is the meaning of the scholion given in note 24.

31 This meaning is corroborated by the scholion, which reads: ὦ γέρον, φησὶν, οὐδὲν ψευσάμενος τὰς ἐμὰς ἀδικίας ἀπηριθμήσω, βλάψαι με βουλόμενος, ὡς ᾤήθης. ἐπὶ δὲ τὸ τέλος τοῦ στίχου στικτέον· τὸ γὰρ φεῦδος ἀντὶ τοῦ ψευδῶς (*Scholia Graeca in Homeri Iliadem*, ed. Dindorf, I 305). Cf. Bremer, *Hamartia*, p. 106.

32 *The Iliad*, ad loc. Dodds, *The Greeks and the Irrational*, p. 19n17, agrees with this. The *Lexicon Homericum*, ed. Ebeling, lists this passage under the definition "stupor, animus sui non compos." Karl Friedrich Ameis and Karl Hentze, *Anhang zu Homers Iliad*, 2 vols. (Leipzig: Teubner, 1879), ad loc., notes: ". . . schwere Verblendung ergriffen hat." An excellent parallel for the sense in which these authors would construe ἄτη here seems to be contained in the *Shield of Heracles* passage (89-94) discussed on p. 26 below.

33 *The Greeks and the Irrational*, p. 5 and note 17. For the reasons given on p. 8 above, it is not possible to agree with Dodds on his interpretation of *Odyssey* 21.302 in this same sense. The *Lexicon Homericum*, ed. Ebeling, also takes ἄτη in this passage to mean "damnum, calamitas."

34 There are 17 such texts, as listed in note 4 above.

35 These texts are *Iliad* 1.412, 16.274, 2.111, 9.18, 8.237.

36 This connotation applies to *Odyssey* 4.261, 23.223; *Iliad* 24.28, 6.356, 3.100.

37 This connotation appears in the plural at *Iliad* 10.391 and 9.115, and in the singular at *Iliad* 24.280.

38 *Odyssey* 12.372.

³⁹ Zeus is the agent at *Iliad* 19.88; 6.356; 2.111; 9.18, 504, 505, 512; 8.237; 19.136, 270; and *Odyssey* 12.372. The other daemonic agents are Aphrodite (*Odyssey* 4.261; *Iliad* 24.28), Apollo (*Iliad* 16.805), and Erinys (*Odyssey* 15.233).

⁴⁰ φρήν is affected in *Iliad* 16.805; 19.88, 126, 129, 136; 6.356; *Odyssey* 15.233; θυμός in *Odyssey* 21.302; 23.223; *Iliad* 19.270; and νόος in *Iliad* 10.391 and 9.115.

⁴¹ *Iliad* 16.805; 8.237; 19.88; 4.261.

⁴² *The Greeks and the Irrational*, pp. 17–18.

⁴³ See above p. 15.

2

HESIOD, THE LYRIC POETS, AND ἄτη

In the almost three hundred years which separate the Homeric poems from the extant works of Aeschylus, ἄτη underwent development both in use and in meaning. The evidence from this period comprises almost as many loci — twenty-four — in which the term appears as the total of such Homeric passages — twenty-six — investigated in the previous chapter. And just as seventh- and sixth-century poets experimented in genres other than the epic, so they employed ἄτη in the non-Homeric objective connotation with greater frequency.

As we continue our investigation and draw closer to the Athenian tragedians' use of the term, we become aware that, in this area, as in so many others in Greek literature, a "tradition" is being created, with Homer as the base, but with ample opportunity for development on the part of subsequent poets. But before turning to the more personalized insights of the lyric poets, we must first investigate Homer's immediate successor in Greek poetic development.

HESIOD

As might be expected, Hesiod's use of ἄτη is both similar and dissimilar to Homer's. The central similarity is that for Hesiod ἄτη has the same basic meaning as it has for Homer, but — and this is one key area of development — Hesiod extends that basic meaning. Hesiod differs from Homer in two respects: he makes no explicit mention of daemonic agency in connection with human ἄτη (the Hesiodic world is not the Mycenaean civilization of the Homeric poems), and he does not link ἄτη with φρήν, θυμός, or νόος.

Works and Days

The first pertinent passage, in the *Works and Days*, employs ἄτη in the sense, rare in Homer, of "ruin" or "destruction." In a section dealing with the just, Hesiod writes:

εἰρήνη δ' ἀνὰ γῆν κουροτρόφος, οὐδέ ποτ' αὐτοῖς
ἀργαλέον πόλεμον τεκμαίρεται εὐρύοπα Ζεύς·
οὐδέ ποτ' ἰθυδίκῃσι μετ' ἀνδράσι λιμὸς ὀπηδεῖ   230
οὐδ' ἀάτη, θαλίης δὲ μεμηλότα ἔργα νέμονται.

There is a chiasmus in these lines which points quite clearly to the meaning of ἄτη in line 231. Just as the tranquil εἰρήνη δ' ἀνὰ γῆν κουροτρόφος is made explicit by θαλίης δὲ μεμηλότα ἔργα νέμονται, so the harsh οὐδέ ποτ' αὐτοῖς ἀργαλέον πόλεμον τεκμαίρεται εὐρύοπα Ζεύς is made explicit by οὐδέ ποτ' ἰθυδίκῃσι μετ' ἀνδράσι λιμὸς ὀπηδεῖ οὐδ' ἀάτη. And thus ἄτη, "ruin," "destruction," is seen as one of the results of war, just as lighthearted cultivation is one of the results of peace.[1]

The application of ἄτη to the agricultural-economic sphere in the preceding passage is a good transition to the other meaning which Hesiod attaches to the word in the *Works and Days*. That meaning is "financial loss," an extension of the sense of "ruin."

At line 352, in a section devoted to pithy generalizations, Hesiod writes:

μὴ κακὰ κερδαίνειν· κακὰ κέρδεα ἶσ' ἀάτῃσιν.

ἄτη is expressly equivalent to κέρδεα ("gains," "profits") here. But they are κακὰ κέρδεα, "financial losses," a meaning clearly supported by the term ζημία in the two scholia on this line.[2]

ἄτη in line 413 has the same meaning. In a series of specific pieces of advice for his brother, Hesiod includes the following:

μηδ' ἀναβάλλεσθαι ἔς τ' αὔριον ἔς τε ἔνηφιν·   410
οὐ γὰρ ἐτωσιοεργὸς ἀνὴρ πίμπλησι καλιὴν
οὐδ' ἀναβαλλόμενος· μελέτη δὲ τὸ ἔργον ὀφέλλει·
αἰεὶ δ' ἀμβολιεργὸς ἀνὴρ ἄτῃσι παλαίει.

Here again the general frame of reference is economic. And it is "financial loss," not necessarily utter ruin, with which the procrastinator must constantly come to grips. And, once more, this is clearly the understanding of the scholiasts.[3] The metaphor of "wrestling" with ἄτη should not pass unnoticed, for it will recur (transformed, to be sure) in Aeschylus.[4]

There is one stylistic point common to all three passages in the *Works and Days* which should be highlighted. In each passage in which ἄτη occurs, a deliberate contrast or an explicit similarity is involved. Thus, εἰρήνη and πόλεμος are contrasted in lines 228–231, as μελέτη and ἀμβολιεργὸς ἀνὴρ are in 410–413, while in 352 ἴσ᾿ makes explicit the similarity between κακὰ κέρδεα and ἄτη.

Theogony

In the *Theogony*, Ἄτη is listed as one of the children of Ἔρις:

αὐτὰρ Ἔρις στυγερὴ τέκε μὲν Πόνον ἀλγινόεντα
Λήθην τε Λιμόν τε καὶ Ἄλγεα δακρυόεντα
Ὑσμίνας τε Μάχας τε Φόνους τ᾿ Ἀνδροκτασίας τε
Νείκεά τε ψευδέας τε Λόγους Ἀμφιλλογίας τε
Δυσνομίην τ᾿ Ἀάτην τε, συνήθεας ἀλλήλῃσιν,   230
Ὅρκον θ᾿, ὃς δὴ πλεῖστον ἐπιχθονίους ἀνθρώπους
πημαίνει, ὅτε κέν τις ἑκὼν ἐπίορκον ὀμόσσῃ.

There is no doubt about the personification of Ἄτη in this context. The overall content of Hesiod's poem makes this clear. But what does Ἄτη mean? Hesiod himself indicates the meaning. First of all, he notes that Ὅρκος is different from the other children of Ἔρις. Among these others, one group stands out as exceptionally homogeneous. This is the group composed of Ὑσμίνη, Μάχη, Φόνος, Ἀνδροκτασία, and Νεῖκος, all five of whom involve violence of one sort or another. But more than that, this group of five sets off two groups of four, one enumerated before and one after it.

Without investigating the significance of the Πόνος, Λήθη, Λιμός, Ἄλγος quartet too closely, it is fair to see in them a group of evils inherent in the human condition. This then leaves the final four, Λόγος ψευδής, Ἀμφιλλογία, Δυσνομία, and Ἄτη. It would be strange if the previous two groups each had something in common and this one did not. But it does, of course, provided Ἄτη is recognized as meaning "blindness," "infatuation," or "folly." This is the basic Homeric meaning, and it is quite akin to Λόγος ψευδής, Ἀμφιλλογία, and Δυσνομία. What is precluded by such kinship is the meaning of "ruin" or "disaster."[5]

The usual interpretation of the phrase συνήθεας ἀλλήλῃσιν is that it applies only to Δυσνομία and Ἄτη. Though this interpretation does not weaken the case for understanding Ἄτη as "blindness," "infatuation," or "folly," that case can be strengthened if the phrase is understood to apply more broadly to all the children of Ἔρις. Thus, Hesiod would claim that all the children of the same mother are συνήθεας ἀλλήλῃσιν (hardly a surprising fact!), and he enumerates those children in a symmetrically arranged order of 4–5–4, with the members of each group particularly συνήθεας ἀλλήλῃσιν.[6]

Shield of Heracles

It is convenient, with the usual reservations about Hesiodic authorship, to consider the *Shield of Heracles* here.[7] ἄτη appears once, at line 93, in a passage in which Heracles is speaking with Iolaus about Iphicles:

> τοῦ μὲν φρένας ἐξέλετο Ζεύς,
> ὃς προλιπὼν σφέτερόν τε δόμον σφετέρους τε τοκῆας   90
> ᾤχετο, τιμήσων ἀλιτήμενον Εὐρυσθῆα,
> σχέτλιος· ἦ που πολλὰ μετεστοναχίζετ' ὀπίσσω
> ἦν ἀάτην ὀχέων· ἦ δ' οὐ παλινάγρετός ἐστιν.

That ἄτη is used in direct discourse helps to create an atmosphere which is quite Homeric,[8] but there are other Homeric reminiscences as well. The phrase φρένας ἐξέλετο Ζεύς combines two Homeric ideas: the agency of Zeus and the association of ἄτη with φρήν. The epithet σχέτλιος, which, in *Iliad* 2.112, Homer applies to Zeus as the author of ἄτη, is transferred here to Iphicles as the victim of ἄτη. Finally, the phrase ἦν ἀάτην ὀχέων is borrowed directly from *Odyssey* 21.302; there the meaning is "blindness" or "folly,"[9] and the same meaning applies here, as the next phrase confirms: ἦ δ' οὐ παλινάγρετός ἐστιν. What "cannot be taken back" is the fact that Iphicles temporarily went "blind," or was deluded, not the fact that he suffered any "disaster" or "ruin."

SOLON

The next author in whose work the word ἄτη appears is Solon. There is thus a gap of perhaps some one hundred and fifty years between the poems of Hesiod and those of Solon in which any use of ἄτη is lost to us.[10] But when the word reappears in Solon the meaning has not changed at all from Homeric and Hesiodic times.

Solon uses ἄτη four times in the fragments which have come down to us. The loci are 4.35 and 13.13, 68, and 75. Three of these passages — 4.35, 13.13, and 13.75 — are more appropriate to the next chapter because they involve the supposed tetralogy of ὄλβος, κόρος, ὕβρις, and ἄτη, and discussion of them will be postponed until then. At line 68 of fragment 13, ἄτη appears as follows:

> ἀλλ' ὁ μὲν εὖ ἔρδειν πειρώμενος οὐ προνοήσας
> ἐς μεγάλην ἄτην καὶ χαλεπὴν ἔπεσεν,
> τῶι δὲ κακῶς ἔρδοντι θεὸς περὶ πάντα δίδωσιν
> συντυχίην ἀγαθήν, ἔκλυσιν ἀφροσύνης.   70

Here the meaning of "ruin," "calamity," or "disaster" is secured for
ἄτη by virtue of the contrast between the two individuals described.
The first ἐς . . . ἄτην . . . ἔπεσεν, while the second is released from
ἀφροσύνης. In this context, ἄτη can only mean "ruin,"[11] and, it would
seem, is caused more by man than by Zeus or some other daemonic
agent.[12]

ALCAEUS

The one fragment of Alcaeus in which ἄτη appears[13] deals with his
feud with Pittacus over power in Mytilene:

> ἐκ δὲ χόλω τῶδε λαθοίμεθ. . [·
> χαλάσσομεν δὲ τὰς θυμοβόρω λύας   10
> ἐμφύλω τε μάχας, τάν τις Ὀλυμπίων
> ἔνωρσε, δᾶμον μὲν εἰς ἀνάταν ἄγων
> Φιττάκωι δὲ δίδοις κῦδος ἐπήρ[ατ]ον.

From what is known from other fragments[14] about Alcaeus' attitude
toward Pittacus, it seems better to interpret ἄτη as "ruin" in this context.
He considers the people's preferring of Pittacus as equivalent to a god's
leading them to ruin, while bestowing on Pittacus its opposite, κῦδος.
It is a brief fragment, but it testifies to the usage on Lesbos in the early-
sixth century in two important respects: (a) the meaning ("ruin") is the
same as that predicated by Hesiod of a group; and (b) the Homeric
daemonic agent is present in the indefinite τις Ὀλυμπίων.[15]

IBYCUS

There is a rather long fragment contained in Oxyrhynchus Papyrus
2081 which is generally attributed to Ibycus.[16] ἄτη appears in line 8 of
this fragment:

> ἀντ.   οἳ κ]αὶ Δαρδανίδα Πριάμοιο μέ-
> γ' ἄσ]τυ περικλεὲς ὄλβιον ἠνάρον
> Ἄργ]οθεν ὀρνυμένοι
> Ζη] νὸς μεγάλοιο βουλαῖς   4
>
> ἐπωιδ. ξα]νθᾶς Ἑλένας περὶ εἴδει
> δῆ]ριν πολύμνον ἔχ[ο]ντες
> πό]λεμον κατὰ δακρ[υό]εντα,
> Πέρ]γαμον δ' ἀνέ[β]α ταλαπείριο[ν ἄ]τα
> χρυ]σοέθειραν δ[ι]ὰ Κύπριδα.   9

There can be no question that the meaning of ἄτη in this context is "ruin"; that is what came upon Troy. Once again a daemonic agent is responsible, this time Aphrodite. Yet the change from Homeric usage is significant. For in Homer, whenever Aphrodite is responsible for ἄτη, ἄτη means "infatuation."[17] Ibycus retains Aphrodite as the cause of ἄτη but shifts the meaning of the ἄτη she produces.

THEOGNIS

The seven occurrences of ἄτη in Theognis appear in two distinct types of passages: the first include the name "Cyrnus," and may, therefore, represent Theognis' own composition;[18] the second are all derived from another poet — in this case, Solon.

There are four Cyrnus passages, and in three of them, although the dependence is not nearly as patent as in the passages derived from Solon, there is a great deal in common with the uses of ἄτη already seen in Homer and Hesiod.

The first of the Cyrnus passages is lines 101 to 104:

μηδείς σ' ἀνθρώπων πείσηι κακὸν ἄνδρα φιλῆσαι
Κύρνε· τί δ' ἔστ' ὄφελος δειλὸς ἀνὴρ φίλος ὤν;
οὔτ' ἄν σ' ἐκ χαλεποῖο πόνου ῥύσαιτο καὶ ἄτης,
οὔτέ κεν ἐσθλὸν ἔχων τοῦ μεταδοῦν ἐθέλοι.

Among the meanings of ἄτη, the context demands "ruin" rather than "blindness," "infatuation," or "folly." The point of the admonition is not to befriend a δειλός, a "low-born" individual, since he would be incapable of freeing one from toil and ἄτη, and even if he should happen to become prosperous he would not willingly surrender any of his prosperity. ἄτη is both the opposite of ἐσθλόν and a synonym of πόνος.

The similarity of this passage to several in Hesiod is striking. The contrast between δειλός and ἐσθλός, though not identical with Hesiod's, is evocative of *Works and Days* 213–218.[19] And Theognis' blunt, pragmatic concern with ὄφελος is quite similar to Hesiod's aphorism in *Works and Days* 412 that μελέτη δὲ τὸ ἔργον ὀφέλλει.[20] Both poets show a "utilitarian" tendency. But for Hesiod the good is work; for Theognis, friendship and its advantages.

The least derivative ἄτη passage in Theognis is the second Cyrnus passage. In two contrasting statements, beginning with line 117, he writes:

κιβδήλου δ᾽ ἀνδρὸς γνῶναι χαλεπώτερον οὐδὲν
Κύρν᾽, οὐδ᾽ εὐλαβίης ἐστὶ περὶ πλέονος.
χρυσοῦ κιβδήλοιο καὶ ἀργύρου ἀνσχετὸς ἄτη
Κύρνε, καὶ ἐξευρεῖν ῥάιδιον ἀνδρὶ σοφῶι.²¹   120

Two considerations point to "infatuation" as the meaning of ἄτη in line 119. First, there is the contrast between ἄτη and qualities of knowledge; for just as it is very difficult to know a base human being, *in spite of a great deal of discretion*, so the ἄτη of base gold and silver is endurable and easy for a *wise* man to discover. Either "infatuation" or "folly," it must be admitted, would fit the context of a non-rational opposition to discretion and wisdom. But what decides the case in favor of "infatuation" is the second consideration, a grammatical one. If ἄτη should be taken to mean "folly," χρυσοῦ κιβδήλοιο καὶ ἀργύρου would be difficult genitives to explain. But if ἄτη is taken to mean "infatuation," then they are readily explicable as objective genitives.

At line 133 ἄτη is again employed, in the third of the Cyrnus passages:

οὐδεὶς Κύρν᾽ ἄτης καὶ κέρδεος αἴτιος αὐτός,
ἀλλὰ θεοὶ τούτων δώτορες ἀμφοτέρων·
οὐδέ τις ἀνθρώπων ἐργάζεται ἐν φρεσὶν εἰδὼς   135
ἐς τέλος εἴτ᾽ ἀγαθὸν γίνεται εἴτε κακόν.

Here the meaning of "loss" is clear; for ἄτη is contrasted with κέρδος, "gain," "profit," in a use recalling Hesiod's juxtaposition of κέρδος and ἄτη in *Works and Days* 352.²² Of interest as well are the parallel between κέρδος – ἄτη and ἀγαθόν – κακόν, and the attribution of the responsibility for ἄτη, as in Homer, to θεοί.

The fourth and final use of ἄτη in a Cyrnus passage occurs at line 631:

ὧιτινι μὴ θυμοῦ κρέσσων νόος, αἰὲν ἐν ἄταις   631
Κύρνε καὶ ἐν μεγάλαις κεῖται ἀμηχανίαις.

ἄτη seems best taken to mean "follies" in this context, for two reasons. There is the general consideration that ἄτη in the plural usually does mean "follies." This is true in both Homer and Hesiod,²³ and, though there are exceptions,²⁴ the plural constitutes a prima facie case for the meaning of "folly." But what corroborates this case in the current passage is that ἄται is closely related to ἀμπλακία, "error," "fault." Theognis is saying that the man of θυμός constantly finds himself in folly and error; there is a moral connotation to the entire concept. Noteworthy, too, in these two lines is the contrast between θυμός and νόος, first adumbrated in Homer,²⁵ and now quite distinct.

Theognis 203ff. is derived from Solon 13.25ff. Solon does not employ ἄτη in the passage, but Theognis does:

ἀλλὰ τάδ᾿ ἀνθρώπων ἀπατᾷι νόον· οὐ γὰρ ἐπ᾿ αὐτοῦ
τίνονται μάκαρες πρήγματος ἀμπλακίας,
ἀλλ᾿ ὁ μὲν αὐτὸς ἔτεισε κακὸν χρέος, οὐδὲ φίλοισιν 205
ἄτην ἐξοπίσω παισὶν ἐπεκρέμασεν·

What is involved here is the standard Greek notion of "blood guilt." Solon expresses the idea positively:

ἀλλ᾿ ὁ μὲν αὐτίκ᾿ ἔτεισεν, ὁ δ᾿ ὕστερον· οἱ δὲ φύγωσιν
αὐτοί, μηδὲ θεῶν μοῖρ᾿ ἐπιοῦσα κίχηι, 30
ἤλυθε πάντως αὖτις· ἀναίτιοι ἔργα τίνουσιν
ἢ παῖδες τούτων ἢ γένος ἐξοπίσω.

Theognis' formulation is negative: whoever has paid for his evil has not extended ἄτη to his descendants. There can be no question in this context, particularly when it is compared with the Solon passage, that ἄτη means "ruin." The very basis of the "blood guilt" concept is that future generations suffer ruin for the unpaid guilt of their ancestors. In this passage, as in the one just discussed, νόος plays a part.

The final two Theognis passages, in each of which ἄτη means "blindness," are derived from Solon.

The first such parallel, Theognis 227–232 and Solon 13.71–76, is more germane to the next chapter, since it contains the ὄλβος, κόρος, and ἄτη triad, and will be discussed there.

Theognis 587–590, on the other hand, contains no mention of ὄλβος or κόρος:

ἀλλ᾿ ὁ μὲν εὐδοκιμεῖν πειρώμενος οὐ προνοήσας
εἰς μεγάλην ἄτην καὶ χαλεπὴν ἔπεσεν·
τῶι δὲ κακῶς ποιεῦντι θεὸς περὶ πάντα τίθησιν
συντυχίην ἀγαθήν, ἔκλυσιν ἀφροσύνης. 590

As is clear, this is almost identical with Solon 13.67–70 discussed earlier.

Theognis' use of ἄτη, therefore, reflects the tradition quite strongly. His debt to Solon in 588 is obvious; yet he is equally indebted to Homer at 119 where ἄτη means "infatuation," and at 631 where not only does it mean "follies" but there is a distinction between θυμός and νόος. Hesiod's use of ἄτη within the tradition is found in Theognis at 103 and 206 ("ruin") and 133 ("financial loss"). Derivative as all this is, there is one element of novelty in Theognis: at 119, where ἄτη means "infatuation," the meaning appears for the first time in a non-erotic context.

PINDAR

The author with whom we may conclude this survey of the use of
ἄτη in Greek lyric poetry is Pindar. He was, to be sure, roughly a
contemporary of the pioneers in the totally different genre of tragedy,
but his cultural background (aristocratic Thebes) was so different from
theirs (democratic Athens). Nevertheless, he presumably inherited the
common Greek poetic tradition with respect to ἄτη, and it is now time
to turn to his use of the term.[26]

In the tenth *Olympian*, ἄτη appears at line 37. This passage concerns
Augeas, king of Elias, whose city was burned by Heracles:

> καὶ μὰν ξεναπάτας
> Ἐπειῶν βασιλεὺς ὄπιθεν   35
> οὐ πολλὸν ἴδε πατρίδα πολυ-
> κτέανον ὑπὸ στερεῷ πυρί
> πλαγαῖς τε σιδάρου βαθὺν εἰς ὀχετὸν ἄτας
> ἵζοισαν ἐὰν πόλιν.

Here Pindar specifies the meaning of "ruin" for ἄτη by including the
means by which the ruin was accomplished: ὑπὸ στερεῷ πυρί πλαγαῖς
τε σιδάρου. The picture of the burning of the city recalls the similar
picture of Troy's destruction in Ibycus where ἄτη also means "ruin."

Another passage in Pindar where ἄτη means "ruin" occurs in the
ninth *Nemean* at line 21. The myth concerns the sons of Talaus march-
ing on Thebes contrary to an omen of Zeus. That omen notwithstanding:

> φαινομέναν δ' ἄρ' ἐς ἄταν σπεῦδεν ὅμιλος ἱκέσθαι   21
> χαλκέοις ὅπλοισιν ἱππείοις τε σὺν ἔντεσιν·

Pindar makes clear in the following lines that ἄτη means "ruin" here,
for he narrates the slaughter of this band near the banks of the Ismenus.

ἄτη occurs twice in the *Pythians*, and each time it means "infatuation."[27] One of the telling reasons for assigning this meaning in both
instances is the erotic context. Discussion of *Pythian* 2.28 more properly
belongs to the next chapter.

ἄτη occurs in *Pythian* 3 at line 24, where the myth involved is that
of Coronis' affair with Ischys, the son of Elatus:

> ἔστι δὲ φῦλον ἐν ἀνθρώποισι ματαιότατον,
> ὅστις αἰσχύνων ἐπιχώρια παπταίνει τὰ πόρσω,
> μεταμώνια θηρεύων ἀκράντοις ἐλπίσιν.
> ἔσχε τοι ταύταν μεγάλαν ἀνάταν
> καλλιπέπλου λῆμα Κορωνίδος·[28]   25

The meaning of "infatuation" for ἀνάταν is indicated not only by the erotic context but by the qualifying ταύταν, which refers to the μεταμώνια and ἀκράντοις ἐλπίσιν of line 23. Of significance too in this passage is that λῆμα is said to have been affected by the ἄτη in question. This is a further differentiation of faculties from the φρήν, θυμός, and νόος originally encountered in Homer.

In sum, there are five points of note in Pindar's use of ἄτη: (a) it always appears in a mythological passage; (b) it is always used in the singular; (c) it means either "ruin" or "infatuation"; (d) with one exception — Olympian 1, to be discussed in the next chapter — no daemonic agent is explicitly mentioned as causing it; and (e) in Pindaric usage λῆμα joins the Homeric and post-Homeric faculties involved with it.

NOTES

¹ But it should be noted that it is *war* which Zeus directly wills unjust men. It is not ἄτη. Thus, the general statement that there is "no explicit mention of daemonic agency in connection with human ἄτη," made on p. 23, is applicable even here.

² The scholion attributed to Proclus is contained in *Scholia vetera in Hesiodi Opera et dies*, ed. Agostino Pertusi (Milan: Vita e pensiero, 1955), p. 118, and reads as follows: τὰς ἄτας ταῖς ζημίαις εἶναι τὰς αὐτὰς φησι, τά δε κέρδη περιποιητικά τινων ὠφελημάτων. ὅσοι οὖν κακὰ κερδαίνουσιν, οὗτοί εἰσιν οἱ αἰσχροκερδεῖς· τὰ δὲ κέρδη ταῖς ζημίαις ἴσα < ἄνθρωποι > κερδαίνουσι διὰ δὴ τὴν αἰσχροκέρδειαν ταύτην, μείζοσιν ἔσθ' ὅτε ζημίαις ἐνίσχονται.

The scholion attributed to Moschopolus is contained in *Poetae minores Graeci*, ed. Thomas Gaisford, 4 vols. (Oxford: Clarendon, 1814–1820), III 190, and reads as follows: μὴ κακὰ κερδαίνειν: μὴ κακὰ κέρδη θέλε κερδαίνειν. τὰ κακὰ κέρδη ἴσα ἄταις, ἀντὶ τοῦ ζημίαις, διὰ γὰρ τὴν αἰσχροκέρδειαν ἔσθ' ὅτε μείζοσι ζημίαις ἐνίσχονται ἄνθρωποι.

³ In ibid., 217–18, Gaisford gives the following two scholia: ... ᾿Αεὶ δ' ὁ ἀμβολιεργὸς ἀνὴρ, ἤγουν ὁ τὸ ἔργον ἀναβαλλόμενος, τὸ ὠφέλιμον δηλονότι, βλάβαις καὶ ζημίαις ἐμπλέκεται. αἰεὶ δ' ἀμβολιεργὸς· διὰ τούτου σαφηνίζει τί καλεῖ ἔργον, ὅτι τὸ ὠφελοῦν ὡς ἔμπροσθεν εἴπομεν, εἴπερ ὁ ἀμβολιεργὸς ἀνὴρ ἀεὶ ἐν ταῖς ζημίαις ἄλλαις ἐξ ἄλλων γίνεται. Διότι γὰρ πᾶν ἔργον ὠφέλιμον, ὅστις ἀναβολαῖς μὴ ἐπὶ τούτῳ χρῆται, τῆς ἀπ' αὐτοῦ ὠφελείας οὐ στέρεται· τῶν δὲ μοχθηρῶν ἔργων αἱ ἀναβολαὶ χρήσιμοι.

For this and the preceding passage, see the remarks of Bremer, *Hamartia*, pp. 112–13.

⁴ See *Suppliants* 468 and *Libation-Bearers* 339.

5 The scholion, in *Poetae minores Graeci*, ed. Gaisford, III 407, says as much: ἕπεται ἡ βλάβη τῇ δυσνομίᾳ. This is followed by F. A. Paley, *The Epics of Hesiod* (London: Whittaker, 1861), ad loc. Friedrich Solmsen, *Hesiod and Aeschylus* (Ithaca, N.Y.: Cornell University Press, 1949), seems to contradict himself, understanding ἄτη correctly, as "infatuation," on p. 29, but taking it to mean "ruin" on p. 97. He also seems to restrict the meaning of συνήθεας ἀλλήλησιν unduly by applying it only to Δυσνομία and Ἄτη.

6 The complete genealogy of Ἄτη as given by Hesiod is: χάος (116), Νύξ (123) Ἔρις (225), Ἄτη (230).

7 For reasons to doubt Hesiod as the author, see M. L. West, "Hesiod," *OCD*, 511. Though uncertain, the date of the *Shield* is usually given as the late-seventh or early-sixth century.

8 See chap. 1, note 6.

9 See above, p. 8.

10 ἄτη does not appear in what remains of: Alcman, Anacreon, Anaximander, Anaximenes, Bacchylides, Callinus, Heraclitus, Hipponax, Homeric Hymns, Mimnermus, Parmenides, Sappho, Simonides, Stesichorus, Pythagoras, Tyrtaeus, or Xenophanes. There is, however, one indirect reference to ἄτη which has come down to us from the seventh century. It is a tetrameter of Archilochus' which, according to Clement of Alexandria, is a variation on *Iliad* 9.116. In a section on plagiarism in his Στρωματεῖς, Clement writes at 6.2.1: ὁ Ἀρχίλοχος τὸ Ὁμηρικὸν ἐκεῖνο μεταφέρων (*Iliad* 9.116) "ἀασάμην οὐδ' αὐτὸς ἀναίνομαι, ἀντὶ νυ πολλῶν," ὧδε πως γράφει· Ἤμβλακον, καὶ πού τιν' ἄλλον ἡ ἀάτη κιχήσατο. Since this is clearly dependent on the *Iliad* passage, there is no reason to take it any differently; the meaning remains "folly."

As was the case with Archilochus, indirect testimony exists that Thales also used ἄτη. Hermann Diels collected citations from Plato (*Charmides* 164D), Stobaeus, and the Suda, all to the effect that Thales employed the proverb ἐγγύα, πάρα δ' ἄτα (*Fragmente der Vorsokratiker*, 6th ed., 3 vols. [Berlin: Weidmann, 1952], I 62, 64, 73, respectively).

11 Ivan M. Linforth, *Solon the Athenian* (Berkeley: University of California Press, 1919), p. 169. translates ἄτη as "misfortune." See also W. Jaeger, "Solons Eunomie," *Sitzungsberichte der Preussischen Akademie der Wissenschaften* (1926), 75–77, and the discussion in Bremer, *Hamartia*, p. 114 and note 4.

12 As will be evident from the discussion of 13.75 in the next chapter, Zeus is also directly responsible for ἄτη in Solon.

13 Ernst Diehl (*Anthologia lyrica Graeca*, 3rd ed., 4 vols. [Leipzig: Teubner, 1949], 1.4.402, in his Fragment 35a, attributes ἄτη to Alcaeus. But different editors have restored this fragment so variously that it cannot validly be taken into account here.

14 Cf. C. M. Bowra, *Greek Lyric Poetry from Alcman to Simonides*, 2nd rev. ed. (Oxford: Clarendon, 1961), pp. 135ff., esp. pp. 151–52, for a treatment of this fragment. Cf. also Denys Page, *Sappho and Alcaeus: An Introduction to the Study of Ancient Lesbian Poetry* (Oxford: Clarendon, 1955), who groups "the political poems" of Alcaeus in one section and treats his relationship to Pittacus passim.

15 Page, *Sappho and Alcaeus*, p. 235, translates ἄτη as "ruin."

16 See Bowra, *Greek Lyric Poetry*, pp. 250–57, for a discussion of the attribution.

17 See above, pp. 14–15.

18 Cf. C. M. Bowra, "Theognis," OCD, 1057.

19 See below, p. 36. Herodotus 1.32.6 offers a parallel for ἄτη in this sense. See also the discussion of *Suppliants* 444 in Appendix C.

20 See above, p. 24.

21 This passage is ably discussed by M. S. Silk, *Interaction in Poetic Imagery* (London & New York: Cambridge University Press, 1974), pp. 123, 125.

22 Cf. p. 24, above. C. M. Bowra, *Early Greek Elegists* (Cambridge: Harvard University Press, 1938), p. 159, translates ἄτη in this sense.

23 *Iliad* 9.115 and 10.391 (see pp. 17 and 16, above); *Works and Days* 216 (see p. 36, below).

24 So in *Iliad* 24.480 ἄτη, in the singular, means "folly" (see p. 17, above). And in *Iliad* 19.270 and *Works and Days* 352 and 413, ἄται, in the plural, means something other than "folly" (see above, pp. 13–14 and 24–25).

25 See above, p. 16. Bremer, *Hamartia*, p. 114, is taken more with the connection of ἄτη with ἀμπλακία.

26 The contemporaneity of Pindar and Aeschylus should be understood in a general sense, since the precise dating of many of Pindar's odes, and of some of Aeschylus' plays, is quite controversial.

27 There are two other *loci* where the MS tradition is uncertain whether ἄτη should be read: *Pythian* 2.82 and 11.55. See any critical edition for the MS evidence and the various emendations proposed. See also R. W. B. Burton's *Pindar's Pythian Odes: Essays in Interpretation* (London: Oxford University Press, 1962), pp. 130 (with references to Wilamowitz and Schroeder) and 74–75, respectively, for commentary on the two passages.

28 For a good treatment of Pindar's dependence on and discrepancy with Hesiod's *Eoiae*, see ibid., pp. 82–84.

3

Ὄ ΛΒΟΣ, ΚΟΡΟΣ, ῝ΥΒΡΙΣ, AND ῎ΑΤΗ

ONE OF THE COMMONPLACES OF CRITICISM with regard to Greek thought is that there existed a canonical tetralogy ὄλβος, κόρος, ὕβρις, and ἄτη, which was inexorably operative in human lives. Thus Basil Gildersleeve, in commenting on Pindar's thought, writes:

> The next point suggested by the first Olympian is the representative position of Pindar as the expounder of Greek ethics. Is Pindar speaking for himself or for his people? Many of his thoughts are not his own. They are fragments of the popular Hellenic catechism, and they became remarkable in Pindar partly by the mode of presentation, partly by the evident heartiness with which he accepts the national creed. So in v. 56, and P.2,28, we find a genealogy which was as popular with the Greeks as Sin and Death in the Christian system. Ὄλβος — Κόρος — ῝Υβρις — ῎Ατη. The prosperity that produces pride and fulness of bread culminates in overweening insolence and outrage, and brings on itself mischief sent from heaven.[1]

In his excellent work on the *Pythians*, a more modern critic, R. W. B. Burton, also presupposes the inexorable tetralogy. He comments on *Pythian* 2.28:

> There is no hint of an intermediate forgiveness, an incident which was perhaps not strictly relevant to the poet's purpose and might have diverted attention from the uninterrupted cycle of ὄλβος, κόρος, ὕβρις, ἄτη.[2]

And even more recently, J. M. Bremer in his study of *Hamartia* states:

> Several times Pindar uses the word *ate* when a hero(-ine) meets disaster after doing wrong. The context, however, is un-homeric in that continual stress is laid upon the connexion between guilt and punishment. The line of thought is most fully expressed in the sequence *olbos — koros — hybris — (amplakia —) ate*: wealth and surfeit lead to wantonness; thus man commits a misdeed and meets with disaster as a heaven-ordained punishment.[3]

Nor is Pindar the only fifth-century author in whose work critics find the ὄλβος, κόρος, ὕβρις, ἄτη tetralogy. Commenting on the first stasimon of Aeschylus' *Agamemnon*, E. T. Owen alludes to "the age-old Ate doctrine."[4]

From these citations it is evident that a number of scholars believe that the Greeks habitually thought in terms of a fundamental and inexorable progression: ὄλβος, κόρος, ὕβρις, ἄτη. In this chapter we shall review the extant literary evidence and show that no such consecrated tetralogy appears. What do appear are three triads: ὄλβος, ὕβρις, and ἄτη; ὄλβος, κόρος, and ἄτη; and κόρος, ὕβρις, and ἄτη. Furthermore, this supposed "traditional" doctrine does not appear, even in its attenuated triadic form, until Hesiod and completely disappears after Aeschylus.

ΟΛΒΟΣ (῾Ο ᾽ΕΣΘΛΟΣ, ῾Ο ΠΛΟΥΤΟΣ), ῞ΥΒΡΙΣ, ᾽ΑΤΗ

Hesiod

Nowhere are ὄλβος, ὕβρις, and ἄτη linked in the Homeric poems. The first such association occurs in Hesiod's *Works and Days*:

> ῏Ω Πέρση, σὺ δ᾽ ἄκουε δίκης, μηδ᾽ ὕβριν ὄφελλε·
> ὕβρις γάρ τε κακὴ δειλῷ βροτῷ· οὐδὲ μὲν ἐσθλὸς
> ῥηιδίως φερέμεν δύναται, βαρύθει δέ θ᾽ ὑπ᾽ αὐτῆς   215
> ἐγκύρσας ἀάτῃσιν· ὁδὸς δ᾽ ἑτέρηφι παρελθεῖν
> κρείσσων ἐς τὰ δίκαια· δίκη δ᾽ ὑπὲρ ὕβριος ἴσχει
> ἐς τέλος ἐξελθοῦσι· παθὼν δέ τε νήπιος ἔγνω.

Several points of this text are of importance for the present study. First, the subject is described, not as ὄλβιος, but as ἐσθλός. The ἐσθλός is contrasted with the δειλός in the typical fashion of an aristocratic society. But there is no question of ὄλβος. Hesiod's target in this passage is ὕβρις, which, he makes quite clear, can afflict the δειλός as well as the ἐσθλός. Hence, there can be no necessary connection postulated between ὄλβος and ὕβρις. Secondly, although ἄτη is linked with ὕβρις, the order of their occurrence should be noted carefully: *after* one has encountered ἄτη, one is weighed down with ὕβρις, not vice versa. Thirdly, the use of the plural ἀάτῃσιν is quite rare,[5] and the meaning applicable to the Homeric passages which employ the plural, that is, "follies," or "false hopes," suits the Hesiodic context admirably. Indeed, ἄτη could hardly mean "ruin" or "disaster" in this context since the ἐσθλός is struggling with ὕβρις, something which would not be likely for a man who has already encountered ruin.[6]

Solon

Solon is the next author is whose extant work ὕβρις and ἄτη are associated. The pertinent passage occurs in fragment 13:

πλοῦτον δ' ὃν μὲν δῶσι θεοί, παραγίγνεται ἀνδρὶ
ἔμπεδος ἐκ νεάτου πυθμένος ἐς κορυφήν·   10
ὃν δ' ἄνδρες τιμῶσιν ὑφ' ὕβριος, οὐ κατὰ κόσμον
ἔρχεται, ἀλλ' ἀδίκοις ἔργμασι πειθόμενος
οὐκ ἐθέλων ἕπεται, ταχέως δ' ἀναμίσγεται ἄτηι·
ἀρχῆς δ' ἐξ ὀλίγης γίγνεται ὥστε πυρός,
φλαύρη μὲν τὸ πρῶτον, ἀνιηρὴ δὲ τελευτᾶι·   15
οὐ γὰρ δὴ< ν> θνητοῖς ὕβριος ἔργα πέλει. . . .

Of special interest in this passage is the appearance for the first time of πλοῦτος in connection with ὕβρις and ἄτη. πλοῦτος is not ὄλβος though they are the same in this context, as the mention of ὄλβος in line 3 makes clear.

But contrary to what is found in Hesiod, ὕβρις precedes ἄτη. The ἄτη which quickly becomes mixed with the ill-gained wealth is "folly." Not only is this consistent with the other instances of Solon's use of ἄτη, but the fact that the person involved in this fragment possesses wealth precludes the notion that ἄτη could mean a "ruin" already accomplished.[7]

Pindar

Chronologically, the next extant piece of evidence is Pindar's second *Pythian*, about which Gildersleeve's and Burton's comments are made. A careful reading of the text, however, substantiates the contention that even Pindar employs only the triad ὄλβος, ὕβρις, and ἄτη, not the supposed tetralogy including κόρος. The passage in question is:

ἔμαθε δὲ σαφές. εὐμενέσσι γὰρ παρὰ Κρονίδαις   25
γλυκὺν ἑλὼν βίοτον, μακρὸν οὐχ ὑπέμεινεν ὄλ-
βον, μαινομέναις φρασίν
Ἥρας ὅτ' ἐράσσατο, τὰν Διὸς εὐναὶ λάχον
πολυγαθέες· ἀλλά νιν ὕβρις εἰς ἀνάταν ὑπεράφανον
ὦρσεν· τάχα δὲ παθὼν ἐοικότ' ἀνὴρ
ἐξαίρετον ἕλε μόχθον.   30

For the first time we have the precise verbal elements under investigation: ὄλβος (neither ἐσθλός as found in Hesiod, nor πλοῦτος as in Solon), ὕβρις, and ἄτη.[8] As in Solon, ὕβρις precedes ἄτη. In this instance it would seem not to exceed the evidence to state that ὕβρις is responsible for ἄτη.

But κόρος is still missing from the supposed tetralogy. And Burton twists the text in order to introduce it when he writes: "Ixion enjoyed a happy life among the sons of Cronus (ὄλβος); he could not withstand it for long (κόρος); he committed sin (ὕβρις), was driven into ἄτη and met his deserts."⁹ κόρος simply is not in Pindar's text.

Yet the real source of misunderstanding in this passage, as indeed in the entire question of the supposed tetralogy, is the misinterpretation of the concept of ἄτη. For the tetralogy to represent some sort of ineluctable process whereby happiness leads to satiety which in its turn leads to proud insolence and then to ἄτη, ἄτη must regularly be understood to mean "ruin," "destruction," or "calamity," i.e., the objective state which is the end product of the downward process.

But in the Hesiodic and Solonic texts already investigated, as well as in the Pindaric passage now under consideration, ἄτη is, not the objective state of "ruin," "destruction," or "calamity," but the subjective state of metaphorical "blindness," "infatuation," or "folly." That this is also true of *Pythian* 2.28 is clear from three indications. The first is the general erotic context of the passage, which is concerned with Ixion's love for Hera. Such contexts involving ἄτη in Homer consistently employ the subjective sense.¹⁰ Secondly, the epithet ὑπεράφανον ("arrogant") simply does not make sense when applied to the objective state of "ruin," "destruction," or "calamity." And, finally, Ixion's ruin is expressly mentioned in the word μόχθον in line 30.

Aeschylus

There are two Aeschylean passages which exhibit the ὄλβος, ὕβρις, ἄτη trilogy.¹¹ The first occurs in the third epeisodion of the *Persians*, in Darius' prophecy of the disaster at Plataea:

ὕβρις γὰρ ἐξανθοῦσ' ἐκάρπωσεν στάχυν
ἄτης, ὅθεν πάγκλαυτον ἐξαμᾷ θέρος.
τοιαῦθ' ὁρῶντες τῶνδε τἀπιτίμια
μέμνησθ' Ἀθηνῶν Ἑλλάδος τε, μηδέ τις
ὑπερφρονήσας τὸν παρόντα δαίμονα   825
ἄλλων ἐρασθεὶς ὄλβον ἐκχέῃ μέγαν.

The absence of κόρος in this passage is very instructive, for lines 824–826 make it quite clear that ὕβρις and ἄτη can afflict one who, far from reaching the point of satiety with regard to ὄλβος, is, as a matter of fact, tempted in the opposite direction — that is, to seek still more. Such, indeed, was the case with Xerxes. But this concept is radically different from the supposed tetralogy which would envision ὕβρις and ἄτη setting in only after κόρος. κόρος is irrelevant here.

Furthermore, the meaning of ἄτη in this passage is of significance in another respect for the present investigation, for although ἄτη here is sometimes interpreted in the objective sense of "ruin" or "sin," there are two excellent reasons for interpreting it in the subjective sense of "blindness," "infatuation," or "folly."

The first argument is based on the use of ὕβρις and ὄλβος together with ἄτη. In the three pre-Aeschylean texts exhibiting the same triad which we have examined thus far, ἄτη consistently means the subjective state of "blindness," "infatuation," or "folly," and such a strong pattern of usage affords strong grounds for expecting the same meaning in *Persians* 822.

This tentative conclusion is confirmed by a second argument: the metaphor of growth employed in the passage. As Broadhead appositely notes:

> . . . ὅθεν introduces a clause that describes the *final* stage along the road to ruin; what precedes describes the earlier stages, first the blossoming, then the ripening of the ear, which represents the full development of ὕβρις, accelerated by the Heaven-sent infatuation (ἄτη). When the ὕβρις-possessed man becomes blindly infatuated, he is unable to see the inevitable result of his actions: he reaps a harvest of calamity.[12]

Not only is this interpretation correct in itself, since it both takes into account the progressive development clearly asserted in the text and denies the poetically less forceful repetition whereby ruin would be both the crop and the harvest, but it is substantiated by other uses of ἄτη in metaphors of growth. So, for example, in Solon's phrase ἄτης ἄνθεα φυόμενα (4.35), ἄτη means "blindness," not "ruin."[13] And in another passage by Aeschylus himself, *Suppliants* 110, in which the metaphor is one of growth, ἄτη means "infatuation" rather than "ruin."

Yet there is one Aeschylean passage in which ἄτη in association with ὄλβος and ὕβρις does mean "ruin," "destruction," or "calamity" — in the third antistrophe and the fourth strophe of the second stasimon of the *Agamemnon*:

ἀντ. παλαίφατος δ' ἐν βροτοῖς γέρων λόγος   750
    τέτυκται μέγαν τελεσθέντα φωτὸς ὄλβον
    τεκνοῦσθαι μηδ' ἄπαιδα θνῄσκειν,
    ἐκ δ' ἀγαθᾶς τύχας γένει   755
    βλαστάνειν ἀκόρεστον οἰζύν.
    δίχα δ' ἄλλων μονόφρων εἰ-

μί· τὸ δυσσεβὲς γὰρ ἔργον
μετὰ μὲν πλείονα τίκτει,
σφετέραι δ' εἰκότα γένναι·   760
οἴκων γὰρ εὐθυδίκων
καλλίπαις πότμος αἰεί.
στρ. φιλεῖ δὲ τίκτειν ὕβρις μὲν παλαι-
        ὰ νεάζουσαν ἐν κακοῖς βροτῶν   765
        ὕβριν, τότ' ἢ τόθ' †ὅταν† τὸ κύριον μόληι
        †νεαρὰ φάους† κότον
        δαίμονά †τε τόν†, ἄμαχον ἀπόλεμον ἀνίερον
        θράσος, μέλαιναν μελάθροισιν ἄταν,   770
        εἰδομέναν τοκεῦσιν.

Though lines 768 and 769 are textually very corrupt,[14] and 770–771 present further problems involving the phrase μέλαιναν . . . ἄταν, εἰδομέναν,[15] there is no question that ἄτη should be read here and a clear indication that, whatever detailed restoration of the text is adopted, ἄτη in line 770 means "ruin," "destruction," or "calamity."

First, ἄτη here is used with two of the customary concomitants for its meaning as "ruin," "destruction," or "calamity." The first is its application to a group — namely, μελάθροισιν (770) — rather than to an individual;[16] the second, its conjunction with some other concept of evil. In the present instance, there are two such concepts: νεάζουσαν ὕβριν (765–766) and θράσος (770).[17]

Secondly, strophe δ is a development of lines 758–760, just as antistrophe δ (772–781) is a development of lines 761–762. Consequently ἄτη in 770 (whether synonymous with νεάζουσαν ὕβριν according to Fraenkel's interpretation, or explanatory of it according to Hermann's) is related to ὕβρις παλαιὰ as πλείονα (759) is related to δυσσεβὲς (758). Just, therefore, as there is a question of impious *deeds* in 758–760, so in 763–772 there is a question of *acts* of insolence resulting in objective ruin, not merely of mental attitudes.

Thirdly, since this passage, as Knox has observed,[18] manifests parallels with and echoes of the second stasimon, it would be strange to find ἄτη in line 770 used in a sense different from that in lines 730 and 735,[19] and since in these two places it means "ruin," "destruction," or "calamity," this is a very good indication that it means the same in 770 as well.

Now that the meaning of ἄτη in 770 has been established, it is possible to focus on the ὄλβος, ὕβρις, ἄτη triad. The most obvious fact is that it is still a triad, since κόρος is not used. Indeed, unless one is predisposed to find κόρος in them, lines 750–756 could much more readily be interpreted as an expression of any one of several proverbial (παλαί-φατος δ' ἐν βροτοῖς γέρων λόγος τέτυκται) Greek concepts: the inexorability of the καιρός, or μηδὲν ἄγαν, or τὸ μέσος. In short, not only is κόρος not present in the Aeschylean text, but the burden of proof lies with those who would introduce it by interpretation.[20]

Yet there is something new in this passage. The chorus go out of their way to state that their opinion is different from others'. And it is precisely here that the meaning of ἄτη in the objective sense of "ruin," "destruction," or "calamity" becomes operative, for in all the extant ὄλβος, ὕβρις, ἄτη texts prior to this, ἄτη means the subjective state of "blindness," "infatuation," or "folly." Here ἄτη is used objectively, as lines 758–759 make explicit. The old opinion was that prosperity bred disaster; the chorus' new opinion is that an evil deed breeds disaster. Hence, there is a parallel between οἰζύς and ἄτη. Thus at *Agamemnon* 770 Aeschylus introduces a new meaning into the triad of ὄλβος, ὕβρις, and ἄτη.

ὌΛΒΟΣ (ΠΛΟΥΤΟΣ), ΚΟΡΟΣ, ἌΤΗ

In our evidence, there exists a second triad, ὄλβος, κόρος, and ἄτη, but this grouping is less frequent than the former, appearing only three times in the extant literature.

Solon

Solon is our earliest witness for this triad. The end of Fragment 13 reads:

> πλούτου δ' οὐδὲν τέρμα πεφασμένον ἀνδράσι κεῖται·
> οἳ γὰρ νῦν ἡμέων πλεῖστον ἔχουσι βίον,
> διπλάσιον σπεύδουσι· τίς ἂν κορέσειεν ἅπαντας;
> κέρδεά τοι θνητοῖς ὤπασαν ἀθάνατοι,
> ἄτη δ' ἐξ αὐτῶν ἀναφαίνεται, ἣν ὁπότε Ζεὺς   75
> πέμψῃι τεισομένην, ἄλλοτε ἄλλος ἔχει.

As in the Solon passage discussed earlier, πλοῦτος is used instead of ὄλβος. And instead of the noun κόρος, Solon employs the verb κορέν-νυμι. Hence, verbally the triad is not exactly derived from the supposed tetralogy.

There are three indications, two textual and one external, that the ἄτη sent by Zeus is, not "ruin," but "blindness." First, the ἄτη results from κέρδεα, a situation scarcely appropriate for someone who is supposed to be ruined. Secondly, in lines 67–70, which immediately precede this passage, Solon has spoken of ἄτη as contrasted with οὐ προνοήσας and ἀφροσύνης. The context, therefore, points to the subjective dispositions involved.

Finally, the derivative passage in Theognis confirms the subjective interpretation. In his first elegy, at lines 227–232, Theognis adapts Solon as follows:

πλούτου δ' οὐδὲν τέρμα πεφασμένον ἀνθρώποισιν·
οἳ γὰρ νῦν ἡμῶν πλεῖστον ἔχουσι βίον,
διπλάσιον σπεύδουσι. τίς ἂν κορέσειεν ἅπαντας;
χρήματά τοι θνητοῖς γίνεται ἀφροσύνη,   230
ἄτη δ' ἐξ αὐτῆς ἀναφαίνεται, ἣν ὁπότε Ζεὺς
πέμψηι τειρομένοις, ἄλλοτε ἄλλος ἔχει.

The dependence on Solon is so obvious that this cannot be considered a separate occurrence of the ὄλβος, κόρος, ἄτη triad. But the ἀφροσύνη in line 230, from which (ἐξ αὐτῆς) ἄτη comes, is an excellent indication of how Theognis understood ἄτη in the Solonic passage: namely, as "blindness" or "folly."

Pindar

The second occurrence of the ὄλβος, κόρος, ἄτη triad is found in Pindar's first *Olympian*, in a passage discussing Tantalus:

εἰ δὲ δή τιν' ἄνδρα θνατὸν Ὀλύμπου σκοποί
ἐτίμασαν, ἦν Τάνταλος οὗτος· ἀλ-   55
λὰ γὰρ καταπέψαι
μέγαν ὄλβον οὐκ ἐδυνάσθη, κόρῳ δ' ἕλεν
ἄταν ὑπέροπλον, ἅν τοι πατὴρ ὕπερ
κρέμασε καρτερὸν αὐτῷ λίθον,
τὸν αἰεὶ μενοινῶν κεφαλᾶς βαλεῖν
εὐφροσύνας ἀλᾶται.

There is no mention of ὕβρις,[21] but for the first time a causal connection is drawn between κόρος and ἄτη. The ἄτη in this instance is the objective state of "calamity," as is made explicit by the next clause, which specifies the "calamity": namely, Zeus' imposition of the rock over Tantalus' head.

Aeschylus

The final text for this triad is the conclusion of the first strophe and the beginning of the antistrophe of the first stasimon in Aeschylus' *Agamemnon*. In highly figurative language the chorus sing:

> οὐ γάρ ἐστιν ἔπαλξις
> πλούτου πρὸς κόρον ἀνδρὶ
> λακτίσαντι μέγαν Δίκας
> βωμὸν εἰς ἀφάνειαν.

ἀντ. βιᾶται δ᾽ ἁ τάλαινα Πειθώ,   385
> προβούλου παῖς ἄφερτος ἄτας.
> ἄκος δὲ πᾶν μάταιον. οὐκ ἐκρύφθη,
> πρέπει δέ, φῶς αἰνολαμπές, σίνος·

There is mention of πλοῦτος (not ὄλβος once again), κόρος, and ἄτη, but not of ὕβρις, though it might be possible to see ὕβρις in the action described in lines 382–384. Even so, the ode is not a forthright expression of the supposed ὄλβος, κόρος, ὕβρις, ἄτη tetralogy; for δίκη and πειθώ are also involved, and their relationship to the other terms renders the entire picture quite complex. Not only is this not an instance of the supposed tetralogy, but ἄτη has consistently been misinterpreted here[22] in spite of three very solid reasons for interpreting it in the subjective sense.

First, the context makes the objective sense highly improbable. The individual described is subject to ἄτη (386), πειθώ (385), κόρος (382), and ἀδικία (375); but the root of them all is ἄτη, for as the genealogical metaphor of lines 385–386 makes clear, it is ἄτη which lays the man open to the persuasion of πειθώ. To be sure, such a man is headed for destruction, but that destruction is the result of, not identical with, the ἄτη which blinds him and results in the pursuit of his disastrous course, that is, ἀδικία.

Aeschylus expresses an analogous idea elsewhere, and that is the second reason for interpreting ἄτη here in the subjective sense. Fraenkel appositely states the parallel:

> The description is given in *Pers.* 97ff. of how Ἄτη carries out her acts of παρασαίνειν . . . on man, whom she entangles in the net, and how all further evil proceeds from this. To this action πείθειν corresponds; thus we can well understand the conception which calls "wretched Peitho" the child of Ate. As a result of ἄτη Peitho overpowers a man by persuading him that he is obliged to do what it is not right for him to do, and at the same time talks him out of his resistance. This is the situation of Agamemnon as it is shown in his words 206ff. and subsequently explained (217ff.).[23]

The third reason for interpreting ἄτη in line 386 in the subjective
sense is the analogous repetition of the same idea in the epode of this
first stasimon. Just as the chorus sing of wealth (lines 374ff.) in the
first strophe and antistrophe, so in the epode they advert to the good
news of Troy's fall (475–477) but warn of the possibility that this may
be a delusion (ψύθος, 478). The irony is pointed and far-reaching, for
Paris' ἄτη ultimately brought him destruction, despite his vast wealth,
and the good news of the success against Troy ultimately proves a
delusion not only to Agamemnon but to Clytemnestra as well.[24]

ΚΟΡΟΣ, ΎΒΡΙΣ, ΆΤΗ

There is only a single example of the third triadic structure. It is the
last occurrence of ἄτη in the fragments of Solon, fragment 4, line 35,
and occurs in a passage in high praise of the effects of Εὐνομίη:

> ταῦτα διδάξαι θυμὸς Ἀθηναίους με κελεύει,   30
> ὡς κακὰ πλεῖστα πόλει Δυσνομίη παρέχει·
> Εὐνομίη δ' εὔκοσμα καὶ ἄρτια πάντ' ἀποφαίνει,
> καὶ θαμὰ τοῖς ἀδίκοις ἀμφιτίθησι πέδας·
> τραχέα λειαίνει, παύει κόρον, ὕβριν ἀμαυροῖ,
> αὐαίνει δ' ἄτης ἄνθεα φυόμενα. . . .   35

The passage, on the whole quite evocative of Hesiod's *Theogony*
226ff., presents the first occurrence of κόρος, ὕβρις, and ἄτη in precisely
that order. ὄλβος is missing, but the other three members of the supposed tetralogy appear together for the first and only time in extant
Greek literature.

The metaphor of Εὐνομίη withering the growing blossoms of ἄτη
is striking, and if ἄτη is taken to mean "folly," this metaphor is consonant with the others in the passage; but if ἄτη should be taken to
mean "ruin," the image of growing blossoms of ruin would be much
too strong. Once again, therefore, Solon uses ἄτη to signify "blindness"
or "folly."[25]

CONCLUSION

Thus, a study of the extant literary evidence leads to five definite conclusions about the supposed ὄλβος, κόρος, ὕβρις, ἄτη tetralogy.

First, the tetralogy simply does not exist. In its place we find three
triads, none of which occurs in Homer: namely, ὄλβος, ὕβρις and

ἄτη in five instances: ὄλβος, κόρος, and ἄτη in three; and κόρος, ὕβρις and ἄτη once. Not only does the tetralogy not exist in our evidence, but the relative infrequency of the three triads lends no support to the common view which sees them as a central doctrine of Greek thought.

Secondly, even on the verbal level there is little evidence for the conclusion that ὄλβος, κόρος, ὕβρις, and ἄτη was a set formula. Perhaps the most graphic way to demonstrate this would be with the following chart, which incorporates the nine passages in the order investigated in this chapter:

	ὄλβος	κόρος	ὕβρις	ἄτη
Hesiod, *Works and Days* 213–218	ἐσθλός	No	x	x
Solon 13.9–16	πλοῦτος	No	x	x
Pindar, *Pythian* 2.25–31	x	No	x	x
Aeschylus, *Persians* 816–826	x	No	x	x
Aeschylus, *Agamemnon* 750–771	x	No	x	x
Solon 13.71–76	πλοῦτος	κορέννυμι	No	x
Pindar, *Olympian* 1.54–59	x	x	No	x
Aeschylus, *Agamemnon* 381–388	πλοῦτος	x	No	x
Solon 4.30–39	No	x	x	x

The discrepancies revealed by this diagram should be enough to demonstrate that, whatever else might be said about ὄλβος, κόρος, ὕβρις, and ἄτη, they were in no legitimate sense "consecrated" pieces of terminology.

Thirdly, even within the triads there is no evidence that any one of them was considered as an ineluctable process rooted in necessary connections between the terms. The evidence points in the opposite direction. So in Hesiod, *Works and Days* 213–218, ἄτη precedes ὕβρις, a fact which would be impossible if ὕβρις *caused* ἄτη.

Fourthly — and this is perhaps the root difficulty of many of the misinterpretations in this whole question — ἄτη is most frequently used, not in the objective sense of "ruin," "destruction," or "calamity," but in the subjective sense of metaphorical "blindness," "folly," or "infatuation." This is the case in seven of the nine pertinent texts: viz., Hesiod, *Works and Days* 213–218; Solon 13.9–16, 71–76, and 4.30–39; Pindar, *Pythian* 2.25–31; Aeschylus, *Persians* 816–826 and *Agamemnon* 381–388. Thus, in the great majority of passages, ὄλβος in conjunction with *either* κόρος *or* ὕβρις (but not both) is seen as leading, not to "ruin" or "destruction," but to "blindness" or "folly." This fact will be most significant in the subsequent chapters on Greek tragedy, and it is perhaps rather on the consequences of this point that future studies might more profitably focus their attention than on the non-existent but supposedly inexorable tetralogy.

Finally, not even the three triads discussed in this chapter ever appear after Aeschylus. The doctrine, if it is one, completely disappears in Sophocles, Euripides, and all later authors.

NOTES

¹ *Pindar: The Olympian and Pythian Odes* (New York: Harper & Brothers, 1885; repr. New York: Arno, 1979), p. xxxi.

² *Pindar's Pythian Odes*, p. 116.

³ P. 115.

⁴ *The Harmony of Aeschylus* (Toronto: Clarke, Irwin, 1952), p. 72. For a slightly different version of the supposed "moral formula," see S. M. Adams, *Sophocles the Playwright* (Toronto: University of Toronto Press, 1957), p. 11; and C. M. Bowra, *Sophoclean Tragedy* (Oxford: Clarendon, 1944; repr. 1965), pp. 31–32. The latter two are particularly misleading because, as the present chapter will show, not even the triadic form appears in Sophocles.

⁵ Of the twenty-six occurrences of ἄτη in Homer, the plural is used only three times: *Iliad* 9.115, 10.391, and 19.270.

⁶ Paley, *Epics of Hesiod*, ad loc., mistakenly understands ἀάτῃσιν to refer to "the misfortunes enumerated inf. v. 239 sqq." Similarly, Bremer, *Hamartia*, p. 112, whose fundamental error is in misinterpreting the sequence and making ἄτη follow ὕβρις, which is *not* what Hesiod says.

⁷ This is the understanding of Bowra, *Early Greek Elegists*, pp. 93–95, 97–98; and of Linforth, *Solon the Athenian*, pp. 108 and esp. 165, where he translates ἄτη as "blind folly." Solmsen seems to contradict himself on this point: on p. 111 of his *Hesiod and Aeschylus*, he seems to understand ἄτη in this sense, yet on p. 107 he takes it to mean "disaster bred of infatuation." For the reasons given, it is necessary once again to disagree with Bremer, *Hamartia*, p. 114, who sees ἄτη as "punishment."

⁸ Pindar is quite late for the first appearance of a dictum from "the popular Hellenic catechism" or a supposed "age-old Ate doctrine."

⁹ *Pindar's Pythian Odes*, p. 116.

¹⁰ There are five such passages: *Iliad* 3.100, 6.356, 24.28, and *Odyssey* 4.261, 23.223. Bremer, *Hamartia*, p. 115, shows himself aware of this when he claims that ἄτη "denotes the foolishness of [Ixion's] desire to be Hera's lover," but changes when he adds "but points also to the subsequent disaster."

[11] A third Aeschylean passage, *Suppliants* 524–530, should be noted for the sake of completeness. But it really does not fall within the scope of the present investigation for several reasons. First, κόρος is not mentioned. Secondly, on the verbal level, the adjective ὄλβιος rather than the noun ὄλβος is used. Finally, and most importantly, in this passage there is such a clear distinction between Zeus, who is ὄλβιος, and men who possess ὕβρις and ἄτη that perhaps not even the champions of the supposed tetralogy would see its presence here.

[12] *The Persae of Aeschylus* (Cambridge: Cambridge University Press, 1960), p. 205.

[13] Incidentally, Solon's use of ἄτη as distinguished from the effects of εὐνομία is quite similar to Darius' use of ἄτη as distinguished from the effects of φρόνησις in the present passage. For a discussion of the Solon passage, see below, p. 44.

[14] As Eduard Fraenkel says (*Aeschylus: Agamemnon*, 3 vols. [Oxford: Clarendon, 1950; repr. 1962] II 352; in addition to the references given by Frankel, see also W. M. Edwards, "*Agamemnon* 767ff.," CR, 56 [1942], 41): "After μόληι begins one of the deeply-rooted corruptions I . . . mentioned on 374ff. . . . It seems pointless to discuss the various attempts at restoration. . . ." Fraenkel is echoing Wilamowitz' opinion: "'The alterations certainly are numerous though slight; the archetype must have been difficult to read, and the Byzantines must have tried to patch it up; . . . here the text of our MSS is so uncertain that corruptions may have taken place which make powerless any criticism that is more than mere trifling'" (Ulrich von Wilamowitz-Moellendorff, *Aeschylos: Interpretationen* [Berlin: Weidmann, 1914], pp. 197–98, as quoted in *Aeschylus: Agamemnon*, ed. Fraenkel, II 352). In view of such skepticism on the part of these two distinguished philologists, it would be rash to try to vindicate any given reading for the two lines in question. Perhaps it is best to accept Fraenkel's reconstruction, with the same hesitation with which he proposes it, as a tentative working basis from which to discuss the two lines. Fraenkel writes: "I regard the following as a possible, though in detail by no means certain, arrangement of the text: †ὅταν† τὸ κύριον μόληι φάος, κότον νεώρη, δαίμονα τίταν, ἄμαχον, continuing with the MS reading" (ibid.).

[15] The problem here is to determine the number and case. The MSS have μελαίνας . . . ἄτας εἰδομέναν, with μελαίνας ἄτας construed as a genitive singular. Fraenkel tentatively adopts the suggestion of Auratus — namely, μέλαιναν ἄταν . . . (εἰδομέναν) — and remarks: "If we adopt it, the result is (assuming the correctness of the very hypothetical rearrangement of the preceding passage as suggested above) a satisfying articulation of the long series of accusatives that (768) follow on φάος, all in apposition to ὕβριν: we get first two parallel elements, κότον νεώρη and δαίμονα τίταν, then the longer element ἄμαχον ἀπόλεμον ἀνίερον θράσος, then after these preparatory periphrases the name of the daemon of evil..., μέλαιναν ... Ἄταν, and finally the closing element εἰδ. τοκ. which emphasizes once again the genealogical relationship by picking up the thought of 760. But this rearrangement cannot be regarded as certain" (ibid., 353).

[16] Fraenkel, ibid., 353–54, remarks: "With regard to the dative μελάθροισιν, many editors have taken it as locative, e.g. Nägelsbach and Wecklein (so too Connington, who, however, understands μελ. μελάθ. ἄτας to mean 'in the halls of black Ate'; which seems to me quite impossible). It is much more natural to take μελάθ. as a genuine dative (so e.g. Schütz, Bothe, Headlam), 'as an Ate for the house,' similar e.g. to 733 ἄμαχον ἄλγος οἰκέταις. To prove that μέλαθρα can stand not only in the

concrete sense of the building but also of the house and its inhabitants (with reference to their destiny) in the same way as οἶκος etc. it is sufficient to compare *Ag.* 1575, *Cho.* 1065."

[17] If Fraenkel's explanation for the passage is accepted, then ἄτη would also be used in connection with κότον in 767. Furthermore, the suggestion of Bernard M. W. Knox, "The Lion in the House (*Agamemnon* 717-36)," CPh, 47 (1952), 18, is probably also correct. In keeping with all the verbal echoes of the second antistrophe contained in the present passage, Knox would maintain that ἄμαχον in 769 recalls ἄμαχον ἄλγος of 733, in which case ἄλγος would be still another concept of evil to which ἄτη in 771 refers.

Bremer, *Hamartia*, p. 125, correctly emphasizes Aeschylus' insistence on "impious trespass and *hybris*" as the cause of evil rather than Troy's wealth.

[18] In "Lion in the House," 18, Knox writes: "The lioncub [of line 717] is a type of the ὕβρις νεάζουσα of the fourth strophe of the stasimon (763-70). Just as the lioncub, when the time comes, χρονισθείς, reveals the temper of its parents, ἀπέδειξεν ἦθος τὸ πρὸς τοκέων, so the new hybris, νεάζουσαν . . . ὕβριν, appears, when the time comes, ὅτε τὸ κύριον μόλῃ φάος τόκου, a spirit invincible, ἄμαχον (769), like the lioncub, ἄμαχον ἄλγος, black ruin for the house, μελαίνας μελάθροισιν Ἄτας, like the lioncub which is a priest of ruin, ἱερεύς τις ἄτας, and this black ruin, like the lioncub, resembles its parents, εἰδομένας τοκεῦσιν (771)."

[19] See below, p. 83, for a discussion of these passages.

[20] Nor is the presence of ἀκόρεστον in 756 enough to justify such an interpretation.

[21] Thus, Burton, in *Pindar's Pythian Odes*, pp. 116-17, is simply wrong in writing: "The process is familiar in Greek literature and may be paralleled exactly for Pindar by his treatment of the story of Tantalus in *Olympian* 1.55f." Similarly, Bremer, *Hamartia*, p. 115, is misleading when he discusses this passage immediately after his "olbos — koros — hybris — (amplakia) — ate" sequence quoted at the beginning of this chapter. The fact remains that ἄτη is not in Pindar's text.

[22] Herbert Weir Smyth, *Aeschylus* (2 vols. [London: Heinemann; Cambridge: Harvard University Press, 1933, 1938]), II 35, translates it as "destruction," and F. Fletcher, *Notes to the Agamemnon of Aeschylus* (Oxford: Blackwell, 1949), p. 18, has "doom." A. Y. Campbell's case in "The Fall of Paris: Aeschylus, *Agamemnon* 373-398," AAL, 28 (1948), 64-82, is built on three false premises: (*a*) that ἄφερτος, which is the reading of all the MSS, should be emended; (*b*) that πειθώ can mean "temptation" (cf. LSJ); and (*c*) that the reading at *Persians* 107-114, which is actually quite disputed, is unquestionably his emended version.

[23] *Aeschylus: Agamemnon*, II 201.

[24] There is another reason for interpreting ἄτη as "infatuation" in 386: namely, the general erotic context of the Paris–Helen myth which is spoken of in this ode and which was common to the five Homeric passages in which ἄτη means "infatuation." See note 10, above. The present passage, incidentally, adds irony to the reference to Thyestes' adultery in 1192.

For the application of 386 to Agamemnon, see R. F. Goheen, "Aspects of Dramatic Symbolism," AJP, 76 (1955), 126-32.

[25] Cf. Bowra, *Early Greek Elegists*, pp. 84-86, and Linforth, *Solon the Athenian*, p. 143, where he translates ἄτη as "wild delusions."

4

THE SUBJECTIVE CONCEPT OF ΆΤΗ
IN AESCHYLEAN TRAGEDY

As Aeschylus inherited the term ἄτη, then, it had appeared most often in his predecessors in its subjective sense of "blindness," "infatuation," or "folly"[1] — a sense which he continued to employ. This chapter will concern itself with an investigation of this usage, studying the continued development of the Greek literary tradition à propos of the term and noting the nuances added by the first of the great tragedians. A chronological consideration of the extant tragedies seems methodologically most proper.

PERSIANS

In his earliest extant tragedy, the *Persians*, Aeschylus employs ἄτη in the traditional, subjective sense in three passages, the first of which appears in the parodos:

στρ. δολόμητιν δ' ἀπάταν θεοῦ
τίς ἀνὴρ θνατὸς ἀλύξει;
τίς ὁ κραιπνῷ ποδὶ δηλή-
ματος εὐπιθοῦς ἀπᾴσσων;   110

ἀντ. φιλόφρων γὰρ παρασαίνει
βροτὸν εἰς ἄρκυας ἄτα,
τόθεν οὐκ ἔστιν ἀλύξαν-
τα φυγεῖν ὕπερθ' ἄνατον.

Though there are significant differences between this text and what appears in the manuscripts for this passage, these differences are dealt with in detail in Appendix B and need not detain us here. What is of immediate concern is the use and meaning of ἄτα in line 112.

The first pertinent consideration is the general context of the passage. Not all critics agree about it. Paley, for example, states: "The whole context, especially compared with *Agamemnon* 1347, ὕψος κρεῖσσον ἐκπηδήματος, shows that the poet has in view a beast inclosed in a net from which there is no escape but by leaping over it."[2] Broadhead, more cautious and more perceptive, carefully notes the similarities and the differences between the first four lines and the last four.

In the first four lines, there is question of escaping from ἀπάτα. But

> the interrogative clauses (107–10) do not imply more than "it is very difficult (well-nigh impossible) to escape the delusion sent by the god." Since the Elders are thinking of Xerxes and the expedition, the questions at least leave open the possibility that he *may* have escaped ἀπάτα and its consequences. . . .

In the last four lines, there is question of escaping from ἄτα. But, Broadhead argues:

> *It is not true that a man may not escape from Ate's toils.* What he can hardly escape is Delusion's onset and the snares of Infatuation, and what he certainly cannot escape is the *consequences* of his infatuation; but that he may free himself from the infatuation itself is obvious from the words of Darius when he charges the Chorus to admonish Xerxes and induce him λῆξαι θεοβλαβοῦνθ' ὑπερκόμπῳ θράσει (831), a task which will be made easier by the fact that calamity has opened his eyes to his folly and sin (cf. γέννα γᾷ τε πατρῴᾳ κακὸν ἆρ' ἐγενόμαν (932)). . . .
>
> That the passage has been widely misunderstood is due partly to the assumption that the "escape" of 108 is the same as that of 114 (a truly banal repetition), partly to the failure to see that what the Chorus fears is the *consequences* of the delusion. They do not say outright that Xerxes has been deluded and ensnared, but the mere fact that they are apprehensive of disaster (116ff.) shows in what direction their thoughts incline.[3]

With this general interpretation of the passage as background, the problem of the relationship between ἀπάτα and ἄτα is brought clearly into focus. This is not the only time Aeschylus indicates a close relationship between the two; he does so as well at *Suppliants* 110–111. If the reading ἄταν δ' ἀπάται is adopted there, it follows that ἄτη is a result of ἀπάτα, not vice versa.[4] And though the connection between the two is not so explicit in the present passage, there are three indications that Aeschylus had the same connection in mind: (*a*) he adverts to the onset of ἀπάτα *initially*, and only then speaks of ἄτα; (*b*) this is precisely the usage inherited from Homer, who consistently used ἄτη as "blindness, infatuation, or folly *caused by delusion* sent by the gods";[5] and (*c*) this use of ἄτη in the sense of "blindness" is confirmed by the presence of φρήν in line 116. This trio of reasons seems to preclude the possibility, still held by some editors and commentators, that ἄτα at *Persians* 112 can mean "ruin."[6]

ἄτη occurs again, in the second stasimon, during the evocation of Darius:

ἀντ. οὔτε γὰρ ἄνδρας ποτ' ἀπώλλυ πολεμοφθόροισιν ἄταις,
θεομήστωρ δ' ἐκικλήσκ-
ετο Πέρσαις, θεομήστωρ δ'   655
ἔσκεν, ἐπεὶ στρατὸν εὖ ποδούχει. ἠέ.

The strong contrast between Darius and Xerxes contained in the juxta-position of ἄταις and the twice-iterated θεομήστωρ provides the reason for understanding ἄτη here as "follies." As "like the gods in counsel," Darius did not destroy his people by acts which were the opposite of counsel, that is, "follies."

Line 822, in the third epeisodion, provides the final instance of the use of ἄτη in the subjective sense in the *Persians*. As an example of the ὄλβος, ὕβρις, ἄτη triad, it was discussed in the previous chapter, and the reasons for understanding ἄτη in the subjective sense are given there.[7]

SEVEN AGAINST THEBES

ἄτη in its subjective meaning appears more frequently in the *Seven Against Thebes*, the next extant Aeschylean tragedy. The only non-lyric use of the word in the play occurs at line 601. The passage is Eteocles' reply to the messenger's report that Amphiaraus is the enemy champion at the sixth gate:

φεῦ τοῦ ξυναλλάσσοντος ὄρνιθος βροτοῖς
δίκαιον ἄνδρα τοῖσι δυσσεβεστέροις.
ἐν παντὶ πράγει δ' ἔσθ' ὁμιλίας κακῆς
κάκιον οὐδέν, καρπὸς οὐ κομιστέος.   600
ἄτης ἄρουρα θάνατον ἐκκαρπίζεται·
ἢ γὰρ ξυνεισβὰς πλοῖον εὐσεβὴς ἀνὴρ
ναύτῃσι θερμοῖς καὶ πανουργίαι τινὶ
ὄλωλεν ἀνδρῶν σὺν θεοπτύστωι γένει,
ἢ ξὺν πολίταις ἀνδράσιν δίκαιος ὢν   605
ἐχθροξένοις τε καὶ θεῶν ἀμνήμοσιν,
ταὐτοῦ κυρήσας ἐκδίκοις ἀγρεύματος,
πληγεὶς θεοῦ μάστιγι παγκοίνωι 'δάμη.

Though a number of arguments have been advanced against the au-thenticity of line 601, none of them conclusive,[8] there are several positive reasons for retention of the line: it is contained in all the man-uscripts; is quite consistent with the imagery of lines 593, 599–600, and 692–694; and when taken in conjunction with lines 692–694, proves quite ironical.[9] Three striking similarities between the use of ἄτη in 601 and the tradition examined thus far lend easy support to the universal contention that the word is used here in the subjective sense. First, the confirmation of the general statement by example (εὐσεβὴς ἀνὴρ ... θερμοῖς καὶ πανουργίαι ... ὄλωλεν and δίκαιος ... ἐχθροξέ- νοις τε καὶ θεῶν ἀμνήμοσιν ... πληγεὶς ... ᾿δάμη) in the present pas- sage is reminiscent of the use of the same device in *Iliad* 9 and 19, in both of which passages ἄτη means "blindness."[10] Secondly, the dichot- omy between δίκαιος ἀνήρ and δυσσέβεστερος in the present passage is analogous to Hesiod's distinction between ἐσθλός and δειλός in *Works and Days* 213–218; and ἄτη in the Hesiod passage means "folly."[11] Finally, the metaphor of growth here recalls two other growth met- aphors involving ἄτη, in Solon 4.35 and *Persians* 822, and in each of them ἄτη means "blindness" or "infatuation."[12]

ἄτη appears once more in the long second epeisodion of the *Seven*. In the first strophe of the kommos toward the end of the epeisodion, the chorus, having heard Eteocles' decision to fight his brother, plead with him:

στρ. τί μέμονας, τέκνον; μή τί σε θυμοπλη-   686
θὴς δορίμαργος ἄτα φερέτω· κακοῦ δ᾿
ἔκβαλ᾿ ἔρωτος ἀρχάν.

That "blindness" or "infatuation" is the meaning for ἄτη here is quite clear from the context. There are overtones of anger and fury con- tained in μέμονας in line 686. The epithet θυμοπληθὴς recalls the pre- Aeschylean association of ἄτη with θυμός, in which ἄτη regularly means "blindness" or "folly."[13] The other epithet, δορίμαργος, which means "raging with the spear," aptly describes a state of "blindness" or "in- fatuation" since its root, μάργος, regularly suggests insatiable greed and is connected with appetite, lust, and the like (cf. Theognis 581, *Suppliants* 741, and *Seven* 380).[14] Finally, the ἄτη of 687 is specified as an ἔρως in 688, an association which is quite valid for a state of "blind- ness" or "infatuation."[15]

The next occurrence of ἄτη is in the lyric passage of lines 951–960:

ἰὼ πολλοῖς ἐπανθίσαντες
πόνοισι γενεάν·
τελευταῖαι δ᾿ ἐπηλάλαξαν
᾿Αραὶ τὸν ὀξὺν νόμον, τετραμμένου
παντρόπωι φυγᾶι γένους·   955
ἔστακε δ᾿ ἄτας τροπαῖον ἐν πύλαις
ἐν αἷς ἐθείνοντο, καὶ δυοῖν κρατή-
σας ἔληξε δαίμων.[16]   960

Two good arguments favor the construing of ἄτη in 956 as "blindness" or "folly": (a) the overall balance of the entire ode (lines 875–960) and (b) the general agreement of this meaning with passages elsewhere in the play.

Analysis reveals that the various elements of the ode carefully echo and balance each other, as the following schema, from lines 875 to 960, indicates:

στρ. α δύσφρονες φίλων ἄπιστοι
       δι μελέους θανάτους ηὕροντο δόμων ἐπὶ λύμηι

ἀντ. α διήλλαχθε σὺν σιδάρωι
       ἀληθῆ πατρὸς . . . πότνι᾽ Ἐρινὺς ἐπέκρανεν

στρ. β ὁμοσπλάγχνων τε πλευρωμάτων
       ἀντιφόνων <ἐκ> θανάτων ἀραί

ἀντ. β διήκει δὲ καὶ πόλιν στόνος
       μένει κτέανα τοῖς ἐπιγόνοις
       ἐμοιράσαντο δ᾽ ὀξυκάρδιοι κτήμαθ᾽

στρ. γ σιδηρόπληκτοι μὲν ὧδ᾽ ἔχουσιν
       τάφων πατρώιων λαχαί
       δαϊκτὴρ γόος αὐτόστονος

ἀντ. γ δυσδαίμων σφιν ἁ τεκοῦσα
       ὑπ᾽ ἀλλαλοφόνοις χερσὶν ὁμοσπόροισιν

στρ. δ ὁ πόντιος ξεῖνος ἐκ πυρὸς συθείς, θηκτὸς σίδαρος
       Ἄρης, ἀρὰν πατρώιαν τιθεὶς ἀλαθῆ

ἀντ. δ ἔχουσι μοῖραν . . . ὦ μέλεοι . . . πολλοῖς ἐπανθίσαντες
       πόνοισι γενεάν
       ἔστακε δ᾽ ἄτας τροπαῖον ἐν πύλαις.

Yet this symmetry is true not only of the ode in general but also of the phrase ἄτας τροπαῖον. As the last phrase in the ode referring to the brothers, it balances the first such phrase, δύσφρονες, φίλων ἄπιστοι, in lines 875–876. In the light of this balance, the concept of ἄτη in 956 is much more intelligible if it is taken to mean "blindness" or "folly," for such "folly" is precisely what the chorus lament in other words in the terms δύσφρονες and φίλων ἄπιστοι.

Furthermore, construing ἄτη here as "blindness" or "folly" is consonant with other passages in the play. Thus at lines 271–279 Eteocles vows that if all should go well and the city should be saved they would offer trophies to the gods of the city. It is ironic that, at line 956, the city has been saved and all has gone well, except for Eteocles personally.[17] There is a τροπαῖον indeed, but it is very different from the one which he had envisioned. It is an ἄτας τροπαῖον. But it is not Eteocles' τροπαῖον alone. Polyneices and the entire house of Laius share in it as well. It is significant, therefore, to recall the following passages. At line 661 Eteocles had characterized Polyneices as σὺν φοί-τωι φρενῶν. At lines 686–688 the chorus had appealed to Eteocles in terms of "folly" (ἄτη) not to fight, and at 800–802 the messenger reported the death of the two brothers in terms of Λαΐου δυσβουλίας. The ἄτας τροπαῖον of 956, then, is a trophy to the folly of the whole house of Laius: to the imprudence of Laius himself, to the curse of Oedipus, to the distraught mind of Polyneices, and to the blind fury of Eteocles. It is not a statue to doom erected at the city gates. It is something much more tragic and poignant, something much more dramatic. It is the two dead bodies of the brothers, slain by each other and recapitulating the tragic folly of their entire family.[18]

The final appearance of ἄτη in the *Seven* occurs toward the end of the antiphonal dirge sung by Antigone and Ismene over the bodies of their dead brothers:

Αντ.	ἰὼ πάντων πολυπονώτατοι.	1000
Ισμ.	ἰὼ δαιμονῶντες ἐν ἄται.	
Αντ.	ἰὼ, ποῦ σφε θήσομεν χθονός;	
Ισμ.	ἰώ, ὅπου τιμιώτατον.	
Αντ.	ἰὼ ἰὼ πῆμα πατρὶ πάρευνον.[19]	

As in all passages of this type, the context is not very helpful for determining the precise meaning of a particular word; the exchanges are so short and the thought shifts so rapidly that it is difficult to argue from any larger frame of reference. The only word which can shed any light on the ἄτη in line 1001 is δαιμονῶντες, yet perhaps it is enough to justify the meaning of "blindness" or "folly" for ἄτη here. To lament Eteocles and Polyneices as "possessed in your folly" is surely consonant with the view of them presented elsewhere in the play, in particular at lines 661, 686–688, 800–802, and 951–960; "possessed in your time of calamity or woe," on the other hand, would mean that the brothers are subject to a δαίμων now that they are dead, a concept not found elsewhere in fifth-century Athenian thought. It is a tenuous argument, perhaps, but all that the passage will allow.

SUPPLIANTS

In the *Suppliants* there are two passages which must be investigated concerning Aeschylean usage of ἄτη in its subjective connotation. The first of these occurs in antistrophe ε of the first stasimon. In the preceding strophe the chorus of Danaids has stated that Zeus destroys men's hopes, not violently or toilfully, but effortlessly. Antistrophe ε then particularizes this thought in terms of the Danaids' plight. They pray that Zeus will look on this outrage, which, although it burgeons with evil thoughts and has its frenzied purpose as an irresistible goad, ἄταν δ' ἀπάται μεταγνούς.[20] The text of the full antistrophe is:

ἀντ. ἰδέσθω δ' εἰς ὕβριν
βρότειον οἷαι νεάζει πυθμὴν   105
δι' ἀμὸν γάμον τεθαλὼς
δυσπαραβούλοισι φρεσίν,
καὶ διάνοιαν μαινόλιν
κέντρον ἔχων ἄφυκτον, †ἄ-   110
ται δ' ἀπάται μεταγνούς†.

Although there are textual difficulties throughout this antistrophe, and particularly in lines 110–111, the fact that ἄτη appears in these lines is beyond dispute.[21] Determination of the meaning must be based on the Danaids' attitude toward the Aegyptiads, i.e., whether they consider them guilty of "infatuation" or of trying to inflict "ruin."

The possibility that the Danaids might consider the Aegyptiads as motivated by a desire to bring about their "ruin" or "destruction," though at first attractive, does not conform to their attitude throughout the play. The loathing (cf. lines 790, 1062–1064) which the Danaids feel, and which makes them want to escape the power of the Aegyptiads (lines 335, 392–393[22]), is based on two recurrent ideas: the Aegyptiads' feelings for them are the "unholy desires of youth," and their attempt to force these feelings is ὕβρις.

The note of youthful lust is initially sounded in the first stasimon (lines 77–82). The Danaids pray that their native gods will not fulfill youth's desires παρ' αἶσαν. Both points are indicative: that the desires belong to youth (ἥβαι) and that they are παρ' αἶσαν. The idea recurs in the description of the Aegyptiads as a μάργον γένος, a "lustful race" (line 741). At this point the Danaids are speaking with their father; it is significant that they add that he is aware of this fact, almost as if to say that this is so fundamental a trait of the Aegyptiads that they had discussed it before and acted accordingly. And, in the fourth stasimon, as the Aegyptiads approach, the Danaids lament that they are being chased μάταισι πολυθρόοις (line 820). This "clamorous lewdness," presumably, is what makes the Aegyptiads ὕβριν δύσφορον, and it is their ὕβρις which must be considered next.

That the Danaids consider the Aegyptiads guilty of ὕβρις is clear from the frequency with which they make the charge (cf. lines 81, 104, 426, 487, 528, 817, 845, and 881). Equally clear, particularly in the light of the preceding considerations, is the fact that this "wanton harassment" is the product of passion. In all but one of the ὕβρις passages, the context is one of lust or passion.[23] Line 81 has already been considered. In line 106, the Danaids hope that Zeus will look on the ὕβρις which is burgeoning δι' ἀμὸν γάμον. Pelasgus, in line 487, reassures Danaus that some of his people will have compassion and detest ὕβριν ἄρσενος στόλου. The Danaids pray, in line 528, that Zeus will ward off ἀνδρῶν ὕβριν. Confronted by the Aegyptiads (or their herald) in line 845, the Danaids wish that their aggressors had perished δεσποσίωι ξὺν ὕβρει. Finally, the overtone of ὕβριν in line 881 is set by the word λύμας, "moral outrage," in line 877. In all these cases, it is clear that the Danaids, by their insistence on the youthful, male, despotic character of the ὕβρις, think of it as wanton harassment arising from sexual passion.

To return, therefore, to the meaning of ἄταν in line 110: if it were to mean "ruin" or "destruction," it would not be consistent with the Danaids' view of the Aegyptiads throughout the rest of the play. That view is quite simple: the Aegyptiads are lustful young men swayed to harassment by their passion. But that is not to say, nor do the Danaids ever say, that they are thereby attempting to accomplish "ruin" or "destruction."[24]

This means, that the other possible meaning of ἄτη in this context, viz., "infatuation," which was standard Homeric usage, must be the correct one.[25] Given the lustful character of the Aegyptiads, the Danaids pray that they will "change their mind about" or "repent of" their infatuation. It is a simple case of youthful, male infatuation, and the Danaids want no part of it.

The word ἀπάται in line 110 presents a difficulty of a different sort. Though it seems best taken as an instrumental dative, and the phrase ἄταν δ' ἀπάται μεταγνούς as meaning "yet changing its mind about infatuation caused by guile," the question arises: Who exercised the guile? It would appear that this is one of the many instances in which Aeschylus is deliberately vague. According to Homeric usage, ἄτη was regularly induced by one of the gods; hence, the explanation would seem to lie along these lines: that is, that the Aegyptiads were beguiled into infatuation by one of the gods.[26] Yet there are no indications elsewhere in the play that this meaning might be intended here. It is tempting to see this explanation behind the use of ἄταν δ' ἀπάται, and the Homeric usage might be quite evocative to an Athenian audience. Unfortunately, Aeschylus never commits himself on this issue.[27]

The text of the *Suppliants* has been maimed between lines 825 and 902.[28] Thus, the next appearance of ἄτη, at line 850, occurs in a section fraught with textual difficulties. Three considerations compound the problem of determining the meaning of ἄτη in this line: (*a*) for lines 836–872 the MSS provide no indication of the identity of the speakers at any given place; quite naturally, this has led (*b*) to varied distribution of the lines by different editors; and (*c*) the antistrophe 859–865, which corresponds to the strophe 847–853, is likewise full of corruptions — with the result that it can be of only limited assistance in any attempt to establish the strophe.

For lines 847–850 M reads:

αἵμονες ὡς ἐπαμίδα
ησυδουτια ἀπιτα
κελεύω βιᾷ μεθέσθαι
ἵχαρ φρενὶ τ' ἄταν.   850

Lines 847–848 are hopelessly corrupt, and have been endlessly emended by editors.[29] Unfortunately, lines 859–860, equally corrupt, can offer no assistance. Some editors also suspect lines 849–850,[30] yet the MSS reading is clear enough, and very definite help is to be derived from the antistrophic lines 861–862 since they are not corrupt.[31] An application of the rules of response between strophe and antistrophe proves disastrous to many of the emendations proposed for lines 848–850,[32] and the remaining proposed emendations, though displaying response, must likewise be rejected.[33] This leaves the reading of M, with Robortelli's easy emendation to βιᾷ in line 849 for response's sake, as the sole valid reading.

According to this reading — which means "I order you by force to put aside the vehement desire and ἄταν in your heart" — the Aegyptiads, or their messenger, display precisely those traits of character which the Danaids feared and which their previous descriptions foretold. The Aegyptiads come "ordering," confident in their own power. And they recognize that the Danaids have a strong determination, a "vehement desire," to escape.

More than that, the Aegyptiads attribute ἄτη to the Danaids. What does this mean? There is strong indication that, joined with ἵχαρ, it means something active, rather than passive, but that meaning is surely not active "guilt" or "sin." The Aegyptiads are not interested in, nor do they try to make a case for, any moral guilt which the Danaids' action might produce. Theirs is not a moral frame of reference, but a physical one, and one of power.[34] In such a framework, ἄτη must mean something like "blindness" or "blind folly," and this meaning is consonant with the Aegyptiads' total view of the Danaids' action: it was "folly" on their part to refuse marriage, to have fled, and now to refuse to surrender.[35]

This first use of ἄτη by the Aegyptiads is "ironic" when juxtaposed with the first use of the word by the Danaids in line 110.[36] There ἄτη means "infatuation";[37] here it means "folly." The irony is significantly more than verbal. At line 110, to the Danaids, the desire of the Aegyptiads *seemed*, there and then, infatuation; to the Aegyptiads their infatuation *was*, then as always, true desire. At line 850, to the Danaids, their flight *seems*, here and now, folly; to the Aegyptiads, the folly *is*, now as always, flight.

Hence, despite the MSS corruption of the immediate context, the association with ἴχαρ and the ironic antithesis with line 100 afford good grounds for taking ἄταν in line 850 to mean "blindness" or "blind folly."[38]

AGAMEMNON

With a total of fifteen (eight lyric and seven non-lyric), the *Agamemnon* alone contains more ἄτη passages than any other play in the Aeschylean corpus. The use and meaning of ἄτη in the *Agamemnon*, therefore, are of cardinal importance in determining Aeschylus' concept of the word. This fact is underscored by the appearance of ἄτη in the speeches of each of the main characters : ἄτη is used by the chorus seven times, by Cassandra four times, by Clytemnestra twice, and by Agamemnon once.[39]

It may seem strange, given the high total of ἄτη passages in this first play of the trilogy, that this chapter will refer to only three of them, but the reason for this is important: namely, the significant shift in the meaning of ἄτη effected in Aeschylean poetry. Of the total fifteen, eleven are in the objective sense of "ruin," "calamity," or "disaster," and will be discussed in the next chapter. For the moment, we must consider three instances in the play of the use of ἄτη in its previously preponderant subjective connotation; the fourth such passage, *Agamemnon* 381–388, has already been examined, in the section dealing with the ὄλβος (πλοῦτος), κόρος, ἄτη triad, in the previous chapter.[40] All three remaining passages are uttered by Cassandra.

As she emerges from her state of possession by Apollo and promises to speak forthrightly to the chorus (line 1178), Cassandra tells them that the house of Atreus is beset by a cacophonous choir:

> καὶ μὴν πεπωκώς γ', ὡς θρασύνεσθαι πλέον,
> βρότειον αἷμα κῶμος ἐν δόμοις μένει
> δύσπεμπτος ἔξω, συγγόνων Ἐρινύων.   1190
> ὑμνοῦσι δ' ὕμνον δώμασιν προσήμεναι
> πρώταρχον ἄτην, ἐν μέρει δ' ἀπέπτυσαν
> εὐνὰς ἀδελφοῦ τῶι πατοῦντι δυσμενεῖς.

Fraenkel's comment on the significance of this passage is worth noting:

> The image of the κῶμος, taken from the homely sphere of everyday life, has here assumed an unexpected and dreadful meaning. . . . The most joyous custom of Attic life is transformed into an object of horror. This κῶμος does not go round from door to door like an ordinary one, but remains resident in the house of the Atridae, and no one can send it away; the drink which inebriates it is human blood, and the song that it sings is ξύμφθογγος οὐκ εὔφωνος.[41]

The magnificence of the passage is increased by the phrase πρώταρχον ἄτην. For Cassandra's vision not only looks forward; it also looks backward to the initial cause of the suffering of the house of Atreus: namely, Thyestes' infatuation with Aerope, the wife of Atreus. Lines 1192–1193 make it evident that "infatuation" is the meaning of ἄτη in line 1192.[42]

This meaning for ἄτη is confirmed by a comparison with the Homeric passages in which ἄτη means "infatuation." All five Homeric texts (*Iliad* 3.100, 6.356, 24.28; *Odyssey* 4.261, 23.223) have the same erotic context found here;[43] and all five are concerned with Paris and Helen (who is in some sense a member of the house of Atreus) just as the present passage is concerned with Aerope and Thyestes (the brother of Atreus). But, most striking of all, each of the Homeric passages, like the present one, speaks of ἄτη, "infatuation," as the cause of suffering.

After a brief lucid interval (lines 1246–1254), Cassandra again becomes subject to Apollo (line 1256). In the course of her speech, she says:

τί δῆτ' ἐμαυτῆς καταγέλωτ' ἔχω τάδε
καὶ σκῆπτρα καὶ μαντεῖα περὶ δέρηι στέφη;   1265
σὲ μὲν πρὸ μοίρας τῆς ἐμῆς διαφθερῶ.
ἴτ' ἐς φθόρον· πεσόντα γ' ὧδ' ἀμείβομαι.
ἄλλην τιν' ἄτης ἀντ' ἐμοῦ πλουτίζετε.⁴⁴

Understanding ἄτη as "blindness" or "folly" is to be preferred here. Cassandra meets her "doom," not because she is a *prophetess* (and it is as prophetess that she is speaking and acting here), but because she is a woman (cf. lines 954–955, 1263, 1440–1443). Hence, it is wrong to imagine her as blaming her "doom" on her prophetic regalia. But what she does blame on her role as prophetess justifies interpreting ἄτη in line 1268 as "folly": Cassandra laments that her prophetic office has made her appear foolish to others. Her appraisal of the foolishness of her office is indicated not only by the juxtaposition of the chorus' misunderstanding in lines 1242–1255 (particularly line 1252 taken in conjunction with her outright statement in line 1246) and her petulant divestiture of her prophetic garb, but most especially by καταγέλωτ' in line 1264 and καταγελωμένην in line 1271.

Cassandra continues, predicting her own death and then exclaiming:

οὐ μὴν ἄτιμοί γ' ἐκ θεῶν τεθνήξομεν·
ἥξει γὰρ ἡμῶν ἄλλος αὖ τιμάορος,   1280
μητροκτόνον φίτυμα, ποινάτωρ πατρός·
φυγὰς δ' ἀλήτης, τῆσδε γῆς ἀπόξενος,
κάτεισιν ἄτας τάσδε θριγκώσων φίλοις·

In establishing the meaning of ἄτη here, it is useful to ask: What is it that Orestes does? He does *not* "complete" the *disasters* of his house, for he perpetrates yet another: he kills his mother.⁴⁵ He *does* "complete" the *follies* of his house: he obeys Apollo. Orestes' action is thus in sharp contrast to the blind, infatuated folly of Thyestes, Atreus, Clytemnestra, and Aegisthus. That his obedience to Apollo constitutes his tragic situation is, of course, in ironic contrast to the previous attitudes of the members of his house.

Furthermore, the general parallelism between the prophecy of Cassandra and the prophecy of Darius at *Persians* 803–822 should not be overlooked.⁴⁶ The *Persians* passage is the only other instance in Aeschylus involving both the use of ἄτη and a prophecy of the future,⁴⁷ and in it ἄτη means "folly."⁴⁸ Likewise φίτυμα (line 1281) is similar to the agricultural metaphor in the *Persians* passage.

LIBATION-BEARERS

As the trilogy proceeds, Aeschylus continues to employ ἄτη in its traditional meaning of "blindness," "infatuation," or "folly." It next appears in that sense in the first antistrophe of the first stasimon of the *Libation-Bearers*. The chorus sing:

ἀντ. ἀλλ' ὑπέρτολμον ἀν-
    δρὸς φρόνημα τίς λέγοι   595
    καὶ γυναικῶν φρεσὶν τλημόνων
    παντόλμους ἔρωτας, ἄ-
    ταισι <   > συννόμους βροτῶν;

Two considerations point to "follies" as the meaning of ἄτη in line 597. First, the association of ἄτη with φρόνημα and φρῆν in this passage is analogous to the frequent Homeric and Aeschylean associations of ἄτη with νοός and φρήν,[49] in which it invariably means "blindness," "infatuation," or "folly." Secondly, the vocabulary of the present antistrophe points much more to the meaning of "follies" for ἄτη in line 597 than to either "ruin" or "calamities." Thus, ὑπέρτολμον φρόνημα in lines 594-595, γυναικῶν τλημόνων in line 596, and παντόλμους ἔρωτας in line 597 indicate that the context is one more of subjective dispositions than of objective disasters.

The next germane occurrence of ἄτη is in the second antistrophe of the third stasimon. The pertinent passage is:

ἀντ. τάχα δὲ παντελὴς χρόνος ἀμείψεται   965
    πρόθυρα δωμάτων, ὅταν ἀφ' ἑστίας
    μύσος ἅπαν ἐλάθῃ
    καθαρμοῖσιν ἀτᾶν ἐλατηρίοις·[50]

Interpreting ἄτη as "follies" in this passage would seem to be more compatible with the notion of "pollution" mentioned in line 967. The pollution infecting the house of Atreus is to be expelled by cleansing rites which dispel, not calamities (since, after all, Orestes has just perpetrated two more), but acts of folly, which are the root cause of the pollution. Orestes' acts of murder, calamitous as they are, are not foolish because they are undertaken at the express command of Apollo. Hence, they are directly contrary to the other acts of violence perpetrated by members of the house, and consequently strike at the root of the pollution: namely, the follies performed by the former members of his line.

The final word of the *Libation-Bearers* is ἄτης. It occurs in the following passage of the exodos:

νῦν δ' αὖ τρίτος ἦλθέ ποθεν σωτήρ,
ἢ μόρον εἴπω;
ποῖ δῆτα κρανεῖ, ποῖ καταλήξει   1075
μετακοιμισθὲν μένος ἄτης;

Perhaps the key to the meaning of ἄτη here is the understanding of the phrase μένος ἄτης. Those who interpret ἄτη as "calamity" understand μένος as "might" or "force," with the resultant meaning "force of calamity" for the phrase as a whole. Yet there is another meaning for μένος, that is, "spirit" or "passion," and an investigation of μένος in this sense proves most interesting. The word is frequently used by both Homer and Aeschylus in this sense, and when it is, either φρήν (or one of its compounds) or θυμός often appears in the immediate context. Thus, Homer has: *Iliad* 1.103, μένεος δὲ μέγα φρένες; 5.470, μένος καὶ θυμόν; 22.312, μένεος δ' ἐμπλήσατο θυμὸν; 23.468, μένος ἔλλαβε θυμόν. And Aeschylus: περίφρονες, *Suppliants* 757; διχόφρονι, *Seven* 899; φρενῶν, *Agamemnon* 1064; φρενῶν, *Libation-Bearers* 452; and παλαιόφρονα, *Eumenides* 873. The pertinence of these texts becomes apparent in the light of the Homeric and Aeschylean association of ἄτη in its subjective sense with exactly the same two words.[51] Is it not probable then that when μένος and ἄτη (each of which is used frequently and separately with φρήν or θυμός) appear together they would be used in a sense compatible with their use with the same common terms? It would seem so, and therefore it would follow that the phrase μένος ἄτης means "spirit of blindness or folly" rather than "force of calamity."

Once such an interpretation for this phrase is admitted as possible, there are three arguments from the context to strengthen it. First, there is the chorus' uncertainty about Orestes; is he a savior or a doom (lines 1073–1074)? That is to say, will he prove to be a person of folly or a savior for the race? They are not uncertain about his performance of a calamitous deed; they were present when he killed Clytemnestra and Aegisthus. Secondly, the chorus' final encounter with Orestes indicated that he too might well be falling victim to the "spirit of folly" plaguing the house of Atreus, for he had fled the stage under incipient possession by the Furies. Finally, there is the chorus' constant preoccupation throughout the play (something, incidentally, which would very fittingly be summed up in the final phrase of the play): their desire to see the house of Atreus purged of the madness and folly which infect it.

In view of all these considerations, then, ἄτη in 1076 should be construed as "blindness" or "folly" rather than as "ruin" or calamity."

EUMENIDES AND PROMETHEUS

There are several interesting aspects to the use and meaning of ἄτη in
the *Eumenides* and the *Prometheus*. Perhaps the most surprising is that
ἄτη is employed only twice in the first play and only three times in the
second. Neither of the passages in the *Eumenides* exhibits ἄτη in its
subjective connotation, and hence both will be discusssed in the next
chapter. In the *Prometheus*, ἄτη is never used by, or in reference to,
Prometheus himself, but when it does appear, it is always in the singular and always in an anapaestic passage. One such, the first appearance of ἄτη in the play, and its only use in its subjective meaning,
occurs at the end of the long third epeisodion. Just before departing,
Io speaks:

> ἐλελεῦ ἐλελεῦ·
> ὑπό μ' αὖ σφάκελος καὶ φρενοπλῆγες
> μανίαι θάλπουσ', οἴστρου δ' ἄρδις
> χρίει μ' ἄπυρος,   880
> κραδία δὲ φόβωι φρένα λακτίζει,
> τροχοδινεῖται δ' ὄμμαθ' ἑλίγδην,
> ἔξω δὲ δρόμου φέρομαι λύσσης
> πνεύματι μάργωι γλώσσης ἀκρατής,
> θολεροὶ δὲ λόγοι παίουσ' εἰκῆι   885
> στυγνῆς πρὸς κύμασιν ἄτης.[52]

Four striking sets of words and phrases in the passage strongly suggest that ἄτη in line 886 means "insanity," "delusion," or "delirium."
First, two words, φρενοπλῆγες in line 878 and φρένα in line 881, recall
the association of ἄτη with φρήν which has been noted frequently both
in pre-Aeschylean usage and at *Persians* 112, *Suppliants* 110–111 and
850, and *Libation-Bearers* 597–598; in each instance ἄτη means "blindness," "infatuation," or "delusion."[53] Secondly, line 882, τροχοδινεῖται
δ' ὄμμαθ' ἑλίγδην, echoes the στρεφεδίνηθεν δὲ οἱ ὄσσε of *Iliad* 16.792.
Next, ἔξω δὲ δρόμου φέρομαι in line 883, finds a parallel expression in
Orestes' statement at *Libation-Bearers* 1022–1023: ὥστερ ξὺν ἵπποις ἡνιο-
στροφῶ δρόμου ἐξωτέρω. The context there makes it quite clear that
Orestes fears delusion, distraction, blindness caused by the onset of the
Furies.[54] Finally, the word εἰκῆι ("without plan or purpose") at the

end of line 885 emphatically strengthens ἄτης at the end of line 886 if the latter is construed as "blindness," "delusion," or "stupor." Such a deliberate reinforcement is made more probable by Aeschylus' use of εἰκῆι in line 450, where the context clearly involves a state of mind rather than a state of fortune. Each of the words or phrases cited, therefore, points to the meaning of "insanity," "delusion," or "delirium" for ἄτη in line 886.

If the meaning of "insanity" or "delirium" is accepted for ἄτη in this passage of the *Prometheus*, a significant point of Aeschylean usage should be noted: the use of ἄτη in similar metaphors cannot *necessarily* be taken as a criterion for establishing the meaning of ἄτη. The sea metaphor of *Prometheus* 886 is fundamentally the same as the sea metaphor of *Suppliants* 470 (ἄτης πέλαγος); yet in the *Suppliants* passage ἄτη means "ruin" or "disaster," while in the *Prometheus* passage it means "insanity," "delusion," or "delirium." In other words, the metaphor remains the same but the meaning of ἄτη does not. Consequently, identical metaphorical usage would not suffice as a valid argument for the identical meaning of ἄτη within the metaphor.

CONCLUSION

This survey of the seventeen Aeschylean passages in which ἄτη appears in its subjective meaning — the fifteen instances treated in the present chapter and *Persians* 822 and *Agamemnon* 386 discussed in Chapter 3 — reveals five general points of contact with the pre-Aeschylean tradition manifesting both Aeschylus' knowledge of the tradition and his consistency in employing ἄτη in this sense within it.

First, and most consistently of all, ἄτη continues in Aeschylean poetry to be associated with various human faculties. Thus, just as it had been associated with φρήν (*Iliad* 6.356; 16.805; 19.88, 126, 129, 136; *Odyssey* 15.233; *Shield of Heracles* 93; and *Pythian* 2.28) and θυμός (*Iliad* 19.270; *Odyssey* 21.302, 23.223; and Theognis 631) in epic and lyric poetry, so it continues to be associated with them in Aeschylus. This occurs at *Persians* 112, *Seven* 687, *Suppliants* 110–111 and 850, *Libation-Bearers* 597, and *Prometheus* 886.

Secondly, there is a consistency of usage with respect to the plural of ἄτη in the sense of "blindness," "infatuation," or "folly." This was the case at *Iliad* 9.115, 10.391, 19.270, *Works and Days* 216, and Theognis

631, and Aeschylus continues it at *Persians* 653, *Agamemnon* 1283, and *Libation-Bearers* 597 and 968.

By this stage of Greek poetic development, thirdly, it is possible to note a certain consistency of appearance of ἄτη in its subjective connotation with given metaphors. Chief among these are the metaphorical expressions involving growth. Solon, at 4.35, uses the metaphor, and Aeschylus apparently thinks it most appropriate, employing it three times: *Persians* 822, *Seven* 601, and *Suppliants* 110–111. At *Prometheus* 886 he uses ἄτη in connection with two vivid associations it had in the earlier tradition: the sea metaphor used with ἄτη at Pindar's *Olympian* 10.37 and the graphic Homeric description of rolling eyes connected with ἄτη at *Iliad* 16.792.

Next, the association of ἄτη with ἀπάτα should be remarked. This usage appeared frequently in Homer — *Iliad* 2.11; 8.237; 9.18, 504–512; 19.88–136, 270, and *Odyssey* 4.261 and 15.233 — and it is taken over precisely by Aeschylus at *Persians* 112 and *Suppliants* 110–111.

Finally, there are two Aeschylean passages which show extraordinary contact with the tradition. At *Seven* 601 ἄτη means "blindness" or "infatuation"; it recalls both Homeric usage insofar as this meaning is developed by examples (as is done in *Iliad* 9 and 19) and a Hesiodic passage, *Works and Days* 213–218, where ἄτη also occurs in a context of contrasted personalities. *Agamemnon* 1192, like *Iliad* 3.100, 6.356, 24.28, and *Odyssey* 4.261 and 23.223, employs ἄτη in the sense of "infatuation" in an erotic context and as a cause of suffering. This Aeschylean passage has an additional similarity to Homeric usage in that the individuals involved are members (or former members) of the house of Atreus.

NOTES

[1] This was the case in thirty-six of the fifty extant passages from Homer to Pindar examined in chaps. 1–3. See also the list in Appendix A.

[2] F. A. Paley, *The Tragedies of Aeschylus* (London: Whittaker, 1855), p. 167.

[3] For this and the other quotations, see his *The Persae of Aeschylus*, pp. 60–61. One of the consequences of this interpretation is another argument in favor of ἄνατον in

line 114 (see Appendix B). As Broadhead states (p. 61): "If the above analysis is correct, and if ἄτα in 112 means 'Infatuation' (not 'ruin,' as Tucker and Sidg.), it follows that the MSS reading ἔστιν ὑπὲρ θνατὸν ἀλύξαντα φυγεῖν gives the wrong meaning. With ἄνατον, however, we get just the sense that is wanted: a man cannot get away from the toils of Ate *unscathed*, he must pay the price for his sin. . . . The stress in the clause falls on ἄνατον, as is indicated by its position."

⁴ See pp. 54–57 below. I am indebted to Professor G. M. Kirkwood of Cornell University for calling my attention to the second stasimon of Sophocles' *Antigone*, where ἐλπίς takes the place of ἀπάτη.

⁵ Cf. *Iliad* 2.111; 8.237; 9.18, 504–512; 19.88–136, 270 and *Odyssey* 4.261, 15.233. See also the remarks of Bremer, *Hamartia*, pp. 118–21.

⁶ Sidgwick, Tucker, and H. J. Rose, *A Commentary on the Surviving Plays of Aeschylus*, 2 vols. in 1 (Amsterdam: Noord-Holland, 1957), p. 97, take ἄτα to mean "ruin."

⁷ See above, pp. 38–39.

⁸ The first argument for rejecting line 601 was advanced by Pieter Groeneboom, *Aeschylus' Zeven tegen Thebe* (Groningen: Wolter, 1938), p. 188, and Gabriel Italie, *Aeschylus: Zeven tegen Thebe* (Leiden: Brill, 1950), ad loc. It is an argument from context: that ἄτη in line 601 does not suit the character of Amphiaraus. J. C. Kamerbeek, in "Aeschylea," *Mnemosyne*, 13, 3rd ser. (1947), 79–80, has answered this objection, by pointing out that line 601 is not restricted to Amphiaraus, and that it is a gnomic statement which fits very well with lines 599 and 600. Kamerbeek also contends that even if one were to restrict line 601 to Amphiaraus Groeneboom's and Italie's argument would not be true, for the fact that Amphiaraus, despite his wisdom, is involved in the evil undertaking cannot be denied: he is at the gate.

Another argument against line 601 was advanced by Paul Mazon, *Eschyle*, 2 vols. (Paris: "Les Belles Lettres," 1955), ad loc. He contended that "death" could not apply to Amphiaraus, and that consequently the line should be rejected. Besides needlessly restricting the application of the line, as Groeneboom's and Italie's do, his argument presupposes that Eteocles knew about Amphiaraus' immortality. But such a supposition is not true. In fact, lines 587–589 would lead Eteocles to think that Amphiaraus believed himself to be mortal. And lines 602–614 surely show that Eteocles believed that Amphiaraus would die at Thebes (see Kamerbeek, "Aeschylea," 79–89).

Dindorf offered two arguments against line 601. The first contends that 601 is a gloss which has crept into the text (*Aeschyli tragoediae superstites et deperditarum fragmenta*, 2 vols. [Oxford: Clarendon, 1832, 1841], II 193), but, as Paley points out (*Tragedies of Aeschylus*, p. 284), it would be a very old gloss indeed, for the Scholion Mediceum comments on the line as follows: λύμης χωρίον ἢ τῶν πονηρῶν φιλία. — γνώμη.

Dindorf's second argument is that "καρπίζομαι nusquam a tragicis in hoc sensu ponitur, sed καρποῦμαι, praeterquam Eurip. *Hipp.* 431" (*Aeschyli tragoediae*, II 193). Paley challenges this and correctly points out that καρπόω ("to form or produce fruit"; cf. *Persians* 821) is to καρποῦμαι ("to have fruit produced for one's own use; to reap the fruit"; cf. *Suppliants* 253, 313; *Prometheus* 851; *Seven* 593; and *Agamemnon* 502, 621) as καρπίζω ("to cause a tree or field to produce fruit"; Euripides, *Helen* 1327; *Bacchants* 408) is to καρπίζεσθαι ("to produce something from itself as fruit"; Euripides, *Hippolytus* 432). "Hence," concludes Paley, "it seems clear that a field may be said ἐκκαρπίζεσθαι in the sense given above, the middle voice referring to the field itself rather than to the owner, as in καρποῦσθαι" (*Tragedies of Aeschylus*, pp. 284–85).

The final argument against admitting line 601 is discussed by T. G. Tucker, *The Seven Against Thebes of Aeschylus* (Cambridge: Cambridge University Press, 1908), ad loc. Without specifying any proponents he asserts that there are some who object to the line because it contains an asyndeton, but he refuses to accept this argument and rightly insists that the gnomic character of the verse is compatible with asyndeton. He compares the agitated tone of this passage with the same tone at *Libation-Bearers* 749ff., and points out that there is asyndeton in both places.

Line 601 is retained by Wecklein, Sidgwick, Tucker, Paley, Smyth, and Jean Dumortier, *Les Images dans la poésie d'Eschyle* (Paris: "Les Belles Lettres," 1935), pp. 159–60.

[9] On this point, see Kamerbeek, "Aeschylea," 79–80.

[10] See above, pp. 8–14 and 16–17.

[11] See above, p. 36.

[12] See p. 44 for a discussion of the Solon passage, and pp. 38–39 for *Persians* 822.

[13] See *Iliad* 19.270, *Odyssey* 21.302 and 23.223, and Theognis 631.

[14] According to F. R. Earp, *The Style of Aeschylus* (Cambridge: Cambridge University Press, 1948; repr. New York: Russell & Russell, 1970), p. 26, δορίμαργος is a ἅπαξ λεγόμενον.

[15] This is in keeping with the general thesis propounded by Friedrich Solmsen, "The Erinys in Aischylos' *Septem*," TAPA, 68 (1937), 197–211. Solmsen maintains that after line 652 Eteocles changes radically because of the presence of the Erinys.

[16] Because of the obscurity in the MSS these lines have been attributed to various characters by the different editors. A full discussion of the problem may be found in *Aeschyli tragoediae*, ed. Ulrich Wilamowitz-Moellendorff (Berlin: Weidmann, 1914), pp. 89–95, and in Hugh Lloyd-Jones, "The End of the *Seven Against Thebes*," CQ, 9 N.S. (1959), 80–114.

[17] Wilamowitz discusses this point in *Aischylos: Interpretationen*, pp. 106–109.

[18] This same idea is mentioned briefly by Dumortier, *Les Images dans la poésie d'Eschyle*, p. 242.

[19] The distribution of the lines in this passage is controverted. See Lloyd-Jones, "The End of the *Seven Against Thebes*," for a discussion of the difficulties.

[20] This is the reading of G² and the Aldine, but not of M. It will be defended below.

[21] In line 105 M reads οἶα, but E, followed by Dindorf, Wecklein, Wilamowitz, Smyth, and Murray, reads οἴα. Page and Schütz have οἷαι. The emendation is made for metrical reasons. Furthermore, as Rose observes, "The text, i.e. the letters, is perfectly sound; accent and word-division are no part of the traditional text, but ancient, mediaeval or modern editors' comment, which may be right or wrong . . . and therefore can seldom be of use in textual criticism" (*Commentary on the Surviving Plays of Aeschylus*, I 23).

In line 107, Bothe's τεθαλὼς, a correction from M's τὸ θάλος (θάλως M¹), has won universal critical acceptance.

Only Tucker has objected to the διάνοιαν μαινόλιν of line 109, which has been accepted by most editors from the reading of the scholiast, claiming that "διάνοιαν μαινόλιν is against the metre, although editors for the most part ignore the fact. φρόνημα of the strophe is past suspicion" (*The "Supplices" of Aeschylus* [London & New York: Macmillan, 1889], p. 29). However, if, with most editors, this is understood as an iambic metron, there is no metrical difficulty.

The most serious textual problem in the entire antistrophe occurs in the crucial lines 110–111. Page prints †ἄται δ' ἀπάται μεταγνούς†.

Textually the μεταγνούς appears sound, and there seems no reason to alter it with Tucker. He would read μεταλγούς, genitive singular of the adjective meaning "bringing sorrow in its train," which would modify his reading of ἄτας. This would make ἀπάταν, which Tucker would also read, in "exegetical apposition to διάνοιαν." There are several objections to this. First, ἀπάταν, accusative, has been shown to be far from satisfactory. Secondly, the word μεταλγής does not occur elsewhere. And, finally, the MSS unanimity regarding μεταγνούς makes this emendation unnecessary. The meaning of the verb μεταγιγνώσκω *with an accusative* is equally sound (cf. LSJ *sub* μεταγιγνώσκω). It means "to change one's mind about, to repent of." The problem here arises with the tense of the participle, the aorist, for, as commentators have long recognized, clearly the Aegyptiads have not *already* seen their error. Though it is a particularly troublesome use of the aorist, given the soundness of the text tradition as well as the well-attested meaning, there seems little other solution than that of A. Y. Campbell, who, in his article "Aeschylea," *Hermes,* 84 (1956), 117, states flatly: "The participle must have had a future reference."

M's reading ἄτᾳ δ' ἀπάταν, however, does not square with the rest of the play, for at no point, either prior to or during the action of the play, is there question of the Aegyptiads' practicing "deceit," "guile," or "treachery." Their whole approach is one of outright violence (cf. lines 104, 335, 350–353, 426–432, 486–487, 609–612, 727–728, 741–745, 812–814, 817–821, and their — or their messenger's — attitude throughout their appearance in the fourth epeisodion, lines 825–952). Consequently, it is unintelligible for the Danaids to pray that they will "change their mind about" their "deceit," "guile," or "treachery." ἀπάταν, therefore, is quite unsatisfactory in the accusative.

[21] G² and the Aldine give what seems to be the preferable reading: ἄταν δ' ἀπάτᾳ. This reading is adopted by Dindorf, Wecklein, Wilamowitz, and Smyth, and with it the Danaids' prayer is that the Aegyptiads will "change their minds about" or "repent of" their ἄτη.

[22] It is interesting to note that in both these instances Pelasgus asks them questions which would be of great help in the present consideration. But each time the Danaids avoid the issues of ἔχθρα, θέμις, and νόμος.

[23] The one exception is line 426, toward the end of the kommos of the first epeisodion. Even here, given all the other similar examples cited, it is possible to interpret ὕβριν ἀνέρων in the wider meaning of male sexual passion, not simply in the restricted contextual sense of the profanation of the right of sanctuary.

[24] This has been expressed for all of Aeschylus' work by Robert Payne, *Hubris: A Study of Pride,* rev. ed. (New York: Harper & Row, 1960), p. 25: "When the gods for their own purposes desire to destroy a hero, they sent down not *hybris* but *ate,* a mental delusion or infatuation which prevents men from foreseeing the consequences of their sins. It is *ate* which makes men reckless, to become the immediate servants of pride."

²⁵ See *Iliad* 3.100 (according to Zenodotus' reading), 6.356, 24.28; *Odyssey* 4.261 and 23.223. Hesiod, *Works and Days* 216 ably illustrates the connection between ὕβρις and ἄτη.

²⁶ See the table in Appendix A.

²⁷ Professor Dodds's opinion is noteworthy. Speaking of ἄτη (*The Greeks and the Irrational*, p. 38), he remarks: "in literature it always, I think, retains the implication that the ruin is supernaturally determined."

²⁸ Some have advanced a plausible explanation that at least part of the cause for this corruption was Aeschylus' attempt to barbarize the Greek in keeping with the "barbaric" character of the Egyptian herald. As Gilbert Murray, *Aeschylus, the Creator of Tragedy* (Oxford: Clarendon, 1962), p. 65, puts it: "the reason of the corruption probably is that Aeschylus had gone so far in the direction of barbarizing his speech that the scribes had failed to understand it." For a similar opinion, see P. T. Stevens, "Colloquial Expressions in Aeschylus and Sophocles," *CQ*, 39 (1945), 96.

²⁹ Thus, for line 847 the following have been proposed: Paley and Murray, following the scholion, read αἷμον' ἔσω σ'; Wilamowitz, Wecklein, Smyth, and Page, following M, retain ἄιμονες ὡς; Dindorf has: ἄιμον ἵζω σ' ἐπ' ἀμίδα; Murray reads: ἐπ' ἀμάδα; Smyth and Page have: ἐπάμιδα; Rose suggests: ἐπ' ἄμαλα.

³⁰ Murray and Paley obelize 850; Smyth does the same to 849 and 850; and Page, to 847–850.

³¹ Rose, *Commentary on the Surviving Plays of Aeschylus*, I 70, is a bit cavalier in condemning the whole antistrophe by saying "the antistrophic verses, *infr.*, 859 *sqq.*, are themselves in too bad a condition to be any guide." For the most part he is correct, but not for lines 861–862.

³² Thus, with lines 861–862 scanning as follows:

σὺ δ' ἐν νᾱῑ νᾱῑ βάσῃ
τᾱχᾰ θέλεος ᾱθἔλἔὄς

the following proposed emendations for lines 849–850 fail to show response in the syllables marked and should be rejected:

849 – Headlam's and Smyth's κελεύω βοᾶν μεθέσθαι
        Weil's κελεύω βίας μεθίεσθᾱῑ

850 – Burges, Headlam's, and Rose's τῐ γαρ; φρενᾱπᾱτᾱν
        Butler's ἰσχυρᾶς φρένος ἀτᾱν

³³ Into this category fall the following suggestions: Tucker proposes τὰν παρφρονά τ' ἰοτᾶτ' or τὰν παρφρονά τ' ἀπάταν, but the palaeographical gymnastics necessary to justify this are beyond credibility; Lobeck proposes either λίχαρ or γλίχαρ, but neither of these words can be found in LSJ or in the *Etymologicon Magnum*.

³⁴ See lines 836–842, 861–863, 882–884, 902–903, 909–910, and 924, where the repetition of βία and κελεύω, as well as the physical threats, are surely intended to be significant. With regard to any moral consideration, the Aegyptiads grandly sweep it aside on two grounds: first, that the Danaids have no right to sanctuary from foreign gods (lines 853, 893–894); and, secondly, that in justice the Danaids rightfully are theirs (lines 916–918).

³⁵ The fact that the Aegyptiads refuse to pursue the question of δίκη at line 924, particularly since it was they who first introduced it at line 916, is significant here. To their minds, the Danaids' action was "folly," not one involving δίκη,

just as, to the Danaids' minds, the action of the Aegyptiads was one of κράτος, when they refused to debate the niceties of νόμος with Pelasgus at lines 392ff.

[36] For an excellent discussion of tragic irony, see G. M. Kirkwood, *A Study of Sophoclean Drama*, Cornell Studies in Classical Philology 31 (Ithaca, N.Y.: Cornell University Press, 1958), pp. 247ff.

[37] See pp. 54–57, above.

[38] There is one other possible occurrence of ἄτη in this play at line 886, but the textual tradition is so poor for lines 885–886 that it is impossible to agree with any certainty with those editors who would read some form of ἄτη here. Hence, it seems best simply to list the MS reading and the proposed emendations, without incorporating this passage as a proper subject for this investigation. Thus: βροτιοσα ροσαται μελδαάγει M. This has led to the following proposals:

(a) Abresch (based on the scholion and Eustathius 1422.19), Wilamowitz, Smyth, Murray, Rose: βρέτεος ἄρος ἀτᾷ.

Enger, Bamberger, Oberdick: βρέτεος ἄρος ματᾷ.

Hartung: βρέτεος ἀποσπάσας.

Tucker: βρότειος ἀρ< κυωρ> ός.

Wecklein: βρέτεος ἄρος ἄτα.

Paley: βρετέων †ἄρος ἄτα

(b) Schütz, Wilamowitz, Smyth, Murray: μ'· ἄλαδ' ἄγει.

Hermann: μ' ἄλαδ' ἄγει μ'.

Hartung: ἀμαλαδ' ἄγει.

Bamberger: ἄμμ' ἄλαδ' ἄγει.

Martin: ἀμύγδ' ἄγει.

Tucker: ἄτα νᾶμα νεῖ.

Wecklein: μάλδα ἄγει.

Paley: ἀμαλάδ ἄγει μ'.

[39] The other use is by the messenger at line 643.

[40] See above, pp. 43–44.

[41] *Aeschylus: Agamemnon*, III 544. See also Benjamin Daube, *Zu den Rechtsproblemen in Aischylos' Agamemnon* (Zurich: Niehans, 1939), pp. 174–76; and Bremer, *Hamartia*, p. 124.

[42] It is interesting to contrast Cassandra's vision of the true cause of trouble for the house of Atreus here with the explanation offered by Aegisthus (himself a victim of ἄτη in the sense of "infatuation," with regard to Clytemnestra) at lines 1583–1602. There, not a word is mentioned about Thyestes' seduction of Aerope.

[43] See above, pp. 14–16. In addition to the Homeric passages discussed, ἄτη meaning "infatuation" is employed twice by Pindar in erotic contexts: *Pythian* 2.28 and 3.24.

[44] The case for ἄτη in line 1268 is controverted. F, followed by Triclinius, Wecklein, Verrall, Paley, and Murray, has ἄτην. Stanley's emendation to ἄτης has been accepted by Wilamowitz, Smyth, George Thomson (*The Oresteia of Aeschylus*, rev. and enl. ed. [Amsterdam: Hakkert; Prague: Academia, 1966]), Rose, Fraenkel, and John Dewar Denniston and Denys Page (*Aeschylus: Agamemnon* [Oxford: Clarendon, 1957]). Fraenkel provides the basic justification for accepting the emendation (*Aeschylus: Agamemnon*, III 585–86): "The ἄτην of the MSS can only be defended by assuming some linguistic monstrosity ('ἄτην πλουτίζετε enrich Destruction, i.e. "be

destroyed"', Verrall; the idea which he finds in the verse is worse than obscure) or else by understanding the expression as meaning that Cassandra terms herself and any successor she may have an ἄτη." In accepting the emendation, however, ἄτης should not be construed as dependent on πλουτίζετε, as Smyth, Rose, and Fraenkel understand it. Smyth, *Aeschylus*, II 111, translates: "Enrich with doom some other in my stead"; Fraenkel, *Aeschylus: Agamemnon*, I 169, has: "Enrich some other in my stead with curse and doom!" According to LSJ πλουτέω may take a genitive, but πλουτίζω, in all the examples cited, governs only accusatives. Hence, ἄτης in 1268 should be understood as a descriptive genitive qualifying ἄλλην τιν'.

45 This is precisely what Cassandra is saying about Orestes in line 1281.

46 For a further discussion of this parallel, see Walter Porzig, *Die attische Tragödie* (Leipzig: Wiegandt, 1926), pp. 51–53.

47 The Hermes passage at *Prometheus* 1071–1078 is, not a prophecy, but a warning.

48 See above, pp. 38–39.

49 ἄτη occurs with νοός at *Iliad* 10.391 and with φρήν at *Iliad* 6.356; 16.805; 19.88, 126, 129, 136, and *Odyssey* 15.233. The Aeschylean association is found at *Persians* 112, 822, *Suppliants* 110, 850, and *Prometheus* 886.

50 It should be noted that line 968 is Schütz's restoration for the metrically unacceptable καθαρμοῖς ἄπαν ἐλατήριον of the MSS.

51 For the passages, see below, pp. 155–59.

52 For a good discussion of this passage, and particularly of its vocabulary of fear, see Jacqueline de Romilly, *La Crainte et l'angoisse dans le théâtre d'Eschyle* (Paris: "Les Belles Lettres," 1958), pp. 23–47, passim. The passage is also discussed in Silk, *Interaction in Poetic Imagery*, pp. 237–38.

53 For the passages, see below, pp. 155–59.

54 See the discussion in Silk, *Interaction in Poetic Imagery*, pp. 119.

5

THE OBJECTIVE CONCEPT OF ἌΤΗ
IN AESCHYLEAN TRAGEDY

THOUGH IT IS TRUE, as the previous chapter has demonstrated, that Aeschylus continued to employ ἄτη in the subjective connotation dominant in the Greek tradition up to his day, it is no less true that with him a fundamental change occurs in the use and meaning of the word.[1] For in Aeschylean tragedy ἄτη begins to be used far more regularly in its objective sense.[2]

More significant, however, than the simple fact of such a change are the reasons behind it. As Greek thought evolved in the fifth century, and as man (particularly Athenian citizens) began to wrestle with such central ideas as human freedom and responsibility, guilt, attribution of motive, human destiny, and all the other problems which emerge in tragedy, one of the concepts employed in this intellectual struggle was ἄτη. As man became more reflexively conscious of his human destiny, and of all that destiny's attendant problems, he tried to express himself in "ethical" terms. One of these terms is ἄτη.

An investigation of Aeschylean tragedy helps to reveal this. If in reading his drama we concentrate on the passages in which ἄτη appears in its objective sense, we find that each of them focuses on one or both of two central Aeschylean ideas: (a) the importance and consequences of human choice; and (b) the relationship of man to the gods. Attention to these ἄτη passages also provides insights into the Aeschylean concepts of δίκη and πάθει μάθος. Thus, ἄτη, δίκη, πάθει μάθος, and several other key terms in Aeschylean poetry are elements of the ethical vocabulary developed by the tragedian. Contemporary thought was posing the problems, and Aeschylus himself was a leader in such thought. The concepts, the vocabulary, even the questions, were not yet totally clear, but a significant turning point in human thought was being reached, and for Aeschylus, at least, ἄτη is at the heart of it.[3]

Let us begin with the Aeschylean ἄτη passages which emphasize the importance and consequences of human choice.

Persians

In the two passages of the *Persians* in which ἄτη is used in the objective sense, some of the consequences of human error are evident. At line 1007 the chorus relate that the δαίμονες have wrought evil like the glance of ἄτη:

στρ. Ξε. βεβᾶσι γὰρ τοίπερ ἀγρέται στρατοῦ.
     Χο. βεβᾶσιν, οἴ, νώνυμοι.
     Ξε. ἰὴ ἰή, ἰὼ ἰώ.
     Χο. ἰὼ ἰώ, δαίμονες,   1005
           †ἔθετ' ἄελπτον κακὸν
           διαπρέπον, οἷον δέδορκεν ἄτα.[4]

ἄτη in line 1007 is clearly "ruin" or "calamity." It is used as a synonym for κακόν and echoes the objective concept of "evil" which κακόν represents. Furthermore, as in the cases in seven of the eight pre-Aeschylean passages in which ἄτη means "ruin,"[5] the disaster here, which the chorus bemoan, is one which has fallen on a group (the army, its commanders, and the entire Persian empire), not simply on an individual. Lastly, the "ruin" is explicitly attributed to δαίμονες, as is usually the case in the pre-Aeschylean texts employing ἄτη in the objective sense.[6] Hence, in both use and meaning Aeschylus here quite closely follows the tradition concerning ἄτη.[7]

At line 1037 the chorus link the disaster suffered by the army on land to the disasters endured at sea:

     Χο. καὶ σθένος γ' ἐκολούθη-   1035
     Ξε. γυμνός εἰμι προπομπῶν.
     Χο. φίλων ἄταισι ποντίαισιν.

The view expressed in these two passages, both of which are taken from the kommos which forms the exodos, is all of a piece: Xerxes allowed himself to become ensnared in action which brought ἄτη, "ruin," on himself and consequently on his people. His choice, indeed, had important consequences.

Suppliants

As the first epeisodion of the *Suppliants* reaches its climax and Pelasgus continues to struggle with his dilemma, he ruminates about the difficulties confronting him. His language is highly figurative:

> †καὶ μὴν πολλαχῆι γε† δυσπάλαιστα πράγματα,
> κακῶν δὲ πλῆθος ποταμὸς ὡς ἐπέρχεται·
> ἄτης δ' ἄβυσσον πέλαγος οὐ μάλ' εὔπορον   470
> τόδ' ἐσβέβηκα, κοὐδαμοῦ λιμὴν κακῶν.

His dilemma is expressed in its harsh reality: either he must surrender the Danaids to the Aegyptiads, thus violating his duty as host and protector and running the risk of pollution for the city, or he must fight the Aegyptiads and endanger the safety of the city. The choice is his, but in either case the result will be ἄτη — "ruin."

As the second stasimon begins, in obedience to Pelasgus' injunction at lines 520–521, the chorus sing:

> στρ. ἄναξ ἀνάκτων, μακάρων
>   μακάρτατε καὶ τελέων   525
>   τελειότατον κράτος, ὄλβιε Ζεῦ,
>   πιθοῦ τε καὶ γένει σῶι
>   ἄλευσον ἀνδρῶν ὕβριν εὖ στυγήσας,
>   λίμναι δ' ἔμβαλε πορφυροειδεῖ
>   τὰν μελανόζυγ' ἄταν.[8]   530

The key to the understanding of ἄτη in this context is the contrast which Aeschylus draws between the "happiness" (ὄλβος) of Zeus and the ἄτη of the Danaids, a contrast highlighted in the epithets πορφυροειδεῖ and μελανόζυγ'.

The two are contrasted, first of all, in the colors involved: purple and black. But the more significant contrast is one of connotation. πορφυροειδής, according to the editors of LSJ, means "purpled." The question here is one of connotation; that is, is the "purpled" sea the bright sea of a serene day or is it a stormy sea? The only other example of the use of the word in tragedy occurs in a passage of Euripides' *Trojan Women*, where Hecuba is speaking:

> πρῷραι ναῶν, ὠκείαις
> Ἴλιον ἱερὰν αἷ κώπαις
>   δι' ἅλα πορφυροειδέα καὶ
>   λιμένας Ἑλλάδος εὐόρμους ...[9]   125

It should be fairly clear from this passage that the sea cannot be stormy since the ships are making swift progress toward Troy. The only other occurrence of this word, in Aristotle, *Col.* 792A17, is an even more convincing confirmation of the connotation of serenity:

τὸ δ᾽ ἁλουργὲς εὐανθὲς μὲν γίνεται καὶ λαμπρόν, ὅταν τῷ μετρίῳ λευκῷ καὶ σκιερῷ κραθῶσιν ἀσθενεῖς αἱ τοῦ ἡλίου αὐγαί. διὸ καὶ περὶ ἀνατολὰς καὶ δύσεις ὁ ἀὴρ πορφυροειδής ἐστιν ὅτε φαίνεται, περὶ ἀνατολὴν καὶ δύσιν ὄντος τοῦ ἡλιοῦ.[10]

Hence, the other two instances of πορφυροειδής preclude the connotation of a stormy sea and indicate that in the *Suppliants* passage the connotation of a bright sea is the proper one.[11]

μελανόζυγ᾽ means "black-benched," and the point of the contrast with πορφυροειδεῖ is clearly carried by the first part of the word, since this is where the contrast in colors occurs. But, again, what is the connotation of μελανόζυγ᾽? There is an interesting metaphorical use of μέλας elsewhere in Aeschylus which should not be overlooked here. In both the *Seven Against Thebes* 833–834 (ὦ μέλαινα καὶ τελεία / γένεος Οἰδίπου τ᾽ ἀρά) and *Agamemnon* 769–770 (μέλαιναν μελάθροισιν ἄταν),[12] μέλας is used in the sense of "hateful" or "dread." Applying such a connotation to the epithet μελανόζυγ᾽ provides a striking contrast to the "serene" overtones of πορφυροειδεῖ, and suggests the possibility of a similar contrast in this element of the strophe. Since the entire strophe manifests meticulous care in its component elements, it would be extremely unlikely that ὄλβιε Ζεῦ . . . ἔμβαλε would not reflect the same meticulousness. And, indeed, the same precise care is manifest if ἄταν, the direct object of ἔμβαλε, means "disaster"; it thereby is set in contrast to the ὄλβος of Zeus, as the serene quality of the sea is contrasted with the "dread" quality of the ship of the Aegyptiads.[13] Thus, understanding ἄτη as "disaster" in line 530 makes excellent sense both in the passage and in the play as a whole: "Happy Zeus, hurl into the purpled sea the black-benched disaster."[14]

Oresteia

Since the importance and consequences of human choice, a choice which could be a wrong one, are fundamental ingredients of the *Oresteia*,[15] the principal point of the following consideration of passages in the trilogy is simply to notice how ἄτη is consistently employed in connection with human choice and its consequences.[16]

Agamemnon. The onset of ἄτη is swift, as the chorus sing in the amoibaion of the fourth epeisodion of the *Agamemnon*:

ποίαν 'Ερινὺν τήνδε δώμασιν κέληι
ἐπορθιάζειν; οὔ με φαιδρύνει λόγος.   1120
ἐπὶ δὲ καρδίαν ἔδραμε κροκοβαφὴς
σταγών, ἄτε καὶ δορὶ πτωσίμοις
ξυνανύτει βίου δύντος αὐγαῖς·
ταχεῖα δ' ἄτα πέλει.[17]

Appearance can conceal ἄτη from the unwary, as in the case of Clytemnestra and Agamemnon related by Cassandra:

νεῶν δ' ἄπαρχος 'Ιλίου τ' ἀναστάτης
οὐκ οἶδεν οἵα γλῶσσα μισητῆς κυνὸς
λέξασα κἀκτείνασα φαιδρόνους δίκην
ἄτης λαθραίου τεύξεται κακῆι τύχηι.[18]   1230

In the fifth epeisodion, after the chorus have threatened her with reprisals, Clytemnestra replies:

καὶ τήνδ' ἀκούεις ὁρκίων ἐμῶν θέμιν·
μὰ τὴν τέλειον τῆς ἐμῆς παιδὸς Δίκην
ἄτην 'Ερινύν θ', αἷσι τόνδ' ἔσφαξ' ἐγώ,
οὔ μοι Φόβου μέλαθρον 'Ελπὶς ἐμπατεῖ,
ἕως ἂν αἴθηι πῦρ ἐφ' ἑστίας ἐμῆς   1435
Αἴγισθος, ὡς τὸ πρόσθεν εὖ φρονῶν ἐμοί·

The context makes it quite improbable that ἄτη could mean "blindness" or "infatuation" here, for to whom would the "blindness" or "infatuation" refer? It might be true that Clytemnestra is, at this point, "infatuated" with Aegisthus, but surely she would not speak of her feeling toward him as "blindness" or "infatuation." Nor is Aegisthus the focus of attention here. Clytemnestra is speaking rather of Iphigenia, τῆς ἐμῆς παιδὸς (1432); but for Clytemnestra to speak of "blindness" or "infatuation" with reference to Iphigenia is quite incomprehensible. Furthermore, in giving the θέμις of her oaths, Clytemnestra makes it quite clear that she joins δίκη, ἄτη, and ἐρινύς very closely, as is brought out not only by their immediate juxtaposition but also by αἷσι (1433); and the notion of "blindness" or "infatuation" makes no sense in conjunction with δίκη and ἐρινύς.

The objective meaning of ἄτη, on the other hand, would seem to suit the context quite well, for to Clytemnestra's mind the one clear fact is that Agamemnon inflicted "ruin" or "destruction" on Iphigenia. Because of this, then, Clytemnestra exacts "justice," and she does so "in a spirit of revenge." Hence, all three concepts (δίκη, ἄτη, ἐρινύς) stem from Agamemnon's treatment of Iphigenia, they all are closely linked, and they focus on no one else but Iphigenia.[19]

At line 1523 Clytemnestra blames Agamemnon for bringing ἄτη on the house by his wanton murder of Iphigenia. Clytemnestra's anapaests from lines 1521 to 1526 appear as follows in the MSS:

οὔτ' ἀνελεύθερον οἶμαι θάνατον
τῶιδε γενέσθαι.
οὐδὲ γὰρ οὗτος δολίαν ἄτην
οἴκοισιν ἔθηκ',
ἀλλ' ἐμὸν ἐκ τοῦδ' ἔρνος ἀερθέν,   1525
τὴν πολύκλαυτον †τ' Ἰφιγένειαν†

Seidler bracketed lines 1521–1522 as a gloss which had crept into the text;[20] but even if the lines are rejected, the meaning of ἄτην in 1523 is quite clear from the context: it means "ruin" or "destruction."[21]

Wilamowitz, taking exception to Seidler's suggestion, argued for retention of the lines, but he indicated a lacuna immediately following them because of hiatus and the lack of a second οὔτε to parallel the one in line 1521.[22] His proposal has been endorsed by Fraenkel and by Denniston and Page.

The hiatus between lines 1522 and 1523 and the absence of the second οὔτε seem a quite conclusive argument for the existence of a lacuna. But if this interpretation of the text is accepted, the meaning of ἄτην in 1523 is not so clear as it previously was, since what precedes line 1523 cannot be known. Thus, Wilamowitz, Kranz, and Fraenkel alike maintain that δολίω μόρω (1519) is answered, not by δολίαν ἄτην (1523), but by some phrase which occurred in the lacuna. But since the ἄτη mentioned in 1523 still is predicated of a group (οἴκοισιν, 1524), and since the context still requires the sense of "ruin" or "destruction" even in this arrangement of the text, it seems best to understand ἄτη in 1523 as "ruin" or "destruction."

Libation-Bearers. After the recognition scene in the first epeisodion of the *Libation-Bearers*, Orestes deliberates the choice he must make,[23] and declares:

οὔτοι προδώσει Λοξίου μεγασθενὴς
χρησμὸς κελεύων τόνδε κίνδυνον περᾶν,   270
κἀξορθιάζων πολλά, καὶ δυσχειμέρους
ἄτας ὑφ' ἧπαρ θερμὸν ἐξαυδώμενος,
εἰ μὴ μέτειμι τοῦ πατρὸς τοὺς αἰτίους
τρόπον τὸν αὐτόν, ἀνταποκτεῖναι λέγων·

The meaning of ἄτη in line 272 is "calamities."[24] It is attributable to Apollo (269) and echoes κακά (277). Orestes' problem is whether to obey Apollo's command of revenge, and thus stand innocent in Apollo's eyes, or to disobey the command and thereby suffer the disaster which the god has threatened.

The lengthy passage of the second stasimon of the *Libation-Bearers* again contains ἄτη in the objective sense and again shows Aeschylus' awareness of the importance of personal choice and its results. The MSS evidence for these lines is quite poor, and, as Smyth observes, "Of verses 829–837 only the general sense is clear."[25] Numerous emendations have been proposed for these lines; the following text is basically Page's, with a few departures underlined for easy recognition. Strophe, mesode, and antistrophe γ, then, are taken to read as follows:

στρ.	καὶ τότ' ἤδη κλυτὸν	
	δωμάτων λυτήριον	820
	θῆλυν οὐριοστάταν	
	ὀξύκρεκτον βοητὸν νόμον	
	μεθήσομεν· πόλει τάδ' εὖ·	
	ἐμὸν ἐμὸν κέρδος αὔξεται τόδ', ἄ-	825
	τα δ' ἀποστατεῖ φίλων.	
μεσωιδ.	σὺ δὲ θαρσῶν ὅταν ἥκῃ μέρος ἔργων,	
	ἐπαύσας πατρὸς αὐδὰν θροοῦσα	
	πρὸς σὲ "τέκνον"	
	καὶ πέραιν' ἀνεπίμομφον ἄταν.	830
ἀντ.	Περσέως δ' ἐν φρεσὶν	
	καρδίαν ἀνασχεθὼν	
	τοῖς θ' ὑπὸ χθονὸς φίλοις	
	τοῖς τ' ἄνωθεν πρόπρασσε χάριν	
	ὀργᾶς λυπρᾶς ἔνδοθεν	835
	φόνιον ἄταν τιθείς, τὸν αἴτιον	
	δ' ἐξαπολλύων μόρον.[26]	

In spite of the condition of the details of the text in the passage, the meaning of ἄτη in lines 825, 830, and 836 can easily be determined. It means "ruin" or "destruction," and there are several reasons for this interpretation, the first of which is provided by the general context. The chorus have just dispatched Orestes' nurse, Cilissa, to summon Aegisthus. The plot for the destruction of Clytemnestra and Aegisthus is on the brink of success, and with its accomplishment Orestes, Electra, and the whole of Argos will escape from evil. Thus, in the mesode and antistrophe at least, the chorus exhort Orestes to kill. The tone established by this exhortation, as well as the chorus' knowledge of and complicity in his intended act, point to the meaning of "ruin," or "destruction," for ἄτη here.

Secondly, there are definite indications in each of the three lyric systems pointing to ἄτη as "ruin" or "destruction." The most important, but at the same time the most nuanced, indication involves the initial occurrence of ἄτη in line 825. It is most important because it establishes the basic meaning which will carry over to lines 830 and 836; it is most nuanced because the meaning of ἄτη in 825 must be determined in two contexts, the original women's song and the applied meaning of that song on the lips of the chorus.

ἄτη is best understood as having meant "loss" in its original framework, for the contrast between "gain" and "loss" seems much more likely to have been the subject of a little everyday tune than the more portentous dichotomy between "gain" and "ruin." Moreover, there are both pre-Aeschylean and Aeschylean precedents for the use of ἄτη meaning "loss" (rather than "ruin") in an economic context such as the present passage provides in the phrase ἐμὸν κέρδος αὔξεται (825): *Works and Days* 413 and *Suppliants* 444, and at line 272 of the present play. Finally, ἄτη is specifically associated with κέρδος in two passages in which the former means "loss" (*Works and Days* 352 and Theognis 133). Thus, there are good indications that in its original setting of the familiar women's song ἄτη meant "loss."

But on the lips of the chorus, ἄτη in line 825 surely assumes the connotation of "ruin" and "destruction," for in the purification of the house the chorus foresee a deliverance, not from "loss," but from "ruin," the ruin which had blighted the house of Atreus and threatened all the citizens of Argos. This becomes clearer as the stasimon progresses.

In the mesode, the adjective ἀνεπίμομφον ("blameless") points to the meaning of "ruin" or "destruction" for ἄτη in line 830. The mesode begins the exhortation to Orestes to kill, and the ἄτη spoken of in line 830 applies not to him, or Electra, or the chorus, but to Clytemnestra. Yet, in accomplishing the ἄτη, Orestes will accomplish an ἀνεπίμομφον ἄταν. The hypallage is significant. It not only indicates that the chorus mean "ruin" by speaking of ἄτη (for what could a "guiltless infatuation" possibly be in this context?); it also shows that the chorus are aware of the possible consequences of Orestes' action. He is liable to be accused as guilty of murder, but not in their eyes, for he will have accomplished an ἀνεπίμομφον ἄταν.[27]

In the antistrophe there are three phrases which secure the meaning of "ruin" or "destruction" for ἄτη. (a) There is the reference in line 831 to Perseus' slaying of Medusa. In recalling the myth the chorus show what they have in mind when they subsequently employ the phrase φόνιον ἄταν τιθείς. (b) The epithet φόνιον can make sense as a modifier of ἄταν only if ἄτη is understood as meaning "ruin" or "destruction." And (c) the last clause of the sentence, τὸν αἴτιον δ' ἐξαπολλύων μόρον, reinforces the concept of "ruin" already expressed in ἄτη.

Eumenides. In the *Eumenides* both the consequences of human choice and the problem of men's relationship to the gods are involved in the two relevant passages.

The first stasimon of the *Eumenides* is the song and dance performed by the chorus to bind Orestes with their spell (lines 306–307). ἄτη occurs in ephymnion γ:

ἐφυμν. μάλα γὰρ οὖν ἁλομένα
    ἀνάκαθεν βαρυπετῆ
    καταφέρω ποδὸς ἀκμάν,
    σφαλερὰ <καὶ> ταννδρόμοις   375
    κῶλα, δύσφορον ἄταν.[28]

Interpreting ἄτη here as "calamities" accords with the context. In this part of the play, the Furies are the sworn enemies of Orestes, and they are determined to make him pay for murdering Clytemnestra.

After the Furies have been transformed into Eumenides, they employ ἄτη in their prayer against στάσις.

ἀντ. τὰν δ' ἄπληστον κακῶν
    μήποτ' ἐν πόλει Στάσιν
    τᾷδ' ἐπεύχομαι βρέμειν,
    μηδὲ πιοῦσα κόνις μέλαν αἷμα πολιτᾶν   980
    δι' ὀργὰν ποινὰς
    ἀντιφόνους ἄτας
    ἁρπαλίσαι πόλεως, . . .

Again the context makes the meaning of "ruin" or "calamities" clear for ἄτη in line 982.

Several aspects of this prayer of the Eumenides that human passion may never again bring ruin, ἄτη, to the city deserve a brief comment. The use of ἄτη in the plural to signify "ruin" has Aeschylean precedents at *Persians* 1037 and *Agamemnon* 730, and the theme of blood on the ground, a theme which Goheen has shown to be developed significantly throughout the trilogy,²⁹ is also associated with ἄτη at *Libation-Bearers* 68, 403, and 404.

Prometheus

Finally, the importance and consequences of human choice appear in the ἄτη passage at lines 1071–1079 of the *Prometheus*. Hermes warns the Oceanids to blame their ἄτη, their ruin, not on Zeus, but on themselves and their own ἄνοια:

> ἀλλ' οὖν μέμνησθ' ἀγὼ προλέγω,
> μηδὲ πρὸς ἄτης θηραθεῖσαι
> μέμψησθε τύχην, μηδέ ποτ' εἴπηθ'
> ὡς Ζεὺς ὑμᾶς εἰς ἀπρόοπτον
> πῆμ' εἰσέβαλεν, μὴ δῆτ', αὐταὶ δ'   1075
> ὑμᾶς αὐτάς· εἰδυῖαι γὰρ
> κοὐκ ἐξαίφνης οὐδὲ λαθραίως
> εἰς ἀπέραντον δίκτυον ἄτης
> ἐμπλεχθήσεσθ' ὑπ' ἀνοίας.

No question has been raised about the meaning of ἄτη in lines 1072 and 1078; it is commonly taken to mean "ruin," "calamity," or "disaster" by all the editors or commentators who discuss it. Nonetheless this passage demands special attention, for the words ὑπ' ἀνοίας (1079) contain the clearest indication yet encountered of the close relationship between ἄτη in its objective sense of "ruin" and in its subjective sense of "blindness." The ruin in which the Oceanids will become enmeshed is directly attributed to their ἄνοια. Hence, ἄτη, meaning "ruin," is still felt to be closely connected with a state of "folly" or "blindness"; and though this state is expressed here by ὑπ' ἀνοίας, it could have been expressed equally well by ἄτη in its subjective sense.

This brief review of fifteen Aeschylean passages reveals the presence of a constant phenomenon: in each instance Aeschylus employs ἄτη in the objective sense of "ruin," "calamity," "disaster," or "destruction" and each time the ἄτη is connected with the importance and consequences of human choice. Clearly, then, this phenomenon was of some importance to Aeschylus.

A second Aeschylean concern, man's relationship to the gods, is the subject of the remaining passages which employ ἄτη in the objective sense.

MAN'S RELATIONSHIP TO THE GODS

Seven Against Thebes

In the first stasimon of the *Seven Against Thebes*, ἄτη appears in the prayer of the chorus to the gods of the country to inflict ruin, ἄτη, on the invaders:

πρὸς τάδ', ὦ πολιοῦχοι
θεοί, τοῖσι μὲν ἔξω
πύργων ἀνδρολέτειραν
καταρρίψοπλον ἄταν   315
ἐμβαλόντες ἄροισθε
κῦδος τοῖσδε πολίταις, ...

There are two reasons for preferring the interpretation of ἄτη as "ruin" or "destruction" here. First, "destruction" is more consonant with the messenger's account, lines 39–68, which told of the invaders' determination to capture the city or to cover it with blood. The chorus know, therefore, of the enemy's intention to take their city or to die in the attempt. Since the chorus are confronted with such resolve, is it not more plausible for them to pray for the implacable enemy's destruction than for his mere panic?

Secondly, the purpose of the chorus is simple and general, not strategic, and to suppose that ἄτη is "panic" here means that the chorus are telling the gods *how* to work things out. Again, this hardly suits the dramatic situation. Consequently, ἄτη at line 315 of the *Seven* is best understood as "calamity" or "destruction."

Oresteia

Relevant passages in the trilogy reveal the same Aeschylean concern for man's relationship to the gods. That Aeschylus is aware of the bilateral nature of any such "relationship" is clear not only from his indications that part of man's relationship to the gods is already established by the gods, but also from his insistence that man could cooperate with the gods, that not all initiative comes from outside man.

Agamemnon. In the anapaestic prelude to the first stasimon, ἄτη appears for the first time in the *Agamemnon*:[30]

ὦ Ζεῦ βασιλεῦ καὶ Νὺξ φιλία,   355
μεγάλων κόσμων κτεάτειρα,
ἥτ' ἐπὶ Τροίας πύργοις ἔβαλες

στεγανὸν δίκτυον, ὡς μήτε μέγαν
μήτ' οὖν νεαρῶν τιν' ὑπερτελέσαι
μέγα δουλείας   360
γάγγαμον, ἄτης παναλώτου.

The use and meaning of ἄτη in line 361 are quite similar to those in other Aeschylean passages. It means "ruin," "calamity," or "disaster." The metaphor of the net, prominent throughout the *Agamemnon*, occurs again with ἄτη at *Prometheus* 1078,[31] and the same word for net, δίκτυον, is used in both passages.

The chorus employ ἄτη twice in the second antistrophe of the second stasimon as they sing of a divinely sent priest of ruin, ἄτη, who was reared in the house and brought destruction, ἄτη, to it:

χρονισθεὶς δ' ἀπέδειξεν ἦ-
θος τὸ πρὸς τοκέων· χάριν
γὰρ τροφεῦσιν ἀμείβων
μηλοφόνοισιν <ἐν> ἄταις   730
δαῖτ' ἀκέλευστος ἔτευξεν,
αἵματι δ' οἶκος ἐφύρθη,
ἄμαχον ἄλγος οἰκέταις,
μέγα σίνος πολυκτόνον·
ἐκ θεοῦ δ' ἱερεύς τις ἄ-   735
τας δόμοις προσεθρέφθη.

Though at line 730 there is a question whether ἄτη should be read at all,[32] and if so what the precise reading is, ἄταισιν can be reasonably well defended here.[33] Meaning "disasters" or "ruins," its usage both is quite consonant with the immediate context and makes excellent sense in a wider context as well, for the image contained in lines 728–731 is expressed analogously of the various disasters encountered by the members of both the house of Pelops and the house of Priam.[34]

At 735, ἄτη clearly means "ruin" or "disaster," and no question has been raised about it.

The final appearance of ἄτη in the *Agamemnon* is in the last antistrophe of the long kommos between Clytemnestra and the chorus:

ὄνειδος ἥκει τόδ' ἀντ' ὀνείδους·   1560
δύσμαχα δ' ἐστὶ κρῖναι.
φέρει φέροντ', ἐκτίνει δ' ὁ καίνων.
μίμνει δὲ μίμνοντος ἐν θρόνωι Διὸς
παθεῖν τὸν ἔρξαντα· θέσμιον γάρ.
τίς ἂν γονὰν ἀραῖον ἐκβάλοι δόμων;   1565
κεκόλληται γένος πρὸς ἄται.

πρὸς ἄται in 1566 is an emendation for προσάψαι of the MSS. The emendation is Bloomfield's and is accepted by all editors without exception.[35] All likewise agree that in this context ἄτη means "ruin," "destruction," or "calamity."

Two features of this passage are worthy of note. The first is the chorus' reminiscence in παθεῖν τὸν ἔρξαντα (1564) of their statement in the parodos:

τὸν φρονεῖν βροτοὺς ὁδώ-   176
σαντα τῶι πάθει μάθος
θέντα κυρίως ἔχειν.

The second is that the notion of inherited evil, which is fundamental to the trilogy and expressed here by the metaphor of the seed (γονὰν ἀραῖον, 1565), has also appeared in connection with ἄτη elsewhere in the *Agamemnon* (see lines 386, 735, 771, and 1283).

Libation-Bearers. The same divine point of reference for the relationship of gods and men is continued in the *Libation-Bearers*. At line 383 Orestes appeals to Zeus of the underworld who sends delayed destruction, ἄτη, upon the wicked. The pertinent passage is strophe δ of the kommos of the first epeisodion:

Ζεῦ Ζεῦ, κάτωθεν ἀμπέμπειν
ὑστερόποινον ἄταν
βροτῶν τλήμονι καὶ πανούργωι
χειρί· τοκεῦσι δ' ὅμως τελεῖται.[36]   385

That ἄτη in line 383 is to be interpreted as "ruin" or "destruction" is obvious from the chorus' next sentence (lines 386–389): they hope to live to glory in the death, that is, the ruin or destruction, of Aegisthus and Clytemnestra.

In lines 403–404, the chorus express Orestes' dilemma:[37] there is a law, they say, that murder demands another destruction, ἄτη. Thus Aeschylus, in powerfully proclaiming the *lex talionis*, shows that "blood vengeance in this play lays claims to being a 'Law' set in the ultimate nature of things":[38]

ἀλλὰ νόμος μὲν φονίας σταγόνας   400
χυμένας ἐς πέδον ἄλλο προσαιτεῖν
αἷμα· βοᾶι γὰρ λοιγὸς Ἐρινὺν
παρὰ τῶν πρότερον φθιμένων ἄτην
ἑτέραν ἐπάγουσαν ἐπ' ἄτηι.

The meaning of the remarkable double use of ἄτη is clear from the context; it means "ruin" or "destruction." In the concrete application of the *lex talionis*, the chorus are thinking of Clytemnestra and Aegisthus, as is shown by the fact that they are answering Electra's question pertaining to κάρανα (line 396), but the generic law enunciated also makes it clear that this type of ἄτη applies to all mankind.

In the next pertinent passage from the *Libation-Bearers*, the chorus show that they also know the implications of the curse upon the house.[39] At 467 they sing of the inbred trouble and bloody stroke of destruction, ἄτη, proper to the house of Atreus:

στρ. ὦ πόνος ἐγγενής,
      καὶ παράμουσος ἄτας
      αἱματόεσσα πλαγά,
      ἰὼ δύστον' ἄφερτα κήδη,
      ἰὼ δυσκατάπαυστον ἄλγος.   470

Three contextual considerations secure the meaning of "ruin" or "disaster" for ἄτη in 467. (*a*) ἄτη applies to a group, as Aeschylus makes clear through the use of ἐγγενής in line 466. (*b*) That daemonic agents, the θεοί κατὰ γᾶς spoken of in line 475, are responsible for the ἄτη is made even clearer when the balance between these concluding lines of the kommos and the words with which the kommos began at lines 306–314 are taken into account. This technique of balance within lyric passages has frequently been noticed in Aeschylus, and ἄτας πλαγά of 467–468 echoes the πληγῆς φονίας φονίαν πληγὴν τινέτω of 312–313 which was to come Διόθεν. And (*c*) ἄτη in 467 reinforces three other words for evil in this passage: πόνος (466), κήδη (469), and ἄλγος (470).

Eumenides. This concept, the divine point of reference for the relationship of man to gods, is also perceptible in the passages in the *Eumenides* already considered.[40] At line 376 the Erinyes, daemonic powers, revel in their boast of bringing calamity, ἄτη, to the opinions of men, and at 982, once they have been transformed into beneficient spirits, they pray that human passion may never again bring ruin, ἄτη, to the city in the new dispensation.

However, some of the passages of the trilogy in which ἄτη is used in the objective sense also reveal Aeschylus' idea that man could cooperate with the gods, that not *all* initiative in effecting or avoiding ἄτη comes from outside man. Sometimes this human cooperation with the divine does not issue in happy results. Thus at *Agamemnon* 643 the herald speaks of war (dear to Ares) which brings ruin, ἄτη, for individuals and the city:

ὅταν δ' ἀπευκτὰ πήματ' ἄγγελος πόλει
στυγνῶι προσώπωι πτωσίμου στρατοῦ φέρηι,
πόλει μὲν ἕλκος ἓν τὸ δήμιον τυχεῖν,   640
πολλοὺς δὲ πολλῶν ἐξαγισθέντας δόμων
ἄνδρας διπλῆι μάστιγι, τὴν ῎Αρης φιλεῖ,
δίλογχον ἄτην, φοινίαν ξυνωρίδα·

ἄτη here means "ruin" or "destruction," as all editors agree.

Sometimes the results are more to an individual's liking. Thus, at 810, at the beginning of the third epeisodion, Agamemnon thanks the gods of Argos, who were equally responsible with him for bringing destruction to Troy; his speech continues:

ἄτης θύελλαι ζῶσι· συνθνήισκουσα δὲ
σποδὸς προπέμπει πίονας πλούτου πνοάς.   820

The irony of such usage, however, should not be overlooked. In the previous stasimon, the chorus had used ἄτη three times with exactly the same meaning, yet in their mouths ἄτη had a multiple application, first in the parable of the lion and then in connection with ὕβρις. Agamemnon is thinking only in terms of Troy when he says ἄτης θύελλαι ζῶσι, but to anyone who has heard the previous stasimon his words assume a wider and ironic significance.[41]

The picture of the blood spilled on the ground, which was discussed in connection with *Libation-Bearers* 400–404, occurred earlier in the same play. The text of the final strophe and antistrophe of the parodos is:

στρ. δι' αἷματ' ἐκποθένθ' ὑπὸ χθονὸς τροφοῦ   66
τίτας φόνος πέπηγεν οὐ διαρρύδαν·
†διαλγὴς† ἄτα διαφέρει τὸν αἴτιον
†παναρκέτας† νόσου βρύειν.

The meaning of ἄτη in line 68 is "ruin," "calamity," or "disaster" — as the scholiast clearly understood: ἡ διαιωνίζουσα ἄτη, τοῦτ' ἔστιν ὁ φόνος — for it echoes φόνος in line 67.[42]

Yet this passage represents a good deal more than just a word-echo. In the choral passage at 400–404, the viewpoint was extrinsic to the murderer and focused on the blood itself; hence it resulted in activity by an exterior agent, the Erinys, who brings ruin (ἄτη). But in the passage from the parodos (lines 66–69) there is a shift in the point of view: the viewpoint is now interior to the murderer.

Dealing with both these passages in yet another manner may help to clarify still more the difference between them. In the Aeschylean ἄτη passages which focus on man's relationship to the gods (*Seven* 312–317; *Agamemnon* 355–361, 726–736, 1560–1566; *Libation-Bearers* 380–385, 400–404, 466–470; and *Eumenides* 368–376 and 976–983), the emphasis is consistently on the activity of the gods in such a relationship. But in the passage from the parodos of the *Libation-Bearers* (lines 66–69), the emphasis is on man's own activity in cooperating with the gods.

The final Aeschylean ἄτη passage occurs at lines 336–339 of the *Libation-Bearers*. Electra pleads with Agamemnon, even though he is dead, to come to their aid and to help to accomplish a deliverance from calamity, ἄτη. The conclusion of antistrophe α of the kommos in the first epeisodion is:

τάφος δ' ἱκέτας δέδε-
κται φυγάδας θ' ὁμοίως·
τί τῶνδ' εὖ, τί δ' ἄτερ κακῶν;
οὐκ ἀτρίακτος ἄτα;   339

The meaning of ἄτη in 339 is clear: "ruin" or "calamity." The group of which it is predicated includes Electra and Orestes (δίπαις in line 334 and ἱκέτας . . . φυγάδας θ' in lines 336–337) in the immediate context, as well as the servants who constitute the chorus and all the citizens of Argos, as the tenor of the whole scene makes clear. And ἄτη in 339 echoes κακῶν in 338.

This second group of texts, like the first, reveals a constant phenomenon: Aeschylus employs ἄτη in the objective sense in each instance, and the subject matter of each passage involves the relationship between the gods and men.

Notice of this consistent use of the objective sense of ἄτη in connection with either the importance and consequences of human choice or the relationship of man and gods affords significant insight into two broad areas of Aeschylean thought: (*a*) the link between moral responsibility and δίκη in the tragic vision of man; and (*b*) the Aeschylean concept of πάθει μάθος.

LINK BETWEEN MORAL RESPONSIBILITY AND ΔΙΚΗ
IN AESCHYLUS' TRAGIC VISION OF MAN

ἄτη and moral responsibility are linked both to δίκη and to retribution in Aeschylean thought. Human choice, Aeschylus shows, has consequences. If the choice is a bad one, then the consequence is one of retribution. It is an ἄτη, a "ruin," "calamity," or "destruction." Moreover, such retribution is just; it involves δίκη.

This concept is perhaps best explained by Aeschylus' tragic vision of man.[43] He sees man as capable of greatness, in both good and evil, yet he also recognizes the supremacy and inscrutability of Zeus. If there is a collision between human choice and Zeus' supremacy, the result is humanly tragic but just nevertheless.

This is the dilemma of Pelasgus: he knows that either to refuse sanctuary or to fight the invaders will involve calamity, ἄτη. This is tragic, but it is not unjust; nor does Pelasgus ever say that it is. The chorus in the *Persians* share the same insight. They lament the delusion, ἄτη, of Xerxes which resulted in personal and national disaster, ἄτη, but know the inevitability of the link between the two. It is to Zeus that the chorus in the *Seven* pray, asking him to inflict disaster, ἄτη, on the invaders; such just retribution comes naturally to them as a subject for petition to Zeus. And Hermes' warning to the Oceanids in the *Prometheus* is explicit: blame your ruin, ἄτη, not on Zeus but on your own ignorance.

In the *Agamemnon* the connection between ἄτη and just retribution is variously presented. Thus, the priest of ruin, ἄτη, who brings destruction, ἄτη, to the house which nurtured him is given one prime characteristic: he is divinely sent. The destruction of Troy, naturally just to a Greek, is celebrated as the work of Zeus by the chorus and by Agamemnon on his return. Yet the terrible side of the war does not escape notice either: the herald sings of war which brings ruin, ἄτη, both on individuals and on the entire city of Argos. It was a just war, but terrible. On a strictly personal level, Clytemnestra glories in having avenged the destruction wrongly inflicted on their daughter; but she also realizes the consequences, as she shows in her indictment of Agamemnon for inducing ruin, ἄτη, on the house by his wanton murder. And the chorus advert to the fact that ὕβρις, a violation of δίκη, leads to ruin, ἄτη. It is a process of retribution within a context of justice.

When Orestes confronts the problem of justice and retribution in the *Libation-Bearers*, he knows the connection with ἄτη. He is faced, he says, with a dilemma: Apollo threatens him with ruin, ἄτη, if he does not exact revenge for his father. He shows implicit trust in the justice of Zeus when he appeals to him as the god who sends destruction upon the wicked. And the chorus exhort him to have the courage to exact satisfaction through revenge. But it is not simply any satisfaction they envisage; rather it will be *blameless* satisfaction, ἀνεπίμομφον ἄταν (830). In other words, his revenge will be just because it will be performed in accordance with the counsels of Zeus and of his messenger Apollo, not under the impulse of human blindness.

In the concluding play of the trilogy, the Eumenides, after their transformation, display this same outlook, for they pray that human passion may never bring ruin, ἄτη, on the city. Now that the horrendous affair of the house of Atreus, simultaneously tragic and just, has been ended, they pray that the divinely sanctioned cycle of just retribution may never again be triggered by human blindness or folly.

In each play, then, human choice does indeed have consequences, and if the choice is a bad one the results are just retribution which ends in human disaster.

Finally, Aeschylus' concept of ἄτη in the objective sense is closely connected with, and at times is almost another expression of, his concept of πάθει μάθος. Thus, in the *Suppliants* the plight of the Danaids and the dilemma of Pelasgus, both expressed in terms of ἄτη, are concrete manifestations of the idea that wisdom comes through suffering. Similarly, the passages of the *Persians* in which ἄτη appears in the objective sense show that Xerxes learned only through catastrophic personal hardship. This is likewise the case of Io in the *Prometheus*. And in the *Seven*, Eteocles learned the harsh lesson only at the price of his life.

The chorus of the *Agamemnon* express the connection most clearly. They state that while Zeus reigns there is a law that one who acts must suffer. And they immediately add, almost as if to say "therefore," that the house of Atreus is mired in ἄτη. This is an echo of one of their earlier reflections: that there is no remedy for a man subject to πειθώ, the child of ἄτη. The same concept is alluded to by the chorus of the *Libation-Bearers* who state that there is a law that ἄτη demands another ἄτη. Knowledge of this law comes at a steep price, as Orestes discovers. And the connection between ἄτη and πάθει μάθος is displayed by the chorus of the Eumenides. Before their transformation they boast of bringing ἄτη to man's opinions. In this case man learns indeed through suffering. After their transformation they pray that never again will the city have to learn through suffering.[44]

Thus a study of Aeschylus' use of the objective meaning of ἄτη reveals the cohesiveness of this concept with several of his other major ideas. In Aeschylean tragedy human choice and responsibility are serious matters. They are capable of profound consequences. It is the tragic situation of man that he must frequently learn this lesson through suffering. But that is the law of Zeus, and, says Aeschylus, it is a just law.

NOTES

[1] In what remains of Greek literature from Homer to Pindar, ἄτη occurs fifty times (see chaps. 1–3 and the list in Appendix A). In the seven extant plays of Aeschylus, however, the word occurs with certainty forty-eight times (again see Appendix A). Thus, in the work of a single author whose extant plays span only about two decades of the fifth century ἄτη is employed approximately as often as it is in the remaining literary tradition of the prior three centuries.

[2] In the pre-Aeschylean tradition ἄτη is used in the objective sense on only eleven occasions out of fifty (Odyssey 12.372; Works and Days 231; Solon 13.68; Alcaeus D 12.12; Ibycus 1.8; Theognis 103, 206 and 588; and Pindar, Olympian 1.57 and 10.37, and Nemean 9.21), the balance of the pertinent passages using the word in its subjective sense. In Aeschylus the situation is significantly changed: of the forty-eight pertinent passages, thirty involve ἄτη in the objective sense.

[3] This is not to pretend that Aeschylus was a "theologian" in the modern sense of the term. Yet he was interested, and profoundly so, in significant human problems.

[4] The question of the personification of ἄτη in line 1007 has basically been answered in two ways. English editors (Paley, Smyth, Page, Murray, and Broadhead) tend to capitalize it. German editors, on the other hand (Dindorf, Wecklein, and Wilamowitz), read ἄτα. Presumably those editors who find personification base their case on the verb δέδορκεν, but δέρκομαι does not necessarily imply a personal agent. Homer uses the verb with animate, though not personal, agents; thus: Γοργὼ . . . δεινὸν δερκομένη and δράκων . . . σμερδαλέον δὲ δέδορκεν (Iliad 11.37 and 22.95, respectively). A similar usage is found in the Seven Against Thebes: λεόντων ὡς ῎Αρη δεδορκότων (53). And Pindar uses the verb with inanimate agents: δέρκεται . . . ὁ μέγας πότμος, and δέδορκεν φάος, and finally δέδορκεν . . . φέγγος (Pythian 3.85, Nemean 3.84 and 9.41). Given such uses of δέρκομαι it seems better to read ἄτα, lower case, in line 1007, in agreement with Dindorf, Wecklein, and Wilamowitz.

[5] Thus, in Odyssey 12.372 it includes Odysseus and his men; in Works and Days 231 it affects farmers generally; in Alcaeus D 12.12 the citizens of Miletus are its victims; in Ibycus 1.8 the Trojans are affected; in Theognis 206 it would affect a man's descendants; in Pindar's Olympian 10.37 the residents of an entire city are its victims; and in Nemean 9.21 it descends upon an entire army. The sole exception is Pindar's Olympian 1.57 where the victim of ruin is Tantalus.

[6] Thus, in Odyssey 12.372: Ζεῦ πάτερ ἠδ' ἄλλοι μάκαρες θεοί; in Hesiod's Works and Days 231: Ζεύς; in Alcaeus: τις 'Ολυμπίων; and in Ibycus 1.8: διὰ Κύπριδα.

⁷ The following table will show how consistent Aeschylean use is with respect to each of these three points. It seems best to gather the evidence into one convenient place in order to avoid needless repetition when discussing each passage. The passages are listed in their order of appearance in this chapter.

Play		Group Affected	Agent	Echoed Evil
Persians	1007	Persian army, commanders, empire	δαίμονες	κακὸν
	1037	Persian fleet		πῆμα 1026 & 1038 ἐπὶ συμφορᾷ κακοῦ 1030
Suppliants	470	City		δύσπάλαιστα πράγματα 468 κακῶν 469
Agamemnon	530	Aegyptiads	Zeus	μελανόζυγ' 530
	1124	γένει 1117 δώμασιν 1119	'Ερινὺν 1119	κροκοβαφὴς σταγών 1121–1122
	1230	a) Agamemnon and Cassandra in immediate context. b) Also Clytemnestra and Aegisthus in context of whole trilogy.		a) οἷα γλῶσσα . . . λέξασα κἀκτείνασα 1228–1229 b) οἷα . . . τεύξεται κακῆι τύχηι 1228–1230
	1433	See pp. 76–77		See pp. 76–77
	1523	οἴκοισιν 1524		(δολίωι μόρωι 1519)
Libation-Bearers	272		Apollo	κακά 277
	825 830 835	φίλων 826		ἐξαπολλύων μόρον 837
Eumenides	376	ταννδρόμοις 375	Furies	ὀρχησμοῖς τ' ἐπιφθόνοις ποδός 371 βαρυπετῆ . . . ποδὸς ἀκμάν 373–374 σθαλερὰ . . . κῶλα 375–376
	982	πόλει 977 πολιτᾶν 980 πόλεως 983	Eumenides	μέλαν αἷμα 980
Prometheus	1072 1078	Daughters of Oceanus as shown by: a) 2nd plural verbs; b) ὑμᾶς 1074 & 1076	Zeus	πῆμα 1075
Seven	315	τοῖσι μὲν ἔξω πύργων 313–314	πολιοῦχοι θεοί 312–313	ἀνδρολέτειραν 314

Play		Group Affected	Agent	Echoed Evil
Agamemnon	361	Τροίας πύργοις 357 ὡς μήτε μέγαν μήτ' οὖν νεαρῶν τιν' ὑπερτελέσαι 358–359	Ζεῦ βασιλεῦ 355	δουλείας 360
	730	τροφεῦσιν 729	ἐκ θεοῦ 735	αἵματι 732
	735	οἶκος 732 οἰκέταις 733		ἄλγος 733 σίνος 734
	1566	γένος 1566 δόμων 1565	Zeus 1563	ἀραῖον 1565
Libation-Bearers	383	βροτῶν 384	Zeus	ποινή root in ὑστερόποινον 383
	403–404	All men	Ἐρινὺν 402	αἷμα & λοιγὸς 402
	467	ἐγγενής 466	θεῶν . . . κατὰ γᾶς 475	πόνος 466 κήδη 469 ἄλγος 470
Eumenides	376⎱ 982⎰	see above, p. 91	see above, p. 91	see above, p. 91
Agamemnon	643	πόλει 638 πόλει 640 πολλοὺς . . . ἄνδρας 641–642	Ares 642	πήματ' 638 ἕλκος 640
	819	πόλις 818	θεοὺς ἐγχωρίους . . . μεταιτίους 810–811 θεοὶ 813	σποδὸς 820
Libation-Bearers	68			φόνος 67
	339	δίπαις 334 ἱκέτας . . . φυγάδας θ' 336–337		κακῶν 338

[8] Notice the similarity to Pindar's *Olympian* 10.37. For a discussion of this passage, see Silk, *Interaction in Poetic Imagery*, pp. 105, 178, 198.

[9] This passage will be discussed in chap. 7, pp. 130–31.

[10] *Aristotle: Minor Works*, trans. W. S. Hett (Cambridge: Harvard University Press; London: Heinemann, 1936), p. 8.

[11] Tucker's note (*'Supplices' of Aeschylus*, p. 109), is both confused and confusing. He is certainly correct in stating that πορφυροειδεῖ is "not otiose"; he is likewise correct in noting that it is "in opposition to the following epithet of colour μελανόζυγα." But he seems to be confused when he tries to make the connotation of the word signify the stormy sea (discussing, as he does, the above passage from Euripides with the comment that "the epithet is idle enough"), and confusing when he cites *Iliad* 14.16 and 21.551 where the word employed is the verb πορφύρω and *Iliad* 17.551 where the word employed is πορφύρεος. As a matter of fact, this last example, if anything, might tend to prove the "serene" rather than the "stormy" overtone: applied to a *cloud* (not the sea) in the passage, it is used to describe that cloud in comparison with a rainbow, which is anything but stormy.

[12] This usage is pointed out by Tucker (ibid.); he also notes that "The former part of the epithet corresponds to the 'black ships (*i.e.*, ships of *war*)' of Homer."

[13] The scholiast is surely correct in recognizing μελανόζυγ' ἄταν as the use of the abstract for the concrete: namely, the Aegyptiads' ship (*Scholia Graeca in Aeschylum quae extant omnia.* I. *Scholia in Agamemnonem, Choephoros, Eumenides, Supplices continens*, ed. Ole Langwitz Smith [Leipzig: Teubner, 1976], p. 75).

[14] It is interesting to note, in passing, that this is as close as Aeschylus comes in this play to employing the supposed consecrated tetralogy ὄλβος, κόρος, ὕβρις, ἄτη. The missing member here, of course, is κόρος. And it should be noted that here, too, ὄλβος is ascribed to a divinity, while ὕβρις and ἄτη are predicated of humans. For these reasons, this passage did not seem to warrant inclusion in chap. 3.

[15] For a discussion of this entire problem, see Hugh Lloyd-Jones, "The Guilt of Agamemnon," CQ, 12 N.S. (1962), 187–99; Alvin Lesky, "Decision and Responsibility in the Tragedy of Aeschylus," JHS, 86 (1966), 78–85; and H. D. F. Kitto, *Poiesis: Structure and Thought*, Sather Classical Lectures 36 (Berkeley: University of California Press, 1966), chap. 1.

[16] The first such passage is *Agamemnon* 750–771, which was discussed on pp. 39–41.

[17] For a good discussion of the general context, particularly of the idea that in this scene Cassandra is a "messenger" of the future to whom the past is also present, see Owen, *Harmony of Aeschylus*, pp. 84–86.

[18] These four lines have been the subject of a good deal of discussion and emendation because, as H. J. Rose remarks, the passage is one "which every modern editor declares more or less corrupt" ("On an Epic Idiom in Aeschylos," *Eranos*, 45 [1947], 98). None of the alleged difficulties, however, involves ἄτης λαθραίου in 1230; Fraenkel's text is quite acceptable, therefore, since it adheres closely to the MSS and avoids many of the radical suggestions proposed.

The proposed emendations may be studied in four articles which, in chronological order, are: A. Y. Campbell, "Aeschylus, *Agamemnon* 1227–30," CQ, 26, No. 1 (January 1932), 45–51; J. C. Lawson, "Aeschylus, *Agamemnon*, 1227–32," CQ, 27, No. 2 (April 1933), 112–14; George Thomson, "Notes on the *Oresteia*," CQ, 28, No. 2 (April 1934), 72–78; A. Y. Campbell, "Aeschylus' *Agamemnon* 1223–38 and Treacherous Monsters," CQ, 29, No. 1 (January 1935), 25–36.

[19] There seems to be no compelling reason to personify the three abstract nouns in 1432–1433 as Fraenkel does. δίκη and ἐρινύς (particularly as echoed in the ἀλάστωρ of 1501) are not necessarily personifications. Nor is ἄτη. Fraenkel's reference to Usener's article is misapplied here, for, as Fraenkel himself admits (*Aeschylus: Agamemnon*, III 675n3), Usener "quotes . . . Sept. 42ff. . . . but does not mention Ag. 1432f."

[20] This suggestion has been followed by Dindorf, Wecklein, Paley, Smyth, Lawson, Thomson, Rose, Fletcher, and Murray.

[21] On this point, see Paley, *Tragedies of Aeschylus*, p. 488.

[22] *Aeschylos: Interpretationen*, p. 74.

[23] Though the MSS do not attribute these lines to any specific character, all editors agree in assigning them to Orestes. This is the only non-lyric occurrence of ἄτη in the play.

[24] De Romilly, *La Crainte et l'angoisse dans le théâtre d'Eschyle*, pp. 86–88, adverts to the notion of "fear" in this passage, and Böhme, *Bühnenbearbeitung Äschyleischer Tragödien*, 1 48–49, points out that Orestes' οὔτοι προδώσει here is echoed by the

words of Apollo to him at *Eumenides* 64. This passage is discussed briefly by Walter Nestle in *Menschliche Existenz und politische Erziehung in der Tragödie des Aischylos* (Stuttgart & Berlin: Kohlhammer, 1934), p. 43. For a good general discussion of Orestes in this play, see Karl Reinhardt, *Aischylos als Regisseur und Theologe* (Bern: Francke, 1949), pp. 112–22.

²⁵ *Aeschylus*, II 239.

²⁶ Although some of the departures from Page's text are significant, none affects the three occurrences of ἄτη in these lines. The reasons for the variances from Page's text are given in Appendix D.

²⁷ It is interesting to note that in their suggested retort, πατρὸς αὐδάν, the chorus justify Orestes' deed on precisely the same ground as Athena does in the *Eumenides*.

²⁸ See the remarks on this passage in Silk, *Interaction in Poetic Imagery*, pp. 129–30.

²⁹ Goheen, "Aspects of Dramatic Symbolism," 120, notes: "We may say, then, that the imagery of dark blood on the ground, which I believe gets its first, visual statement in the carpet of the *Agamemnon*, helps to develop within the trilogy one of its thematic ideas — namely, since bloodshed is irredeemable, bloodshed is not an adequate solution; legal process and a willingness to reach understanding offer more hope."

For a possible historical allusion in this passage, see R. Livingstone, "The Problem of the *Eumenides* of Aeschylus," JHS, 45 (1925), 129, and Anthony J. Podlecki, *The Political Background of Aeschylean Tragedy* (Ann Arbor: The University of Michigan Press, 1966), pp. 85–86.

³⁰ The MSS read ἄτα at line 131, but this has been universally rejected, on metrical grounds, in favor of Hermann's emendation, ἄγα. The same correction has been made at *Suppliants* 164.

³¹ See William Chase Green, "Dramatic and Ethical Motives in the *Agamemnon*," HSPh, 54 (1943), 25–31, esp. 25–26. The *Prometheus* passage is treated above, p. 81.

³² The problem is posed by the MS reading μηλοφόνοισιν ἄταις. As Fraenkel observes (*Aeschylus: Agamemnon*, II 340): "In itself the MS μηλοφόνοισιν ἄταις would be perfectly satisfactory, cf. *Pers*. 652 . . . , 1037. . . . But the metre shows that a short syllable is lacking." The missing short syllable is needed for responsion to ἐν βιότου προτελείοις in line 720. Among the editors only Wecklein retains the MS reading.

³³ To remedy the metrical deficiency, two basic types of emendations have been made. The first group retains ἄτη in some form. Thus, ἄταισιν (given by Triclinius), [ἐν] ἄταις (suggested by Bothe and adopted by Wilamowitz, Smyth, Thomson, and Fraenkel), and [σὺν] ἄταις (read by Lawson, Fletcher, Denniston and Page) have all been proposed. The second rejects ἄτη in favor of some other word. Thus, ἄσαισιν (put forward by Paley), ἄγαισιν (adopted by Hermann and Dindorf), and μάταισιν (read by Murray following Schneider) have been suggested as possible emendations. The various proposals of this second group are ingenious but unnecessary, since the retention of some form of ἄτη can be defended.

The case for the validity of ἄτη as a reading here is based on analogous appearance of lines 728–731 elsewhere in the play, as Knox has so admirably pointed out in "The Lion in the House." Thus, if Triclinius' reading ἄταισιν is adopted — as it should be, not only because it is good Greek in itself and less awkward than either ἐν or σὺν ἄταις but also because, in what follows, the local force of ἐν or the accompaniment involved in σύν is not always verified and would be positively mis-leading in some instances — lines 728–731 mean: "For in gratitude for its upbringing, though unbidden, [the lion] prepared a banquet by means of disasters which destroy the flocks."

34 In these analogous references, whenever there is a question of disasters to the families of either Pelops or Priam, the pastoral language and imagery are striking. See, for the Pelopidae, lines 655–657, 795–798, 895–896, and 1415-1418, which involve Menelaus, Agamemnon, Iphigenia, and Thyestes, respectively; and referring to Priam, lines 529–532, for the destruction of Troy in general, and 1296–1298, addressed to Cassandra.

35 As Conington wrote: " 'ἀραῖον and πρὸς ἄτᾳ . . . are both so indisputable that it is hardly requisite to particularize them as departures from the reading of the MSS'. . ." (quoted in Fraenkel, Aeschylus: Agamemnon, III 737). Fraenkel points out that "κεκόλληται . . . πρὸς ἄται is a drastic intensification of the Homeric expression in B 111 (= I 18) Ζεύς με . . . ἄτηι ἐνέδησε, which (as Reisig saw) Sophocles takes over word for word in Oed. C. 525f." (ibid.).

36 For lines 380–585 — with the exception of line 479, which is ascribed to Elec-tra — the MSS give no indication which actor is speaking at any given place. This circumstance has led, naturally, to a certain discrepancy among the editors in assigning various passages. In the current instance, however, most editors — namely, Portus, Wecklein, Wilamowitz, Smyth, Thomson, Murray, and Page — agree that this strophe should be attributed to Orestes. Dindorf and Paley, though, follow the scholiast in assigning it to Electra, but this seems less satisfactory, in view of the construction of the entire kommos. For a good discussion of this point, see W. Scha-dewaldt, "Der Kommos in Aischylos Choephoren," Hermes, 67 (1932), 312–45.

37 All editors ascribe these lines to the chorus.

38 Goheen, "Aspects of Dramatic Symbolism," 120. He also remarks: "the image of blood on the ground, reiterated and modulated like a motif in music, leads from this point on [i.e., Agamemnon 1018–1021] through the entire Oresteia. In the Choeph-ori it appears three times: 48, 400–2, 520–1; and in the most fully delineated of these the figure is adapted to crystallize the vengeful ethos of that play" (p. 119). As will be seen below, it seems possible to add line 467 to this list.

39 Most editors — namely, Wecklein, Dindorf, Paley, Wilamowitz, Smyth, Thom-son, Murray, and Page — attribute these lines to the chorus. The scholiast assigned them to Orestes and Electra. Kirchhoff and O. Mueller attribute them to Orestes, Electra, and the chorus. The imagery of the passage is discussed by Silk, Interaction in Poetic Imagery, p. 110.

40 See above, pp. 80–81.

41 See Silk's analysis of lines 818–820 in Interaction in Poetic Imagery, pp. 184–85.

42 For a discussion of line 67, see ibid., p. 100; for the general context, see N. B. Booth, "The Run of the Sense in Aeschylus, Choephoroi 22–83," CPh, 54 (1969), 111–13.

43 See the excellent remarks of Alvin Lesky, Greek Tragedy, trans. H. A. Frankfort, 2nd ed. (London: Benn; New York: Barnes & Noble, 1967), pp. 13ff., on this point.

44 See Lloyd-Jones, Justice of Zeus, pp. 87–88, for the notion that πάθει μάθος does not necessarily imply that the sufferer learns. Learning does indeed occur, but perhaps to others. This, if true, makes ἄτη an even more reasonable form of πάθει μάθος.

6

THE CONCEPT OF *ATH
IN SOPHOCLEAN TRAGEDY

THE RELATIVELY CLEAR-CUT DISTINCTION between the subjective and objective meanings of ἄτη which appears in Aeschylean tragedy disappears in Sophocles' extant work. The use and meaning of ἄτη in Sophocles are marked by ambivalence.* Though he shows himself conscious of the differences in meaning which Aeschylus had so sharply emphasized, in a brilliant extension of his propensity for dramatic irony, Sophocles most often employs ἄτη in contexts where it carries the overtones of *both* "blindness" and "ruin." This, of course, is quite consonant with so much else in his dramatic style and way of thought.

Yet more is involved. The Sophoclean ambivalence toward ἄτη reflects a further sharpening of the Greek consciousness of the tension between human freedom and divine destiny. In Sophocles ἄτη is employed with other terms which, in the fifth century, were becoming increasingly important in the consideration of man's freedom and responsibility. Thus, it appears with: μόρος at *Ajax* 848; ὄνειδος at *Ajax* 1189; μοῖρα at *Trachinian Women* 850; οἶτον, πότμος, and δύσμορος at *Antigone* 864; ἁμαρτάνω at *Antigone* 1260; and ἀνάγκη at *Electra* 224. Human ἄτη is seen not only as more ambivalent, but also as more nuanced.

AJAX

The earliest extant Sophoclean tragedy, most scholars agree, is the *Ajax*.[1] The study of ἄτη in this play is particularly important because, as has been said, we are "presented with an illustration of the power of Ate in its most extreme form: those whom the gods would destroy

---

* As used here and in similar contexts, "ambivalence"/"ambivalent" does not carry its customary denotation of "vagueness," "inconsistency," or "vacillation." Rather, reflecting its Latin roots, the word indicates that in a single instance both (*ambi*) meanings of ἄτη are operative (*valens*).

they first make mad.''² The combination of the two notions, destruction and madness, in the single term ἄτη summarizes the predominant Sophoclean usage.

In the only Sophoclean prologue in which a god appears, Athena shows Ajax to Odysseus, who, despite their enmity, is moved at the sight of his demented foe. After Ajax has retired from the stage, Odysseus and Athena discuss the situation; to Athena's question whether he could have found a "more prudent" (προνούστερος) man, Odysseus replies:

> ἐγὼ μὲν οὐδέν' οἶδ'· ἐποικτίρω δέ νιν   121
> δύστηνον ἔμπας, καίπερ ὄντα δυσμενῆ,
> ὁθούνεκ' ἄτη συγκατέζευκται κακῇ, ...³

Both aspects of ἄτη are present here. Not only is the subjective meaning indicated by the association with προνούστερος in line 119, but the idea of the "blindness" or "folly" of Ajax — his "madness" — is found throughout the prologue. It is the subject of Athena's report in lines 51–65, underlies her purpose in showing Ajax to Odysseus (see line 85),

> δείξω δὲ καὶ σοὶ τήνδε περιφανῆ νόσον,   66
> ὡς πᾶσιν Ἀργείοισιν εἰσιδὼν θροῇς.

and provides the basis for her taunt of Odysseus:

> μεμηνότ' ἄνδρα περιφανῶς ὀκνεῖς ἰδεῖν;   81

Though τήνδε περιφανῆ νόσον (line 66) is a fine description of someone afflicted with ἄτη in the sense of "blindness," lines 91–117 offer the best contextual indication for the subjective meaning: by his very appearance Ajax shows just how "blind" he is to reality and how "foolish" his supposed victory is. The objective note of "ruin" or "calamity" is introduced in the present passage by Odysseus' remark in line 124. In looking at Ajax, he is afraid, not of "folly," but of "disaster." The yoke of blindness which has come upon his former enemy also portends disaster.⁴

ἄτη occurs next toward the end of the parados, as the chorus sing:

> ἐπ.   ἀλλ' ἄνα ἐξ ἑδράνων
> ὅπου μακραίωνι
> στηρίζει ποτὲ τᾷδ' ἀγωνίῳ σχολᾷ,
> ἄταν οὐρανίαν φλέγων.⁵   195

Again, Sophoclean ambivalence with respect to ἄτη is operative in this passage. The subjective connotation of "blindness," "madness," or "folly" is reflected in the context. The chorus enter singing of slaughter (lines 141ff.), but lacking the surety which Athena had given Odysseus, they start to inquire (at line 172) from which one of the gods Ajax had received his mad inspiration (θεία νόσος, 185) to slaughter the flocks.[6] Thus far, the argument from context indicates a certain parallel between Odysseus and the chorus in their attitude toward Ajax at this moment of the play: both are disturbed by the slaughter of the cattle and both wish to know the source of the act. This is an interpretation supported by the ancient scholiast.[7]

Yet the objective notion of "ruin" or "disaster" is also contained in the phrase ἄταν οὐρανίαν φλέγων. By his absence Ajax is permitting the disaster to grow in strength, and this evokes the chorus' exhortation to him.

ἄτη appears again at line 307, in the first epeisodion, as Tecmessa describes Ajax after his encounter with Athena at the door:

> κἄπειτ' ἐπᾴξας αὖθις ἐς δόμους πάλιν   305
> ἔμφρων μόλις πως ξὺν χρόνῳ καθίσταται,
> καὶ πλῆρες ἄτης ὡς διοπτεύει στέγος,
> παίσας κάρα 'θώυξεν·

Although in this passage ἄτη is more the objective "ruin" or "disaster" afflicting Ajax, this "ruin" is closely connected with the blind "folly" of his act. Hence, once again, Sophoclean ambivalence with respect to ἄτη.

Sophoclean ambivalence is also present in the next occurrence of ἄτη, in the second kommos of the first epeisodion:

> Αι.   ἰώ,
>   γένος ναΐας ἀρωγὸν τέχνας,
>   ἅλιον ὃς ἐπέβας ἑλίσσων πλάταν,
>   σέ τοι σέ τοι μόνον δέδορ-
>   κα πημονὰν ἐπαρκέσοντ'.   360
>   ἀλλά με συνδάιξον.
> Χο. εὔφημα φώνει· μὴ κακὸν κακῷ διδοὺς
>   ἄκος πλέον τὸ πῆμα τῆς ἄτης τίθει.

Perhaps the necessity for an ambivalent interpretation may most easily be seen in the two opinions contained in the ancient scholion on the passage. Commenting on line 362, the scholiast wrote:

> εὔφημα φώνει· μὴ κακόν : τὸ ἑξῆς, μὴ κακὸν κακῷ διδοὺς ἄκος μεῖζον
> ποίει τῆς ἄτης τὸ πῆμα (ἄτην δὲ τὴν μανίαν, πῆμα δὲ τὸν θάνατον) ὅ
> ἐστι χεῖρον τῆς μανίας· τοῦτο δέ φησιν
> ἐπεὶ ὁ Αἴας λέγει τῷ χορῷ ἀλλά με συνδάιξον.

ἄλλως : μὴ θεραπείαν κακοῦ ἕτερον κακὸν ἐπεισαγάγῃς οἷον μὴ τῷ
θανάτῳ διαλύσῃς τὸ ὄνειδος· πῆμα δὲ ἄτης κατὰ περίφρασιν τὴν ἄτην,
μὴ τὴν ἄτην πλείονα ποιήσῃς· ἀρκεῖ γὰρ ἡ παροῦσα.[8]

J. C. Kamerbeek's commentary illustrates well the ambivalent meaning of ἄτη here, for although his detailed discussion, in remarking on lines 362–363, quotes the second interpretation of the scholion with approval,[9] his introductory essay contains the following description of this scene: "The way in which Ajax is depicted in this lyric scene renders the *mental derangement* by which he had been struck psychologically comprehensible; though he has come to his senses again, he gives the impression of a mono*maniac* of ambition and vindictiveness."[10] This quotation is quite patently in agreement with the first part of the scholion. One can see μανία behind the italicized words.[11]

At the end of the first stasimon, ἄτη occurs again. This choral ode, begun with the mention of Salamis (line 596), concludes with a lament addressed to Telamon:

ὦ τλᾶμον πάτερ, οἷ-
αν σε μένει πυθέσθαι
παιδὸς δύσφορον ἄταν,
ἃν οὔπω τις ἔθρεψεν
αἰὼν Αἰακιδᾶν ἄτερθε τοῦδε.   645

Since the chorus have echoed the preceding epeisodion consistently throughout this stasimon,[12] their general attitude would suggest that ἄτη is used subjectively in this instance, in keeping with their confrontation with the maddened Ajax of the first epeisodion. This interpretation is strengthened by the vocabulary of the stasimon. A number of references to Ajax reflect the picture of his "madness"— θείᾳ μανίᾳ ξύναυλος (line 611), φρενὸς οἰοβώτας (lines 614–615), νοσοῦντα φρενοβόρως (lines 625–626), and κρείσσων γὰρ Ἅιδᾳ κεύθων ὁ νοσῶν μάταν (line 635) — and indicate that when the chorus sing of ἄτη in line 643 ἄτη should be consonant with these expressions of subjective dispositions.

Yet the Sophoclean penchant for irony is also reflected in this passage. Though the ἄτη referred to in line 643 is, literally, "blindness" or "folly," by the time the news of Ajax's misadventures *does* reach Telamon it will include a report of objective ἄτη: Ajax's catastrophic death.

Just before that death occurs, ἄτη appears again. Toward the end of the third epeisodion, as he steels himself to commit suicide, Ajax prays:

σὺ δ', ὦ τὸν αἰπὺν οὐρανὸν διφρηλατῶν   845
Ἥλιε, πατρῴαν τὴν ἐμὴν ὅταν χθόνα
ἴδῃς, ἐπισχὼν χρυσόνωτον ἡνίαν
ἄγγειλον ἄτας τὰς ἐμὰς μόρον τ' ἐμὸν
γέροντι πατρὶ τῇ τε δυστήνῳ τροφῷ.

Both the context and the character of Ajax point to the objective connotation of "ruin" or "disaster" for ἄτη here. Not only is it used in conjunction with μόρος, which Sophocles consistently uses to signify "death,"[13] but for Ajax to refer to his "follies" would be out of character. Still, ultimately, his death, his "ruin," has been brought on by a series of blind follies: his slaughter of the cattle, his suicide, and the resultant widowing of Tecmessa and orphaning of Eurysaces.[14] Consequently, even when speaking of his death as ἄτη, Ajax evokes the overtones of the term in its subjective connotation.

The only non-ambivalent Sophoclean use of ἄτη in its subjective meaning occurs in the kommos following the epiparodos, as the chorus sing:

ὤμοι ἐμᾶς ἄτας, οἷος ἄρ' αἱμάχθης,
ἄφαρκτος φίλων·   910
ἐγὼ δ' ὁ πάντα κωφός, ὁ πάντ' ἄιδρις,
κατημέλησα.

The "context shows that ἄτα has here the full force of 'blind folly'," as one critic has observed,[15] the presence of ἄιδρις κατημέλησα underscores the subjective element, and the association with κωφός recalls the original meaning of ἄτη, "physical blindness," and its use in this sense in *Iliad* 16.805.[16]

Teucer's cry of anguish opens the fourth epeisodion, and evokes the next appearance of ἄτη:

Τε.   ἰώ μοί μοι.
Χο.   σίγησον· αὐδὴν γὰρ δοκῶ Τεύκρου κλύειν   975
           βοῶντος ἄτης τῆσδ' ἐπίσκοπον μέλος.

Teucer immediately recognizes the import of Ajax's death for Tecmessa, for himself, and for the Salaminian sailors of the chorus: for them all, that death is indeed a "calamity."[17]

The final appearance of ἄτη in the *Ajax* occurs at the start of the concluding stasimon. After Teucer's confrontation with Menelaus, the chorus sing:

στρ. τίς ἄρα νέατος ἐς πότε λή-   1185
ξει πολυπλάγκτων ἐτέων ἀριθμός,
τὰν ἄπαυστον αἰὲν ἐμοὶ δορυσσοή-
των μόχθων ἄταν ἐπάγων
τάνδ' ἀν' εὐρυεδῆ Τροίαν,   1190
δύστανον ὄνειδος Ἑλλάνων;

The poetry of this stasimon makes the ambivalent use of ἄτη most appropriate.[18] As the antistrophe (1192–1198) shows, the chorus are extremely incensed with Menelaus; after all, he has just forbidden the burial of their heroic leader. In their anger they reproach the "ceaseless calamity" which his original summons to war has become. They are sick and tired of the war, as their ode goes on to show.

But war, of course, can be both "calamity" and "folly," as ἄτη can in Sophoclean usage. If ἄτη is understood here also in the sense of "folly," then the chorus are attributing to Menelaus precisely the quality consistently attributed to Ajax throughout the play, and in virtue of which he met his own destruction. Much has been written about the diptych nature of this play,[19] and it is surely a part of Sophocles' highly polished technique to have the chorus, early in the "second part" of the play, underscoring the original "folly" of Menelaus in calling the Greek nation to this tiresome and devastating war, in a parallel position to the emphasis placed on Ajax's "folly" early in the "first part" of the play. The opposed ideals, the "aristocratic" of Menelaus and the "heroic" of Ajax, Sophocles is subtly pointing out, are equally susceptible of "folly."[20]

TRACHINIAN WOMEN

The controversy concerning the precise chronology of the extant Sophoclean tragedies notwithstanding, it seems appropriate to consider the *Trachinian Women* next since scholars with increasing unanimity are advancing an early date for it.[21]

Like the *Ajax*, the *Trachinian Women* is a diptych play. Only one of the five appearances of ἄτη in this play occurs in the "first part." In the second strophe of the third stasimon, the chorus sing:

ἁ δ' ἐρχομένα μοῖρα προ-
φαίνει δολίαν καὶ μεγάλαν ἄταν.   850

Although the context underscores the objective connotation for ἄτη here, several other considerations point to Sophoclean ambivalence yet once again. The first of these is the importance of the verb προφαίνει for a proper understanding of the passage. In commenting on lines 849–850, J. C. Kamerbeek rightly observes that προφαίνει means, not "portends" or "foreshadows," but "shows forth"; consequently, he argues, "ἄτη is the blindness or infatuation and its consequences, bane or ruin."[22] It is the crafty and tremendous deception of Nessus and its consequences which μοῖρα is now displaying.

This association of ἄτη with μοῖρα is the second consideration hinting at the double significance for ἄτη in this passage. ἄτη and μοῖρα were associated once before, at *Iliad* 19.88, and in that context ἄτη meant "blindness." Moreover, the *Iliad* passage is in a context which, strikingly, also deals with Heracles. Though explicit echoing is difficult to prove, the suspicion is strong that Sophocles might well have had the Homeric lines in mind while composing the current passage.

The next three passages, all from the "second part" of the play, share two features which will prove helpful in establishing the connotation of ἄτη in each instance. In each case, the speaker is Heracles, and in each case, the fundamental metaphor involves medical terminology. It will be useful simply to quote the three passages consecutively and then to attempt an analysis.

The first passage occurs at the end of the anapaestic section beginning the exodos. Heracles, who has been carried on stage, says:

τίς γὰρ ἀοιδός, τίς ὁ χειροτέχνης   1000
ἰατορίας, ὃς τήνδ᾿ ἄτην
χωρὶς Ζηνὸς κατακηλήσει;[23]

After a μέλος ἀπὸ σκηνῆς,[24] Heracles has a long speech in trimeters in which ἄτη appears twice:

ἔθαλψέ μ᾿ ἄτης σπασμὸς ἀρτίως ὅδ᾿ αὖ,
διῇξε πλευρῶν, οὐδ᾿ ἀγύμναστόν μ᾿ ἐᾶν
ἔοικεν ἡ τάλαινα διάβορος νόσος.   1084

νῦν δ᾿ ὧδ᾿ ἄναρθρος καὶ κατερρακωμένος
τυφλῆς ὑπ᾿ ἄτης ἐκπεπόρθημαι τάλας,
ὁ τῆς ἀρίστης μητρὸς ὠνομασμένος,   1105
ὁ τοῦ κατ᾿ ἄστρα Ζηνὸς αὐδηθεὶς γόνος.

As the medical terminology used in these three passages suggests, the ἄτη afflicting Heracles is a destructive disease. This disease is both the blind "infatuation" of love, and a love which is a dark destructive power — in other words, an ἄτη in both its subjective and objective meanings.[25] The suffering which Heracles undergoes is indeed a "disaster."

ἄτη occurs for the final time in the *Trachinian Women* toward the close of the exodos.[26] After commanding the attendants to lift Heracles and carry him off for the journey to Mount Oeta, Hyllus adds some generalizations, among which are:

τὰ μὲν οὖν μέλλοντ᾽ οὐδεὶς ἀφορᾷ,   1270
τὰ δὲ νῦν ἑστῶτ᾽ οἰκτρὰ μὲν ἡμῖν,
αἰσχρὰ δ᾽ ἐκείνοις,
χαλεπώτατα δ᾽ οὖν ἀνδρῶν πάντων
τῷ τήνδ᾽ ἄτην ὑπέχοντι.

The context makes it clear that the ἄτη referred to in line 1274 is the impending death of Heracles on the funeral pyre which he had commanded; there seems to be no reason to understand it here in any sense other than in its objective meaning of "ruin," "calamity," or "disaster."

ANTIGONE

One of the textually most controverted passages in the Sophoclean corpus is the opening of the *Antigone*:

Ὦ κοινὸν αὐτάδελφον Ἰσμήνης κάρα,
ἆρ᾽ οἶσθ᾽ ὅ τι Ζεὺς τῶν ἀπ᾽ Οἰδίπου κακῶν
ὁποῖον οὐχὶ νῷν ἔτι ζώσαιν τελεῖ;
οὐδὲν γὰρ οὔτ᾽ ἀλγεινὸν οὔτ᾽ ἄτης ἄτερ
οὔτ᾽ αἰσχρὸν οὔτ᾽ ἄτιμόν ἐσθ᾽, ὁποῖον οὐ   5
τῶν σῶν τε κἀμῶν οὐκ ὄπωπ᾽ ἐγὼ κακῶν.

These initial words of Antigone's involve two principal difficulties. The first, in line 2, is not crucial to our discussion;[27] but the second is most germane since it involves the phrase οὔτ᾽ ἄτης ἄτερ in line 4. Many emendations have been proposed, and though Jebb took the somewhat pessimistic view that "no emendation [is] sufficiently probable to be admitted,"[28] V. Coulon has advanced three good reasons vindicating the MSS reading.[29]

Remarkably, although Jebb was not pleased with οὔτ᾽ ἄτης ἄτερ as a reading, his calling attention to the way in which "αἰσχρόν in a manner balances the subjective ἀλγεινόν, as the external ἀτιμία corresponds with the ἄτη,"[30] is quite helpful in arriving at an understanding of the meaning of ἄτη here. For the *external* character of ἄτη is precisely what is called for when the word is used in its objective sense.

After the chorus enter and sing the parodos, Creon enters at the start of the first epeisodion and states his general principle that patriotism is the prime criterion. In the course of this speech, he says:

> ἐγὼ γάρ, ἴστω Ζεὺς ὁ πάνθ᾽ ὁρῶν ἀεί,
> οὔτ᾽ ἂν σιωπήσαιμι τὴν ἄτην ὁρῶν   185
> στείχουσαν ἀστοῖς ἀντὶ τῆς σωτηρίας, . . . [31]

The context, the vocabulary, and the dramatic moment in the play indicate that ἄτη is used here in the objective connotation of "ruin," "disaster," or "calamity."[32]

As Ismene enters in the second epeisodion, Creon addresses a vicious question to her:

> σὺ δ᾽, ἣ κατ᾽ οἴκους ὡς ἔχιδν᾽ ὑφειμένη
> λήθουσά μ᾽ ἐξέπινες, οὐδ᾽ ἐμάνθανον
> τρέφων δύ᾽ ἄτα κἀπαναστάσεις θρόνων,
> φέρ᾽, εἰπὲ δή μοι, καὶ σὺ τοῦδε τοῦ τάφου
> φήσεις μετασχεῖν, ἢ ᾽ξομῇ τὸ μὴ εἰδέναι;   535

The parallel concepts indicated by the parallel construction of the two participles τρέφων and ἀπαναστάσεις suggest that ἄτη is to be understood here in its objective sense. Creon's whole position in the play thus far has made it abundantly clear that he would consider the ἀπαναστάσεις θρόνων as "disaster" not just for himself, but for the entire state.[33]

The second stasimon of the *Antigone* is not so famous as the first, the celebrated "hymn to man," or the third, the "hymn of Eros," but it is important for present considerations because ἄτη occurs four times (lines 584, 614, 624, and 625) within the span of two strophes and antistrophes.[34]

> στρ. α   εὐδαίμονες οἷσι κακῶν ἄγευστος αἰών.
> οἷς γὰρ ἂν σεισθῇ θεόθεν δόμος, ἄτας
> οὐδὲν ἐλλείπει γενεᾶς ἐπὶ πλῆθος ἕρπον·   585
> ὅμοιον ὥστε πόντιον
> οἶδμα δυσπνόοις ὅταν
> Θρῄσσησιν ἔρεβος ὕφαλον ἐπιδράμῃ πνοαῖς,
> κυλίνδει βυσσόθεν κελαινὰν   590
> θῖνα καὶ δυσάνεμοι
> στόνῳ βρέμουσιν ἀντιπλῆγες ἀκταί.

ἀντ. α ἀρχαῖα τὰ Λαβδακιδᾶν οἴκων ὁρῶμαι
πήματα φθιμένων ἐπὶ πήμασι πίπτοντ',   595
οὐδ' ἀπαλλάσσει γενεὰν γένος, ἀλλ' ἐρείπει
θεῶν τις, οὐδ' ἔχει λύσιν.
νῦν γὰρ ἐσχάτας ὕπερ
ῥίζας ἐτέτατο φάος ἐν Οἰδίπου δόμοις·   600
κατ' αὖ νιν φοινία θεῶν τῶν
νερτέρων ἀμᾷ κοπίς,
λόγου τ' ἄνοια καὶ φρενῶν Ἐρινύς.
στρ. β τεάν, Ζεῦ, δύνασιν τίς ἀνδρῶν ὑπερβασία κατάσχοι;   605
τὰν οὔθ' ὕπνος αἱρεῖ ποθ' ὁ παντογήρως
οὔτ' ἀκάματοι θεῶν
μῆνες, ἀγήρως δὲ χρόνῳ δυνάστας
κατέχεις Ὀλύμπου
μαρμαρόεσσαν αἴγλαν.   610
τό τ' ἔπειτα καὶ τὸ μέλλον
καὶ τὸ πρὶν ἐπαρκέσει
νόμος ὅδ'· οὐδὲν ἕρπει
θνατῶν βιότῳ πάμπολύ γ' ἐκτὸς ἄτας.
ἀντ. β ἁ γὰρ δὴ πολύπλαγκτος ἐλ-
πὶς πολλοῖς μὲν ὄνασις ἀνδρῶν,   616
πολλοῖς δ' ἀπάτα κουφονόων ἐρώτων·
εἰδότι δ' οὐδὲν ἕρπει,
πρὶν πυρὶ θερμῷ πόδα τις προσαύσῃ.
σοφίᾳ γὰρ ἔκ του   620
κλεινὸν ἔπος πέφανται,
τὸ κακὸν δοκεῖν ποτ' ἐσθλὸν
τῷδ' ἔμμεν ὅτῳ φρένας
θεὸς ἄγει πρὸς ἄταν·
πράσσει δ' ὀλίγιστον χρόνον ἐκτὸς ἄτας.   625

Several general observations are in order before a more detailed analysis is undertaken. As a whole, this stasimon illustrates the Sophoclean propensity for employing ἄτη at the beginning (e.g., line 584) or at the end (e.g., line 614) of a lyric system or of an entire stasimon (e.g., lines 624 and 625).[35] But in this instance even more emphasis is given to ἄτη by its position each time it occurs, for in each of the four places it occurs at the end of a line.

The first strophe introduces the familiar theme of recurrent disaster within a given family, while antistrophe α is surely best understood as a concrete application to the house of Labdacus of the general principle enunciated in lines 581-585 and strengthened by the simile of lines 586-591. In this context, it is difficult to understand ἄτη in line 584 in any way other than as connected with the ἀρχαῖα . . . πήματα of lines 594–595, that is, as "ruin," "calamity," or "disaster."

The close connection between strophe and antistrophe, already manifest in the first pair of this stasimon, is present as well in strophe and antistrophe β, and is clarified through the use of the γάρ in line 615.[36] Moreover, just as strophe and antistrophe α are linked conceptually as a statement of a general principle (lines 581–585), a simile exemplifying this principle (lines 586–591), and a concrete application of the principle within the context of the tragedy (all of antistrophe α), so the second system is similarly linked. Thus, we have the statement of a general principle (all of strophe β), and a metaphor (rather than a simile) explaining this principle within the context of the tragedy (lines 621–625). Furthermore, the gnomic quality of the νόμος in line 613 and of the ἔπος in line 621 reinforces the interconnection of strophe and antistrophe. Finally, the verbal echo ἐκτὸς ἄτας (line 614) and ἐκτὸς ἄτας (line 625) clearly indicates that ἄτη has the same meaning in each instance.

That ἄτη in line 625 is to be differentiated from ἄτη in line 624 is indicated by the adversative δ'. The reason for taking ἄτη in 624 to mean "blindness" will be explored in the next paragraph. If it is accepted, the differentiated ἄτη of 625 must mean "ruin," "calamity," or "disaster." To be sure, if ἄτη in 625 should also be understood to mean "blindness," the thought would be reduced to banality. And the interpretation of ἄτη in 625 in the objective sense is completely consonant with the ἄτη in 614 understood as "disaster" (also used in the phrase ἐκτὸς ἄτας, it will be recalled), which then becomes but another expression of the traditional Greek belief in the καιρός.[37]

That ἄτη in line 624 carries its subjective meaning of "blindness," "infatuation," or "folly" is suggested not only because of its differentiation from the objective meaning in 625 but also because of the presence of φρένας in line 623. A god working on human φρήν must refer primarily to the ἄτη which is god-sent as affecting some subjective disposition of the human.[38]

Toward the end of the kommos of the fourth epeisodion, Antigone sings:

> ἰὼ ματρῷαι λέ-
> κτρων ἄται κοιμήματά τ' αὐ-
> τογέννητ' ἐμῷ πατρὶ δυσμόρου ματρός,   865
> οἵων ἐγώ ποθ' ἁ ταλαίφρων ἔφυν·

Both the general context and the dramatic reality of the tragedy at this point indicate the objective meaning of "disaster" for ἄτη in line 864. Yet Sophoclean ambivalence toward the word is also operative here, and the overtone of "infatuation" can also be justified by two considerations. The first is the general erotic context in which ἄτη appears. This kommos occurs immediately after the "hymn of Eros," the third stasimon, and the mention of λέκτρων and κοιμήματα recalls the use of ἄτη in similar contexts.[39] Secondly, not only is the general focus interiorized by Antigone's mention of μερίμνας in 857, but the rest of the passage contains several words pointing to internal concerns or qualities: οἶτον (858), πότμον (860), and δυσμόρου (865). The association of ἄτη with such terms has occurred elsewhere in Sophocles,[40] but here this association, underlined by a threefold use of words connected with human destiny, would seem to point to a connotative association of ἄτη with concepts involved in man's destiny. This is Antigone's sentiment in the present passage, and the inevitability of μοῖρα forms the choral reflections of the fourth stasimon.

The fifth epeisodion contains the confrontation between Creon and Teiresias. The old prophet tells the king that the gods are angry because of his refusal to bury Polyneices, but Creon, refusing to budge, accuses Teiresias of venal motives. Thus goaded, Teiresias reveals to Creon that Haemon will also die in order to avenge Antigone's murder. As Teiresias stalks off the stage, the chorus try to persuade Creon to capitulate and to free Antigone, arguing that they have never known the prophet's warning to deceive the city (1094). To this Creon replies:

> ἔγνωκα καὐτὸς καὶ ταράσσομαι φρένας·   1095
> τό τ' εἰκαθεῖν γὰρ δεινόν, ἀντιστάντα δὲ
> ἄτῃ πατάξαι θυμὸν ἐν δεινῷ πάρα.

The dramatic tension of the play at this moment, as well as the entire context, point to the objective meaning for ἄτη in line 1097. Yet there are several indications that Sophocles is again using the word ambivalently, and that its subjective, interiorized, meaning is also intended here.

First, Creon's basic dilemma is signaled by the antithetical τ' ... δὲ, and by the parallel δεινόν and ἐν δεινῷ.[41] The internal quality of his dilemma should be quite obvious: εἰκαθεῖν is something which takes place interiorly, and so, it should be presumed, should the other half of the dilemma, ἄτῃ πατάξαι θυμὸν. This interior quality is, of course, strengthened by the presence of both φρήν and θυμός in the passage. The use of these terms here must not go unnoticed, for in pre-Sophoclean usage, φρήν and θυμός were consistently used with ἄτη only in its subjective sense.[42] But Sophocles, manifesting the shifting ambivalence associated with the evolving concept of ἄτη, does not hesitate to employ words previously restricted to the subjective connotation of the term in a context in which its objective connotation is paramount.

The trimeters of the exodos conclude with the following remarks by the coryphaeus:

καὶ μὴν ὅδ᾽ ἄναξ αὐτὸς ἐφήκει
μνῆμ᾽ ἐπίσημον διὰ χειρὸς ἔχων,
εἰ θέμις εἰπεῖν, οὐκ ἀλλοτρίαν
ἄτην, ἀλλ᾽ αὐτὸς ἁμαρτών.　　　　　　　1260

The tragic procession bringing Haemon's corpse clearly marks the ἄτη in line 1260, referring to the dead body, as a "ruin," "calamity," or "disaster."

But this climactic moment in the play raises some fundamental questions about the interpretation of the tragedy as a whole rather than of just ἄτη as it appears in line 1260. And these questions will show that, yet once more, ἄτη is used in a double sense here and carries with it as well the overtones of its subjective meaning.

The core of this argument, encapsulated in Jebb's brief observation that "the corpse is an ἄτη because the death was caused by Creon's infatuation,"[43] has been expanded upon by Adams:

> it was in a final seizure of ate, mental blindness, that [Creon] acted as he did both here and at the tomb; and that is how and why the fate foretold for him came to pass. The gods took him in hand, blinding him. That is precisely his own verdict (1271–1274). . . . And well may the coryphaeus refer to Haemon's body, when the diversion caused by Eurydice's exit is past, as οὐκ ἀλλοτρίαν ἄτην, the work of Creon's own infatuation.[44]

One further element must be considered for completeness' sake in the treatment of this passage. Without wishing to revert to nineteenth-century scholarship which saw ἁμαρτία, particularly as it occurs in the famous discussion of tragedy in Aristotle's *Poetics*, as a moral fault of some sort, it is nevertheless worth adverting to the use of ἄτη with ἁμαρτάνω in this context, as an example of yet another fifth-century term frequently used in the discussion of human freedom and responsibility associated with ἄτη.[45]

OEDIPUS TYRANNOS

ἄτη appears only three times in the *Oedipus Tyrannos*. The first appearance is in the first antistrophe of the parados, when, as they enter, the chorus of Theban elders sing:

> τρισσοὶ ἀλεξίμοροι προφάνητέ μοι,
> εἴ ποτε καὶ προτέρας ἄτας ὕπερ
> ὀρνυμένας πόλει   165
> ἠνύσατ' ἐκτοπίαν φλόγα πήματος,
> ἔλθετε καὶ νῦν.

The synonymous use of ἄτη and φλόγα πήματος, together with the entire dramatic mood of the chorus, indicates the objective meaning for ἄτη in line 164.[46] In strophe β of the fourth stasimon, the chorus sing:

> στρ. τανῦν δ' ἀκούειν τίς ἀθλιώτερος ;
> τίς ἄταις ἀγρίαις, τίς ἐν πόνοις   1205
> ξύνοικος ἀλλαγᾷ βίου ;[47]

Line 1205 has been the source of considerable controversy among editors. The difficulty is basically metrical, since the MSS reading does not respond to line 1214 in the antistrophe. The above text is Hermann's suggestion, and has been adopted by many editors; but whatever detailed reconstruction of the line is adopted, no one doubts the presence of ἄταις.[48] Nor is its meaning difficult to determine. As Oedipus' entire catastrophe becomes known, and as the chorus manifest in referring to it with the synonymous ἐν πόνοις, ἄτη in 1205 refers to the savage "disasters," or "calamities," which have overwhelmed him.

The final appearance of ἄτη in the *Oedipus Tyrannos* occurs during the messenger's description of Oedipus' self-blinding in the exodos. His report concludes:

> ὁ πρὶν παλαιὸς δ' ὄλβος ἦν πάροιθε μὲν
> ὄλβος δικαίως, νῦν δὲ τῇδε θἠμέρα
> στεναγμός, ἄτη, θάνατος, αἰσχύνη, κακῶν
> ὅσ' ἐστὶ πάντων ὀνόματ', οὐδέν ἐστ' ἀπόν.   1285

As the portrait of the blinded Oedipus in general, the use of κακά in line 1281, and lines 1284-1285 make clear, ἄτη in this context is used in its objective sense.

The use of irony in connection with ἄτη is superb in the *Oedipus Tyrannos*.[49] At lines 164 and 1205, ἄτη is used objectively by the chorus and pertains to a past disaster; yet the words can be applied to the future and be understood to refer to the impending self-blinding of Oedipus (ἄτη in its subjective sense). Conversely, in the messenger's speech in the exodos, ἄτη is used in its objective sense of "ruin," but this use occurs in the report of the physical blindness which Oedipus has inflicted on himself! Once again, Sophocles has shown his consummate genius with words, a genius which will reappear with the same type of ironic ambivalence in the passages in the *Oedipus at Colonus* containing ἄτη.

ELECTRA

The kommos of the parodos to the *Electra* contains three appearances of ἄτη. The final antistrophe and the beginning of the epode of this kommos are:

ἀντ. Χο. φράζου μὴ πόρσω φωνεῖν.
οὐ γνώμαν ἴσχεις ἐξ οἵων
τὰ παρόντ'; οἰκείας εἰς ἄτας   215
ἐμπίπτεις οὕτως αἰκῶς.
πολὺ γάρ τι κακῶν ὑπερεκτήσω,
σᾷ δυσθύμῳ τίκτουσ' αἰεὶ
ψυχᾷ πολέμους· τὰ δὲ τοῖς δυνατοῖς
οὐκ ἐριστὰ πλάθειν.   220
Ηλ. δείν' ἐν δεινοῖς ἠναγκάσθην·
ἔξοιδ', οὐ λάθει μ' ὀργά.
ἀλλ' ἐν γὰρ δεινοῖς οὐ σχήσω
ταύτας ἄτας,
ὄφρα με βίος ἔχῃ.   225
τίνι γάρ ποτ' ἄν, ὦ φιλία γενέθλα,
πρόσφορον ἀκούσαιμ' ἔπος,
τίνι φρονοῦντι καίρια;
ἄνετέ μ' ἄνετε παράγοροι.
τάδε γὰρ ἄλυτα κεκλήσεται·   230
οὐδέ ποτ' ἐκ καμάτων ἀποπαύσομαι
ἀνάριθμος ὧδε θρήνων.
ἐπ. Χο. ἀλλ' οὖν εὐνοίᾳ γ' αὐδῶ,
μάτηρ ὡσεί τις πιστά,
μὴ τίκτειν σ' ἄταν ἄταις.   235

This passage is a splendid example of Sophoclean ambivalence with respect to the use and meaning of ἄτη. The objective notion of "ruin," "calamity," or "disaster" can readily be established for ἄτη in lines 215, 224, and 235, for the passage contains more than enough synonymous expressions for ἄτη interpreted in this sense — πολὺ τι κακῶν (217), πολέμους (219), and καμάτων (231) — to make it clear that Sophocles had such a meaning in mind.

But each of these phrases is also connected with a mental state of Electra's which issues in laments. The specific πολέμους of line 219 clearly refer to this, since they are mental (ψυχᾷ, 219) and result at most in *verbal* wrangling (ἐριστά, 220). Moreover, there are other indications that the focus of this kommos is Electra's mental state at this dramatic moment, as she is on her way to being steeled for the terrible events to follow:[50] γνώμαν ἴσχεις (214), δυσθύμῳ (218), ὀργά (222), φρονοῦντι (228), θρήνων (232), and εὐνοίᾳ (233).

The next occurrence of ἄτη is in the long second epeisodion. Chrysothemis has returned joyfully from the tomb of Agamemnon to tell Electra of discovering a lock of Orestes' hair there. Electra then informs her that a messenger has come telling of Orestes' death, and Chrysothemis cries:

> ὢ δυστυχής· ἐγὼ δὲ σὺν χαρᾷ λόγους
> τοιούσδ' ἔχουσ' ἔσπευδον, οὐκ εἰδυῖ' ἄρα   935
> ἵν' ἦμεν ἄτης· ἀλλὰ νῦν, ὅθ' ἱκόμην,
> τά τ' ὄντα πρόσθεν ἄλλα θ' εὑρίσκω κακά.[51]

This ἄτη is explicitly connected with ἀλλὰ ... κακά in 936–938, and consequently clearly means "ruin," "calamity," or "disaster" in this context.

The second stasimon continues, and Electra asks Chrysothemis' help in slaying Aegisthus. Chrysothemis demurs, and the heart of her argument is:

> τίς οὖν τοιοῦτον ἄνδρα βουλεύων ἑλεῖν   1001
> ἄλυπος ἄτης ἐξαπαλλαχθήσεται;
> ὅρα κακῶς πράσσοντε μὴ μείζω κακὰ
> κτησώμεθ', εἴ τις τούσδ' ἀκούσεται λόγους.

The use of ἄτη is again straightforward in this passage; it means "ruin," "calamity," or "disaster," as is clear from its synonym κακά in line 1003. The wrestling metaphor echoes the same metaphor used with ἄτη at *Suppliants* 470 and *Libation-Bearers* 339, in both of which instances ἄτη is also used in its objective sense.

In the third epeisodion, after he has identified himself to his sister, Orestes cautions her about revealing the deception to Clytemnestra:

οὕτως δ' ὅπως μήτηρ σε μὴ 'πιγνώσεται
φαιδρῷ προσώπῳ νῦν ἐπελθόντοιν δόμους·
ἀλλ' ὡς ἐπ' ἄτῃ τῇ μάτην λελεγμένῃ
στέναζ'· ὅταν γὰρ εὐτυχήσωμεν, τότε
χαίρειν παρέσται καὶ γελᾶν ἐλευθέρως.[52]   1300

The ἄτη τῇ μάτην λελεγμένῃ of line 1298 refers, of course, to the false report of the supposed death of Orestes given by the paedagogus in lines 680–763. That Orestes' death is considered an "evil" is precisely what gives dramatic tension to the play. Hence, the ἄτη of the current passage is clearly meant to be understood in its objective sense.

From these four ἄτη passages in the *Electra*, it is possible to draw some general conclusions. Significant concepts connected with the evolving fifth-century concern with human freedom and responsibility appear in each instance. Thus ἠναγκάσθην occurs at line 221 in the midst of the long passage from the kommos of the parodos; and some form of τύχη is used in each of the three other passages: δυστυχής at 934, εὐτυχεῖ at 999, and εὐτυχήσωμεν at 1299. What is important here is the association of ἄτη and τύχη in these last three passages, and the association of ἄτη with other "ethical" terms elsewhere in Sophocles, viz., μόρος (*Ajax* 848), ὄνειδος (*Ajax* 1189), μοῖρα (*Trachinian Women* 850), οἶτος, πότμος, δυσμόρος (*Antigone* 864), ἁμαρτία (*Antigone* 1260) and ἀνάγκη (*Electra* 224).[53]

If this distinction is cast in terms of culpability, the results are startling. By his very word-associations, Sophocles declares that whenever the subjective meaning of "blindness," "infatuation," or "folly" attaches to ἄτη even in the ambivalent sense, then such ἄτη is attributable to an individual's μοῖρα, πότμος, ἁμαρτία, or ἀνάγκη; and that non-ambivalent "ruin," "calamity," or "disaster" is attributable more to τύχη. The implications about a person's control with respect to his own μοῖρα, as opposed to his lack of control over his τύχη, are profound. τύχη as an impersonal, objective force, independent of human volitional control, remains "out there," sometimes resulting in "ruin," etc., if the τύχη happens to be *bad* luck. But — and this is the significant advance adumbrated by the association and usage — μοῖρα, πότμος, ἁμαρτία, and ἀνάγκη are interiorized, subjective (even when ambiguously so) qualities of "blindness," "infatuation," or "folly," and are therefore *not* "out there," completely independent of man; somehow they are within his control. We are much more accustomed to thinking of such concerns as Euripidean, particularly, perhaps, the "necessity" involved in such things as the power of Eros (*Hippolytus*) or Dionysiac frenzy (*Bacchae*), yet clearly such concerns were also Sophoclean!

PHILOCTETES

In the *Philoctetes*, as Neoptolemus is still attempting the deception which Odysseus counseled, the chorus, in the course of the first stasimon, employ ἄτη in its sole occurrence in the play:

εἶρπε δ' ἄλλοτ' ἀλλ<αχ>ᾷ
τότ' ἂν εἰλνόμενος,
παῖς ἄτερ ὡς φίλας τιθή-
νας, ὅθεν εὐμάρει' ὑπάρ-
χοι πόρου, ἀνίκ' ἐξανεί-   705
η δακέθυμος ἄτα·

The ἄτη suffered by Philoctetes, as is manifest in the play, is his physical handicap. Hence, it is best to understand ἄτη in line 706 as referring, primarily, to this "ruin," "calamity," or "disaster" which has come upon him.

Nonetheless, there are indications that, although rooted in his physical handicap, his ἄτη is not restricted to it, and that the other, the subjective, meaning for ἄτη is also intended. First, the medical terminology in the passage echoes the medical vocabulary associated with ἄτη at *Trachinian Women* 1082 and 1104, where the Sophoclean propensity for the ambivalent notion of ἄτη is likewise manifest. Secondly, an interior, subjective, disposition is consonant with one of the major images of the play: namely, the companionship–loneliness dichotomy.[54] Furthermore, the rare epithet δακέθυμος for ἄτη in this passage echoes both the loneliness and the interiorization which Knox envisions, who, in describing the dramatic function of this stasimon, writes that it "is to set before us all those feelings of sympathy and admiration for Philoctetes which Neoptolemus has suppressed and hidden beneath the brilliant surface of his lying improvisations, all that is soon to burst out and overpower him."[55] Once again it becomes obvious that ἄτη is used ambivalently at a crucial moment in a play, for the struggle of Philoctetes, with which Neoptolemus is about to help him, is far more than merely physical. It is precisely this level of intent which adds greatness to the Sophoclean drama.

OEDIPUS AT COLONUS

After the departure of the ξένος in the prologue of the *Oedipus at Colonus*, Oedipus speaks:

ὦ πότνιαι δεινῶπες, εὖτε νῦν ἕδρας
πρώτων ἐφ᾽ ὑμῶν τῆσδε γῆς ἔκαμψ᾽ ἐγώ,   85
Φοίβῳ τε κἀμοὶ μὴ γένησθ᾽ ἀγνώμονες,
ὅς μοι, τὰ πόλλ᾽ ἐκεῖν᾽ ὅτ᾽ ἐξέχρη κακά,
ταύτην ἔλεξε παῦλαν ἐν χρόνῳ μακρῷ,
ἐλθόντι χώραν τερμίαν, ὅπου θεῶν
σεμνῶν ἕδραν λάβοιμι καὶ ξενόστασιν·   90
ἐνταῦθα κάμψειν τὸν ταλαίπωρον βίον,
κέρδη μὲν οἰκήσαντα τοῖς δεδεγμένοις,
ἄτην δὲ τοῖς πέμψασιν, οἵ μ᾽ ἀπήλασαν·

That the meaning of ἄτη in line 93 is "ruin," "disaster," "calamity" is clear from two contextual considerations. (*a*) ἄτη is clearly opposed to κέρδη in line 92, as the antithetical μὲν . . . δὲ in lines 92–93 indicates. This antithesis also occurs at *Works and Days* 352, Theognis 133, and *Libation-Bearers* 825, and in all three places ἄτη is used objectively. (*b*) Although it is not explicitly stated, the ἄτη of line 93 is synonymous with other disasters befalling the house of Labdacus at Thebes, the siege of the city at the seven gates, in particular.

During the spirited exchange between Oedipus and the chorus in the parodos, the following outburst occurs:

Οι.   ἰώ μοί μοι
Αν.   χεραὸν ἐς χέρα σῶμα σὸν   200
       προκλίνας φιλίαν ἐμάν.
Οι.   ὤμοι δύσφρονος ἄτας.
Χο.   ὦ τλάμων, ὅτε νῦν χαλᾷς,
       αὔδασον, τίς ἔφυς βροτῶν;[56]

Providing a discussion of the context in which ἄτη is used here is, naturally, quite difficult since the word appears in a one-line remark. Still, a survey of the preceding development of the parodos would suggest that ἄτη here refers to the "calamity" or "disaster" of Oedipus' blindness. The idea of physical blindness has been very prominent throughout this scene prior to Oedipus' cry at line 202: at line 141 the chorus' initial reaction to the first sight of Oedipus is one of horror at his physical appearance; at lines 145–147 Oedipus laments his blindness, and in the next two lines the chorus inquire about its duration; at lines 173ff. Antigone leads Oedipus, and at 182–183 she encourages him as they walk. Finally, in the passage under consideration, Oedipus is being seated with the help of Antigone, and once again the focus of attention is on his "calamity," his physical blindness, ἄτη in its objective connotation.

Yet Sophocles also introduces several notes of ambivalence. First, the epithet δύσφρων in conjunction with ἄτη points to the subjective connotation for ἄτη. And the "calamity" of physical blindness, the original meaning of ἄτη at *Iliad* 16.805,[57] cannot help but remind us of the many subsequent uses of ἄτη in its subjective meaning of metaphorical "blindness," "infatuation" or "folly."

The next two instances of the use of ἄτη occur in a lyrical interchange between Oedipus and the chorus, in the first antistrophe of the kommos in the first epeisodion:

ἀτν. Οι.   ἤνεγκ᾽ οὖν κακότατ᾽, ὦ ξένοι, ἤνεγκ᾽
            ἀέκων μέν, θεὸς ἴστω,
            τούτων δ᾽ αὐθαίρετον οὐδέν.
Χο.   ἀλλ᾽ ἐς τί;
Οι.   κακᾷ μ᾽ εὐνᾷ πόλις οὐδὲν ἴδριν   525
            γάμων ἐνέδησεν ἄτᾳ.
Χο.   ἦ ματρόθεν, ὡς ἀκούω,
            δυσώνυμα λέκτρ᾽ ἐπλήσω;
Οι.   ὤμοι, θάνατος μὲν τάδ᾽ ἀκούειν,
            ὦ ξεῖν᾽· αὗται δὲ δύ᾽ ἐξ ἐμοῦ < μὲν >   530
Χο.   πῶς φῄς;
Οι.   παῖδε, δύο δ᾽ ἄτα. . . .

In a brilliant example of his gift for irony, Sophocles has employed ἄτη in both its objective and its subjective senses simultaneously in these two instances. The objective connotation is validated by the presence of κακότατ᾽ in line 521 and the description of incest in lines 527–528. Thus, ἄτη means "ruin," "calamity," or "disaster" at both 526 and 532. Yet the subjective connotation is suggested by the similarity of expression here with two earlier passages, in both of which ἄτη means "blindness," "infatuation," "folly": *Iliad* 2.111 (Ζεύς με μέγα Κρονίδης ἄτη ἐνέδησε βαρείῃ) and *Antigone* 863 (ματρῷαι λέκτρων ἄται).[58] These two literary echoes, together with the generally "erotic" context of the passage, would seem to indicate that the second, the subjective, meaning for ἄτη is also present in this passage.

The final appearance of ἄτη in the Sophoclean corpus occurs in the epode of the third stasimon of the *Oedipus at Colonus*. The chorus conclude their brief song with:

ὣς καὶ τόνδε κατ' ἄκρας
δειναὶ κυματοαγεῖς
ἆται κλονέουσιν ἀεὶ ξυνοῦσαι,
αἱ μὲν ἀπ' ἀελίου δυσμᾶν,   1245
  αἱ δ' ἀνατέλλοντος,
αἱ δ' ἀνὰ μέσσαν ἀκτῖν',
αἱ δ' ἐννυχιᾶν ἀπὸ 'Ριπᾶν.

The effect of total buffeting which the simile, in its power and beauty
a fine example of Sophoclean art, produces provides the concomitant
contextual "evil" and clearly indicates that ἄτη here is used in its
objective sense.

CONCLUSION

As fifth-century thought continued to evolve, the seven extant plays
of Sophocles provide more and valuable evidence for our consideration
of the use and meaning of ἄτη within the Greek poetic tradition. A
comparison of Sophoclean with pre-Sophoclean usage reveals both
his adherence to the tradition and his nuanced originality within that
tradition.

In only two instances, *Ajax* 909 and *Antigone* 624, does Sophocles
employ ἄτη unambivalently in its subjective sense, the meaning which
has been predominant prior to Aeschylus.[59] Rather, Sophocles follows
his dramatic predecessor and prefers to employ ἄτη in its objective sense
on sixteen occasions.[60] Indeed, he follows the Aeschylean introduction of a new association with ἄτη objectively construed by introducing
his own new association: namely, words signifying sight or sound, in
ten of the sixteen passages in which he employs ἄτη in its objective
connotation.[61]

But the major development with respect to the use and meaning of
ἄτη in Sophoclean poetry is analogous to his dramatic technique of irony
and ambivalence. In twenty-two passages, by far the majority, both
meanings of ἄτη, "blindness" and "ruin," are present.[62] This ambivalence is significant for the Sophoclean outlook.

The favorite Sophoclean metaphor employed with ἄτη in its ambivalent usage, in nine of the twenty-two passages in which it appears in this sense, is connected with medicine.[63] But of greater significance than the number of times the metaphor is used are the manner
of its use and the implications.

At *Ajax* 195, 363, and 909, ἄτη appears with medical terminology, as if to reinforce the notion that the "mental" blindness, the ἄτη, inflicted on Ajax by Athena, also has "physical" overtones in that he lost sight of his ideals and his τιμή. At lines 1001, 1082, and 1104 of the *Trachinian Women*, ἄτη and a medical phrase appear in highly erotic contexts in a play treating love as a "disease" which has infected the house. The same medical association with ἄτη appears at *Philoctetes* 706, appositely in a play concerned with a protagonist whose physical malady is dramatically central. And, finally, much the same situation is true of Oedipus at line 302 of the *Oedipus at Colonus*. For Sophocles ἄτη in its ambivalent connotation is a "disease" of some sort; modern man would call it a "sickness" of the spirit or a mental "disorder," but the fifth-century Athenian did not have available our contemporary psychological terminology.

These considerations gain even greater significance through the second major, and highly important, innovation which Sophocles makes with respect to the use of ἄτη in its ambivalent sense of both "blindness" and "ruin." He uses it with nine different concepts which by the mid-fifth century were beginning to acquire definite "moral" connotations as the Athenians grew more and more conscious of the problem of human freedom and responsibility *vs.* the notion of guilt and accountability.[64]

Thus, at *Ajax* 848 ἄτη is found with μόρος; with ὄνειδος at *Ajax* 1189; with the term which became so central to this whole problem, μοῖρα, at *Trachinian Women* 850; with the remarkable trio οἶτος, πότμος, and δυσμόρος at *Antigone* 864; with ἁμαρτία at *Antigone* 1260; with ἀνάγκη at *Electra* 224; and, finally, with ἀέκων at *Oedipus at Colonus* 526 and 532. None of his predecessors had employed ἄτη with such an array of ethical concepts. Clearly Sophocles sees some importance in such an association.[65]

Since it is the ambivalent, subjective *and* objective, meaning of ἄτη which is associated with these terms, it is reasonable to see a Sophoclean indication that he makes some connection between human responsibility and divine destiny in all this. For if ἄτη means the subjective, interiorized concept of human "blindness," "infatuation," or "folly," while simultaneously meaning some "ruin," "disaster," or "calamity" inflicted on man from outside himself, and such a concept is frequently associated with man's fate, destiny, or end (μόρος, ὄνειδος, μοῖρα, οἶτος, πότμος, δύσμορος, ἁμαρτία, and ἀνάγκη), then in some valid, though as yet only half-articulated sense, man's external destiny and his interior dispositions are interconnected. We would say that man, according to the Sophoclean view, is in some valid sense "responsible" for his destiny.

The repercussions of this for human culpability are profound, and the profundity of such concerns is precisely what gives greatness to Sophoclean tragedy. He might not agree with the Sophistic view of man as the measure, but he surely has a far more complex concept of man, his destiny, and his responsibility toward that destiny than is manifested in the Homeric poems. And to say that the ethical and moral associations of ἄτη in Sophocles simply outstrip all such associations in his predecessors is not to overstate the evidence.

NOTES

[1] J. C. Kamerbeek, *The Plays of Sophocles: Commentaries.* I. *The Ajax* (Leiden: Brill, 1953), pp. 15–17, rehearses most of the pertinent arguments.

[2] Herbert Musurillo, *The Light and the Darkness: Studies in the Dramatic Poetry of Sophocles* (Leiden: Brill, 1967), p. 9.

[3] In addition to the Pearson text, the following editions have been consulted: *Sophocles: Tragoediae septem*, ed. R. F. P. Brunck (Oxford: Bliss, 1808); *Sophoclis tragoediae superstites*, ed. Wilhelm Dindorf, 2 vols. (Leipzig: Teubner, 1863); *Sophocles*, ed. F. H. M. Blaydes, 2 vols. (London: Bell, 1859); *Sophocles: Tragoediae septem*, ed. Gottfried Hermann, 2 vols. (London: Black, Young & Young, 1825); *Sophocles*, ed. Lewis Campbell, 2 vols. (Oxford: Clarendon, 1879, 1881); *Sophocles: The Plays and the Fragments*, ed. R. C. Jebb, 7 vols. (Cambridge: Cambridge University Press, 1900–1928; repr. Amsterdam: Hakkert, 1962–1965); *Sophocle*, ed. Paul Masqueray, 2 vols. (Paris: "Les Belles Lettres," 1922, 1924); *Sophocles*, ed. Alphonse Dain, trans. Paul Mazon, 3 vols. in 1 (Paris: "Les Belles Lettres," 1955–1960); J. C. Kamerbeek, *The Plays of Sophocles: Commentaries*, 6 vols. (Leiden: Brill, 1953–1980). Dawe, "Some Reflections on Ate and Hamartia," 116, notes the presence of the Aristotelian "pity and fear" here.

[4] Kamerbeek's remark, *Ajax*, p. 43, ad loc., that "the idea of ἄτη = 'distraction' (with ruin following), sent to man by the wrathful gods, can hardly be realized more sharply than in a situation like this" is correct. But the interpretation of Adams, *Sophocles the Playwright*, pp. 26–29, is superb. See also Bremer, *Hamartia*, p. 136.

[5] The archaic structure of the entire parodos is ably discussed by Kamerbeek, *Ajax*, p. 9.

6 Athena describes Ajax to Odysseus twice as a victim of νόσος, in lines 59 and 66. When the tale is told again by Tecmessa, she not only uses νόσος (line 271) but even more explicitly describes Ajax as a victim of μανία (line 216).

7 *Scholia in Sophoclis tragoedias*, ed. Petros N. Papageorgios (Leipzig: Teubner, 1888), ad loc.

8 Ibid., ad loc.

9 His *reason* for this approval — namely, the supposed parallel to πῆμα κακοῦ of *Odyssey* 3.152 — would seem to be a *petitio principii* (*Ajax*, pp. 85–86).

10 Ibid., p. 10; emphasis added. Perhaps another contradiction is contained in the remark on p. 84 that "On account of the prevalence of the dochmiacs the rhythms are expressive of the pathetic state of Ajax."

11 Bowra, *Sophoclean Tragedy*, pp. 31–32, is also ambiguous, for although he translates ἄτη as "doom" he goes on to agree with the first part of the scholion.

12 As Adams, *Sophocles the Playwright*, p. 33, expresses it: "They have taken their cue from the preceding episode."

13 In addition to the present passage, the *Lexicon Sophocleum*, ed. Friedrich Theodor Ellendt, 2nd rev. ed. Hermann Franz Genthe (Berlin: Barntraeger, 1872; repr. Hildesheim: Olms, 1958), lists the following instances in which Sophocles employs μόρος in the sense of "sors ultima fatalis, mors": *Ajax* 1059; *Trachinian Women* 357, 1042; *Antigone* 56, 489, 629, 769, 1266, 1292, 1313; *Electra* 860; and *Oedipus at Colonus* 1510, 1563. For a good discussion of the scene, as well as a review of the bibliography on it, see Ignacio Errandonea, s.j., "Les quatre monologues d'*Ajax* et leur signification dramatique," LEC, 26, No. 1 (January 1958), 21–40.

14 See lines 646–692 for the "deception speech" and lines 652–653, in particular, for the Tecmessa and Eurysaces issues.

15 Kamerbeek, *Ajax*, p. 184, ad loc.

16 See above, pp. 7–8, as well as *Ajax* 363, discussed on pp. 98–99 above.

17 In commenting on this passage, Lewis Campbell incisively calls the ἄτη in line 976 "'calamity', i.e., the sudden cry of Teucer shows that his eye has been arrested by the dead body and the group surrounding it" (*Sophocles*, ad loc.); while Adams acutely observes that Teucer's very appearance here shows that Ajax's first prayer, the one to Zeus, discussed on p. 100 above, was answered (*Sophocles the Playwright*, p. 37).

18 The remark by Dain & Mazon, *Sophocles*, ad loc., is worth quoting in order to correct it: "Le mot ἄτη qui signifie chez Homère *délire, aveuglement d'esprit*, est pris ici dans l'acception plus générale de *malheur*, qui devient fréquente à partir de Sophocle (Tournier)." As chap. 5 above amply demonstrates, this shift began with Aeschylus, not with Sophocles.

19 See, for example, Kirkwood, *Study of Sophoclean Drama*, pp. 42–54. The term, as applied to Sophocles, originated with T. B. L. Webster (see his *An Introduction to Sophocles* [Oxford: Clarendon, 1936], pp. 102–103).

20 It is Kirkwood's insight (*Study of Sophoclean Drama*, p. 48), therefore, which is correct: Odysseus (not Menelaus or Agamemnon) recognizes this, and this contrast is what the play is concerned with.

21 For a representative sample of opinion, see ibid., pp. 289–94. Adams feels the question of chronology so strongly that he denies Sophoclean authorship to the play; see his *Sophocles the Playwright*, pp. 124–26.

22 "Sophoclea IV: Notes, Critical and Exegetical, on the *Trachiniae*," *Mnemosyne*, 10, 4th ser. (1957), 123.

23 In virtue of the presence of *both* ἄνθος *and* μανία in this passage, the remarks of Musurillo, *The Light and the Darkness*, pp. 69–70, become even more pertinent to an appreciation of the imagery.

24 For a discussion of it, see A. H. Coxon, "The μέλος ἀπὸ σκηνῆς in Sophocles' *Trachiniae* (ll. 1004–1043)," CR, 51, No. 3 (December 1947), 69–72.

25 For studies of these passages, see Musurillo, *The Light and the Darkness*, pp. 77–78; Cedric H. Whitman, *Sophocles: A Study of Heroic Humanism* (Cambridge: Harvard University Press, 1951), pp. 115–16; and A. A. Long, *Language and Thought in Sophocles*, University of London Classical Studies 6 (London: Athlone, 1968), pp. 56, 130, 134.

26 The attribution of the final four lines (1275–1278) of the play to Hyllus or to the chorus remains a subject of controversy. For a good review of the arguments, see Paul Mazon, "Notes sur Sophocle," RPh, 25 (1951), 7–17.

27 It is a question of whether to read ὅ τι or ὅτι. In the best (though still unconvincing) treatment of the question, V. Coulon, "Observations critiques et exégétiques sur divers passages controversées de Sophocle," REG, 52 (1939), 1–18, has opted for ὅτι, following Boeckh's argument that ὅ τι . . . ὁποῖον is grammatically impossible.

28 *Sophocles: The Plays and Fragments. III. The Antigone* (Cambridge: Cambridge University Press, 1900; repr. Amsterdam: Hakkert, 1962), p. 9, ad loc.

29 Coulon's first reason is the one advanced by Brunck: namely, that Antigone could not escape mentioning, among the misfortunes of the house of Labdacus, the famous ἄτη which the poet recalls later on in *Oedipus Tyrannos* 1283–1285. As a second reason, Coulon points out the obvious exigencies of the meter which would prohibit ἀτηρόν. Coulon's third reason is based on the interpretation of Didymus contained in the ancient scholion on this passage.

For an opposite view and an attempt to vindicate the reading οὔτ' ἄκης ἄτερ, see J. D. Meerwaldt, "Ad Antigones Exordium," *Mnemosyne*, 1, 4th ser. (1948), 284–93; I find his arguments — namely, consonance, parallelism, grammar, and Sophocles' propensity for medical metaphors — singularly unconvincing.

30 *Antigone*, p. 9, ad loc.

31 These lines are part of the passage (175–190) quoted by Demosthenes against Aeschines in XIX.247.

32 See B. M. W. Knox's fine discussion of Creon's entire speech in *The Heroic Temper: Studies in Sophoclean Tragedy*, Sather Classical Lectures 35 (Berkeley: University of California Press, 1964), pp. 84–87, and Robert F. Goheen's illuminating remark, in *The Imagery of Sophocles' Antigone: A Study of Poetic Language and Structure* (Princeton: Princeton University Press, 1951), p. 116, that "in the *Antigone* Sophocles trades to a considerable extent on the sea and its storms as concrete referents for trouble (e.g., 162ff., 541, 584ff.)."

33 The quality of the language here, particularly the use of the dual to show the close bond perceived between the sisters, and the use of metonymy display Sophocles' artistry once again. For the use of the dual, see Knox, *Heroic Temper*, pp. 79–80; for the metonymy, see Long, *Language and Thought in Sophocles*, pp. 10–11, 121.

34 For a fine discussion of the importance of this stasimon, see Goheen, *Imagery of Sophocles' Antigone*, pp. 47–48. See also Bremer, *Hamartia*, pp. 141–42, and Dawe, "Some Reflections on Ate and Hamartia," 111–13.

³⁵ See, for example, *Ajax* 909 and *Oedipus Tyrannos* 1205 for the beginning of a lyric system; *Trachinian Women* 850, 1274, *Antigone* 1260, *Oedipus Tyrannos* 165, *Electra* 215, 224, 235, *Philoctetes* 706, and *Oedipus at Colonus* 202, 526, and 532 for the end of a lyric system; and *Ajax* 643, 1189, and *Oedipus at Colonus* 1244 for the end of a stasimon.

³⁶ See the note on lines 615–625 in *Antigone*, ed. Jebb, pp. 118–19.

³⁷ It should also be noted that in both instances, with typical Sophoclean ambivalence, the "ruin" also suggests god-sent "blindness."

³⁸ Except for the association of ἄτη and ὄλβος at *Oedipus Tyrannos* 1284, this association of ἐσθλός with ἄτη is the only Sophoclean echo of the supposed ὄλβος, κόρος, ὕβρις, ἄτη tetralogy purportedly so prevalent in ancient Greek thought. For a general treatment of this stasimon, see Dietmar Korzeniewski, "Interpretationen zu Sophokleischen Chorliedern," RhM, 104 N.S. (1961), 193–201; and Musurillo, *The Light and the Darkness*, pp. 48–52. Goheen, *Imagery of Sophocles' Antigone*, pp. 56–64, also has a fine treatment of this stasimon. His remarks on ἄτη are generally excellent, particularly his notion (p. 59) of the shift in meaning. See also Bowra's treatment of this stasimon, *Sophoclean Tragedy*, pp. 87–90, which he appears to contradict somewhat on pp. 114–15.

A similar frequency of the use of ἄτη recurs in Sophocles in the parodos of the *Electra*, lines 215, 224, 235 bis.

³⁹ Thus, the generally erotic picture here echoes the use of ἄτη in *Iliad* 3.100, 6.356, 24.28; *Odyssey* 4.261, 23.223; *Pythian* 2.28; *Suppliants* 110, 850; and *Agamemnon* 386, 1192.

⁴⁰ We find ἄτη in connection with μόρος at *Ajax* 848, with ὄνειδος at *Ajax* 1189, and with μοῖρα at *Trachinian Women* 850.

⁴¹ See Jebb's excellent note on the phrase ἐν δεινῷ πάρα in *Antigone*, pp. 194–95, ad loc. Dawe, "Some Reflections on Ate and Hamartia," 113n40, speaks of the "crisp antithesis" in these lines.

⁴² ἄτη is associated with these concepts at *Iliad* 6.356, 16.805, 19.88, 126, 129, 136, 270; *Odyssey* 15.233, 21.302, 23.223; *Shield of Heracles* 93; *Persians* 112, 822; *Seven Against Thebes* 687; *Suppliants* 110, 850; *Libation-Bearers* 597; and *Prometheus* 886.

⁴³ *Antigone*, p. 222, note on lines 1259f.

⁴⁴ *Sophocles the Playwright*, pp. 57–58.

⁴⁵ The collocation of ἁμαρτία and ἄτη is precisely the focus of the two fine studies frequently referred to in these notes, Bremer's *Hamartia* and Dawe's "Some Reflections on Ate and Hamartia."

⁴⁶ B. M. W. Knox has treated this antistrophe in some detail in "The Date of the *Oedipus Tyrannus* of Sophocles," AJP, 77 (1956), 133–47, esp. 140ff. For a discussion of the imagery of this antistrophe, see Musurillo, *The Light and the Darkness*, pp. 88–89.

⁴⁷ The following textual variants occur:

1205 — τίς ἄταις ἀγρίαις, τίς ἐν πόνοις	Hermann
— τίς ἄταις ἐν ἀγρίαις, τίς ἐν πόνοις	
servato in antistr. 1214 τον	Gleditsch
— τίς ἐν πόναις τίς ἄταις ἀγρίαις	L, Campbell
— τοσούτοισιν ἐν πόνοις τίς ἀγρίοις	Brunck
— τίς ἐν πόνοισιν, τίς ἄταις ἀγρίαις	Hermann, Seidler.

In addition, V. Coulon, in "Note sur Sophocle, *Oed. R.* 1204–1206 et 696," REG, 69 (1956), 446–48, reads τίς ἄταις, τίς ἀγρίοις < ιν> ἐν πόνοις, and J. C. Kamerbeek, in "Sophoclea V," *Mnemosyne,* 15, 4th ser. (1962), 24–30, very tentatively suggests τίς < ὧδε> πόνοις, τίς ἄταις ἀγρίαις.

This stasimon, and particularly the first occurrence of βασιλεύς as applied to Oedipus in 1201, figures prominently in B. M. W. Knox's excellent article "Why Is Oedipus Called Tyrannos?" CJ, 50 (1954), 97–102.

[48] The articles by Coulon and Kamerbeek mentioned in the preceding note contain discussions of the problem.

[49] For some penetrating remarks on Sophoclean irony, see Kirkwood, *Study of Sophoclean Drama*, pp. 247–87.

[50] For the relationship between the chorus and Electra, see the excellent article by Ignacio Errandonea, s.j.: "Le chœur dans l'*Electre* de Sophocle," LEC, 23, No. 4 (October 1955), 369–70.

[51] It should be noted with Adams, *Sophocles the Playwright*, p. 73, that this is the peripeteia of the tragedy.

[52] For the difficulty posed by this passage vis-à-vis a fixed mask, see Roy C. Flickinger, *The Greek Theatre and Its Drama*, 4th ed. (Chicago: The University of Chicago Press, 1936), p. 222.

[53] See the preliminary discussion of this point on p. 96 above.

[54] See Musurillo, *The Light and the Darkness*, pp. 122–23.

[55] *Heroic Temper*, pp. 129–30.

[56] Although none of the other textual variants for this passage is significant, Jebb, *Sophocles: The Plays and Fragments.* II. *The Oedipus Coloneus* (Cambridge: Cambridge University Press, 1900; repr. Amsterdam: Hakkert, 1965), p. 42, and Dain and Mazon, *Sophocles*, introduce, at line 199, the line βάσει βάσιν ἅρμοσαι without a single word of explanation!

See the good analysis of this entire scene given by Adams, *Sophocles the Playwright*, p. 167, and the remarks of Bremer, *Hamartia*, p. 172.

[57] See above, pp. 7–8.

[58] *Iliad* 2.111 is discussed on p. 13 above; *Antigone* 864, on pp. 106–107.

[59] See chaps. 4 and 5.

[60] *Ajax* 976; *Trachinian Women* 1274; *Antigone* 4, 185, 533, 584, 614, 625; *Oedipus Tyrannos* 164, 1205, 1284; *Electra* 936, 1002, 1298; *Oedipus at Colonus* 93, 1244.

[61] *Trachinian Women* 1274; *Antigone* 4, 185, 533; *Oedipus Tyrannos* 1284; *Electra* 936, 1002, 1298; *Oedipus at Colonus* 93, 1244.

[62] *Ajax* 123, 195, 307, 363, 643, 848, 1189; *Trachinian Women* 850, 1001, 1082, 1104; *Antigone* 864, 1097, 1260; *Electra* 215, 224, 235 bis; *Philoctetes* 706; *Oedipus at Colonus* 202, 526, 532.

[63] This is the case at *Ajax* 195, 363, 643, 909; *Trachinian Women* 1001, 1082, 1104; *Philoctetes* 706; and *Oedipus at Colonus* 202.

[64] This has been admirably treated by A. W. Adkins, *Merit and Responsibility* (Oxford: Clarendon, 1960).

[65] As indicated above on pp. 112–13, this is particularly interesting when contrasted with his use of ἄτη in its objective sense with τύχη at *Electra* 936, 1002, and 1298.

7

EURIPIDES AND ᾿ΑΤΗ

FOR EURIPIDES, ἄτη was obviously not so important a concept as it had been for Aeschylus and Sophocles. In the eighteen or nineteen extant Euripidean plays, ἄτη appears in only thirty-one passages. Not only is the proportionate appearance of ἄτη significantly lower than it is in his two predecessors, but frequently ἄτη appears only once in a play. This renders interpretation from the context — a significant factor in dealing with the two earlier tragedians — all but impossible. Nevertheless, through other considerations, it is possible to undertake an investigation of ἄτη in the drama of Euripides.

To maintain the parallel with the procedure used in dealing with his predecessors, this investigation will follow the chronological order of Euripides' productions — though Euripides does not develop the concept of ἄτη so much as try to make it more expressive through such devices as metonymy, alliteration, final position, and striking imagery.

ALCESTIS

In the *Alcestis* ἄτη appears only in the parodos. As the chorus of the elders of Pherae make their unusual entrance in two semi-choruses, the first strophe sung is:

στρ. κλύει τις ἢ στεναγμὸν ἢ
χειρῶν κτύπον κατὰ στέγας
ἢ γόον ὡς πεπραγμένων;
οὐ μὰν οὐδέ τις ἀμφιπόλων στα-
τίζεται ἀμφὶ πύλας. εἰ   90
γὰρ μετακύμιος ἄτας,
ὦ Παιάν, φανείης. ¹

The use of ἄτη here is evocative of both Aeschylean and Sophoclean usage. As is frequently the case in Aeschylus (and often repeated in Sophocles), ἄτη as "ruin," "disaster," or "calamity" is symptomatic of other expressions of "evil" in the immediate context: στεναγμὸν (line 86), χειρῶν κτύπον (line 87), and γόον (line 88). Like Sophocles,

Euripides associates ἄτη in the objective sense with words connected with sound; thus lines 86–88, replete with concepts involving sound, frame the question which is answered by the other semi-chorus in the lines directly involving ἄτη. The striking metaphor μετακύμιος ἄτας in line 91, which is drawn from the sea and has been characterized as "an obscure phrase," recalls the similar association of ἄτη in its objective sense with the sea metaphor in Aeschylus' *Suppliants* 470.[2]

MEDEA

One of the Euripidean tragedies in which ἄτη does appear more than once is the *Medea*. In this drama of "infatuation" turned to hatred, ἄτη occurs four times, yet, remarkably, in none of the four passages is it used in the subjective sense.

At the end of the prologue, ἄτη appears for the first time, spoken by the nurse:

> τὰ δ' ὑπερβάλλοντ'
> οὐδένα καιρὸν δύναται θνητοῖς·
> μείζους δ' ἄτας, ὅταν ὀργισθῇ
> δαίμων οἴκοις, ἀπέδωκεν.[3]   130

The ἄτη of line 129 is associated with another concept denoting "evil" — namely, ὀργισθῇ — in the same line. The metaphorical expression in lines 127–128 is drawn from the realm of finance,[4] and if the meaning of καιρός as "profit" is accepted in this context, the conceptual echo of κέρδεα in association with ἄτη in its objective sense is quite plain and recalls the association of the two words in Hesiod, *Works and Days* 352, Theognis 133, *Libation-Bearers* 825, and *Oedipus at Colonus* 93.

As the first epeisodion unfolds, Creon arrives and decrees banishment for Medea. As Conacher observes, "the dramatist endows her with the insight and skill to twist what should most tell against her — her reputation as 'a wise one' and Creon's protective love for his own daughter — to serve her purpose."[5] Here, then, is the beginning of Medea's cunning reply:

> αἰαῖ· πανώλης ἡ τάλαιν' ἀπόλλυμαι.
> ἐχθροὶ γὰρ ἐξιᾶσι πάντα δὴ κάλων,
> κοὐκ ἔστιν ἄτης εὐπρόσοιστος ἔκβασις.
> ἐρήσομαι δὲ καὶ κακῶς πάσχουσ' ὅμως·   280
> τίνος μ' ἕκατι γῆς ἀποστέλλεις, Κρέον;

That the objective concept of ἄτη is operative in line 279 is clear from the context: it is synonymous with other expressions for "evil" in the passage — ἀπόλλυμαι in line 277, all of line 278, and κακῶς πάσχουσ' in line 280[6] — and the metaphor involving it with ἔκβασις recalls its association with λιμήν in Aeschylus' *Suppliants* 470, where it also was used objectively.[7]

The final two occurrences of ἄτη in the *Medea* are in the first strophe and antistrophe of the fourth stasimon. Jason and the children have just exited, and the chorus, in a masterfully dramatic heightening of suspense, sing:

στρ.   νῦν ἐλπίδες οὐκέτι μοι παίδων ζόας,
        οὐκέτι· στείχουσι γὰρ ἐς φόνον ἤδη.
        δέξεται νύμφα χρυσέων ἀναδεσμῶν
        δέξεται δύστανος ἄταν·
        ξανθᾷ δ' ἀμφὶ κόμᾳ θήσει τὸν Ἅιδα   980
        κόσμον αὐτὰ χεροῖν. [λαβοῦσα.]

ἀντ.   πείσει χάρις ἀμβρόσιός τ' αὐγὰ πέπλων
        χρυσέων τευκτὸν στέφανον περιθέσθαι·
        νερτέροις δ' ἤδη πάρα νυμφοκομήσει.   985
        τοῖον εἰς ἕρκος πεσεῖται
        καὶ μοῖραν θανάτου δύστανος· ἄταν δ'
        οὐχ ὑπεκφεύξεται.[8]

Although the punctuation varies in lines 979 and 987, the verbal echo of δύστανος ἄταν, coupled with the usual supposition that ἄτη repeated in close proximity retains the same connotation, prompts the consideration of these twin appearances as a single occurrence. That ἄτη is meant here in its objective sense is clear from its use as a synonym for other expressions for "evil" in the immediate context: φόνον in line 977, Ἅιδα κόσμον in lines 980–981, ἕρκος in line 986, and μοῖραν θανάτου in line 987.

There is a significant difference between Euripidean usage, as evidenced in this passage, and Sophoclean usage in *Trachinian Women* 849–850. In Sophocles, as we have seen,[9] μοῖρα and ἄτη were joined when ἄτη was used ambivalently in both its objective sense, as here, and in its subjective sense of "blindness," "infatuation," or "folly." But here Euripides associates μοῖρα with ἄτη only in its objective sense. Thus in this instance, at least, Euripides conceives μοῖρα, not as something partially interior to man and over which he has some control, but as something outside man and beyond his ability to determine.[10]

HERACLIDAE

The only appearance of ἄτη in the *Heraclidae* occurs at the end of the second epeisodion. After Macaria has rejected selection by lot and insisted on dying for all, she exits, and Iolaus' subsequent remarks conclude with:

> ὡς οὔτε τούτοις ἥδομαι πεπραγμένοις,   605
> χρησμοῦ τε μὴ κρανθέντος οὐ βιώσιμον·
> μείζων γὰρ ἄτη· συμφορὰ δὲ καὶ τάδε.[11]

The contrast between the totality of ἄτη and the mitigated συμφορά in line 607 is the initial indication that ἄτη is used here in its objective sense. Iolaus, to be sure, has tried to dissuade Macaria from assuming the sole responsibility of dying for all the children of Heracles (lines 544–546), but he was unsuccessful and, hence, could legitimately utter line 605 and refer to Macaria's death as συμφορά. Yet he knows that far greater catastrophe, ἄτη, awaits them if they fail to fulfill the oracle (line 606).

The context corroborates this objective connotation, for ἄτη in line 607 is synonymous with other expressions of "evil" in the immediate context: οἰχόμεσθα in line 602, λύπη in line 603 and τούτοις ... πεπραγμένοις in line 605 (which, in the concrete, is Macaria's death).

HIPPOLYTUS

In the *Hippolytus* there are four passages to be considered, and in each of them ἄτη is used by a different character.

In the first epeisodion, Phaedra, who has been brought outdoors by the nurse, speaks wildly (lines 212–214; παράφρων, 232; φρένας, 238) to her about the hunt. As she comes to her senses, she says:

> δύστηνος ἐγώ, τί ποτ' εἰργασάμην;
> ποῖ παρεπλάγχθην γνώμης ἀγαθῆς;   240
> ἐμάνην, ἔπεσον δαίμονος ἄτῃ.

That ἄτη in line 241 is used simultaneously in both its objective and its subjective meanings is obvious from several features in the context. First, the passage is replete with indications of Phaedra's subjective, interior, state of mind; γνώμης ἀγαθῆς in 240, ἐμάνην in 241, αἰδούμεθα in 244, ἐπ' αἰσχύνην in 246, μαινόμενον in 248, and μὴ γιγνώσκοντ' in 249 are expressions consonant with ἄτη interpreted subjectively.[12]

Secondly, the general context of the play up to this point indicates a subjective interpretation for ἄτη in 241, since from the prologue we know that Aphrodite is attempting to destroy Hippolytus through the unnatural "infatuation" which she causes in Phaedra. But that infatuation itself is, of course, a "calamity" not only for Hippolytus but also for Phaedra, and, hence, it is possible to see the other, objective, meaning of ἄτη involved here. Thus ἄτη is precisely what Barrett characterized it: a simultaneous disastrous deterioration of one's wits and one's fortunes.[13]

The next appearance of ἄτη in the *Hippolytus* is also in the first epeisodion. As the stichomythy between the nurse and the chorus progresses, the following exchange occurs:

> Xo. ὡς ἀσθενεῖ τε καὶ κατέξανται δέμας.
> Τρ. πῶς δ' οὔ, τριταίαν γ' οὖσ' ἄσιτος ἡμέραν;   275
> Xo. πότερον ὑπ' ἄτης ἢ θανεῖν πειρωμένη;[14]

The ἄτη of line 276 is something less than the final calamity of death, as the antithesis makes clear. Once again, as so often in this play, the interdependence of mental and physical illness is involved and ἄτη expresses it well.[15] The folly of her infatuation for Hippolytus has pushed Phaedra to the brink of exhaustion, so much so that the chorus are not sure whether her illness will stop there or culminate in death. Hence, they characterize her behavior as an ἄτη, a simultaneous mental and physical deterioration.

After the exile of Hippolytus decreed by Theseus in the third epeisodion, the chorus conclude the third stasimon:

> ἰὼ ἰώ·
> συζύγιαι Χάριτες, τί τὸν τάλαν' ἐκ πατρίας γᾶς
> οὐδὲν ἄτας αἴτιον
> πέμπετε τῶνδ' ἀπ' οἴκων;[16]   1150

The dramatic moment makes it clear that in protesting the innocence of Hippolytus the chorus have uppermost in their minds his lack of complicity in the death of Phaedra. Hence, ἄτη here is to be understood in its objective meaning.

At the beginning of the exodos, Artemis enters and makes these remarks to Theseus:

> Θησεῦ, τί τάλας τοῖσδε συνήδῃ,   1286
> παῖδ' οὐχ ὁσίως σὸν ἀποκτείνας,
> ψευδέσι μύθοις ἀλόχου πεισθεὶς
> ἀφανῆ; φανερὰν δ' ἔσχεθες ἄτην.[17]

The context, the dramatic moment, and the vocabulary used with ἄτη in line 1289 make it clear that here too ἄτη must be understood in its objective sense.

HECUBA

The only occurrence of ἄτη in the *Hecuba* is in the third epeisodion. After she has lost her appeal to Odysseus for the life of Polyxena, Hecuba is confronted, as the third epeisodion opens, by a servant bringing more tragic news. As the cover is removed from the corpse, the following exchange takes place:

> Ἑκ.   οἴμοι, βλέπω δὴ παῖδ᾽ ἐμὸν τεθνηκότα,
> Πολύδωρον, ὅν μοι Θρῂξ ἔσῳζ᾽ οἴκοις ἀνήρ.
> ἀπωλόμην δύστηνος, οὐκέτ᾽ εἰμὶ δή.
>   ὦ τέκνον τέκνον,
>   αἰαῖ, κατάρχομαι γόων,   685
>   βακχεῖον ἐξ ἀλάστορος
>   ἀρτιμαθῆ νόμον.
> Θε.   ἔγνως γὰρ ἄτην παιδός, ὦ δύστηνε σύ;
> Ἑκ.   ἄπιστ᾽ ἄπιστα, καινὰ καινὰ δέρκομαι.

The servant's question in line 688 clearly employs ἄτη in the objective sense, since the reference is to Polydorus' death. This interpretation is corroborated by the mention of a δαίμων, the ἀλάστωρ of line 686, and by the synonyms for "evil" contained in lines 690 and 693. But, as she shows in lines 689 and 690, Hecuba sees ἄτη as pertaining to more than one of her children, and to more than one calamity. She has been overwhelmed by the destruction of Troy, the death of Hector, her reduction to servitude, and now the deaths of her daughter and son. Indeed, before she was shown the corpse, she had steeled herself to see possibly the corpse of Polyxena (line 671) or even Cassandra (line 677); thus, her thoughts are shown to embrace multiple disaster, even when she confronts but a single concrete instance of it.[18]

    This passage is noteworthy for the collocation of ἄτη with γιγνώσκω, a far cry from the Homeric and archaic lyric association of ἄτη with φρήν, θυμός, etc.[19]

ANDROMACHE

Toward the end of the prologue in the play named for her, Andromache engages in an elegiac lament, the first six lines of which are:

Ἰλίῳ αἰπεινᾷ Πάρις οὐ γάμον ἀλλά τιν' ἄταν
ἠγάγετ' εὐναίαν εἰς θαλάμους Ἑλέναν.
ἇς ἕνεκ', ὦ Τροία, δορὶ καὶ πυρὶ δηιάλωτον   105
εἷλέ σ' ὁ χιλιόναυς Ἑλλάδος ὠκὺς Ἄρης
καὶ τὸν ἐμὸν μελέας πόσιν Ἕκτορα, τὸν περὶ τείχη
εἷλκυσε διφρεύων παῖς ἁλίας Θέτιδος·[20]

As P. T. Stevens has observed in his commentary on lines 103–104, "It is better to take γάμον (and ἄταν) in apposition to the sentence ἠγάγετ' . . . Ἑλέναν. . . . It is, as Barrett says, a special form of the internal accusative, the force of which is here 'he brought Helen home, not marriage-wise but disastrously.' "[21]

The context secures this objective sense of "disaster" for ἄτη on two levels: one involving the whole of Troy; the other, Andromache personally. The synonymous descriptions for other κακά are, with respect to Troy, δορὶ καὶ πυρὶ δηιάλωτον / εἷλέ σ', in lines 105–106, and, for Andromache herself, the horrible vision of her husband being dragged around the city, in lines 107–108.

This passage is the Euripidean equivalent of the Aeschylean metaphor of Helen as a ἱερεύς τις ἄτας in the famous lioncub image in the second stasimon of the *Agamemnon*.[22] Yet Euripides, in a brilliant piece of poetic technique, expands the Aeschylean concept by changing a metaphor into a metonymy. Thus, if Helen's γάμος is a disaster, an ἄτη, for the Trojans, Helen is also ill-fated for them. Through the metonymy, a person who is ruinous for people becomes fatal for people! This concept will become explicit in the *Electra*, but it is not premature to see its root in this passage of the *Andromache*.

HERCULES FURENS

In the play named for him, Heracles has arrived home to save his father, Amphitryon, his wife, Megara, and his sons from the death intended for them by the usurper Lycus. After killing Lycus (line 753), Heracles is immediately beset by Λύσσα (lines 815ff.), at the command of Isis and Hera, and kills his own sons and his wife under this influence. In the third epeisodion, the following exchange occurs between the chorus and the messenger:

Αγ.   οὐκ ἄν τις εἴποι μᾶλλον ἢ πεπόνθαμεν.
Χο.   πῶς παισὶ στενακτὰν ἄταν ἄταν
      πατέρος ἀμφαίνεις;

λέγε, τίνα τρόπον ἔσυτο θεόθεν ἐπὶ
μέλαθρα κακὰ τάδε,   920
τλήμονάς τε παίδων τύχας;

In its twin appearance in line 917, ἄτη is used in its ambivalent sense
of objective "calamity" and subjective "blindness." The immediate
context focuses on the objective meaning, with the synonymous expressions of disaster in κακὰ in line 920 and τλήμονάς ... τύχας in
line 921. That Heracles acted in a fit of madness, however, cannot help
but color the meaning of ἄτη with its subjective connotation of "blindness" or "folly." The repetition of ἄτη in a single line recalls Sophocles'
Electra 235.[23]

The only other appearance of ἄτη in the *Hercules Furens*, at line 1284
in the exodos, marks the final use of the word in a non-lyric passage in
the extant works of Euripides. Theseus is trying to dissuade Heracles
from committing suicide. To counter his argument, Heracles reviews
his life and says:

ἥκω δ᾽ ἀνάγκης ἐς τόδ᾽· οὔτ᾽ ἐμαῖς φίλαις   1281
Θήβαις ἐνοικεῖν ὅσιον· ἢν δὲ καὶ μένω,
ἐς ποῖον ἱερὸν ἢ πανήγυριν φίλων
εἶμ᾽; οὐ γὰρ ἄτας εὐπροσηγόρους ἔχω.

As the context makes clear, the meaning of ἄτη in line 1284 is "calamities" or "disasters," which are enumerated in the passage under consideration. Thus, the murder of his sons will render Heracles a religious
and social outcast.

TROJAN WOMEN

As the *Trojan Women* opens, Poseidon and Athena set aside their enmity and agree to cooperate in creating a difficult return voyage for the
Greeks (line 75) because of Ajax' desecration of Athena's shrine (line
69). After they exit, Hecuba awakens and begins her lyrical lament.
This highly emotional passage contains ἄτη twice, at lines 121 and
137:

μοῦσα δὲ χαὔτη τοῖς δυστήνοις   120
ἄτας κελαδεῖν ἀχορεύτους.

πρῷραι ναῶν, ὠκείαις
῎Ιλιον ἱερὰν αἳ κώπαις
δι᾽ ἅλα πορφυροειδέα καὶ
λιμένας ῾Ελλάδος εὐόρμους   125

αὐλῶν παιᾶνι στυγνῷ
συρίγγων τ' εὐφθόγγων φωνᾷ
βαίνουσαι πλεκτὰν Αἰγύπτου
παιδείαν ἐξηρτήσασθ',
αἰαῖ, Τροίας ἐν κόλποις   130
τὰν Μενελάου μετανισόμεναι
στυγνὰν ἄλοχον, Κάστορι λώβαν
τῷ τ' Εὐρώτᾳ δυσκλείαν,
ἃ σφάζει μὲν
τὸν πεντήκοντ' ἀροτῆρα τέκνων   135
     Πρίαμον, ἐμέ τε μελέαν Ἑκάβαν
     ἐς τάνδ' ἐξώκειλ' ἄταν.²⁴

In addition to the personal physical woes outlined in lines 112ff., Hecuba's lament goes on to describe in broader perspective the "evils" associated with the first occurrence of ἄτη in its objective sense at line 121. Thus, the complicated sentence from line 122 to line 136 details from the Trojan point of view three specific "evils" which befell them: (1) πρῷραι ναῶν; (2) τὰν Μενελάου μετανισόμεναι στυγνὰν ἄλοχον; and (3) ἃ σφάζει μὲν τὸν πεντήκοντ' ἀροτῆρα τέκνων Πρίαμον. With the mention of Priam's name, of course, Hecuba is reminded of her personal "calamity," and for the second time ἄτη occurs in her lament. That the word is again employed in the objective sense is indicated not only by its conceptual continuation of all that has preceded, but also by the use of τάνδ' in line 137 and the metaphor contained in the verb ἐξώκειλ' (line 137), which is relevant to the πρῷραι ναῶν mentioned in line 122. The nautical metaphor, of course, recalls the use of a similar metaphor with ἄτη at *Alcestis* 91.

At the conclusion of Hecuba's lament, the chorus of Trojan women enter, and the parodos begins at line 153. The following brief lyrical exchange takes place between Hecuba and a semi-chorus of women:

Εκ.   ὦ τέκν', Ἀργείων πρὸς ναῦς ἤδη ...
          κινεῖται κωπήρης χείρ;   160
      οἲ ἐγώ, τί θέλουσ', ἦ πού μ' ἤδη
      ναυσθλώσουσιν πατρίας ἐκ γᾶς;
Εκ.   οὐκ οἶδ', εἰκάζω δ' ἄταν.

Besides echoing the nautical metaphor of the last occurrence of ἄτη at line 137, the appearance of ἄτη in line 163 continues the objective use of the word, consistent with the emotional tone of the previous lament. The choral question in lines 161–162 — ἦ πού μ' ἤδη ναυσθλώσουσιν πατρίας ἐκ γᾶς; — with its synonymous specification of the concrete application they fear will be the "calamity" about to come on them all corroborates the interpretation.

The first stasimon begins with the chorus proclaiming that, under the inspiration of the Muse, they will sing the dirge of Troy's destruction. Their song immediately turns to a narrative of the incident of the wooden horse, in which the first strophe ends and the first antistrophe begins as follows:

> κεχαρμένοι δ' ἀοιδαῖς
> δόλιον ἔσχον ἄταν.   530
> ἀντ.   πᾶσα δὲ γέννα Φρυγῶν
> πρὸς πύλας ὡρμάθη,
> πεύκᾳ ἐν οὐρείᾳ ξεστὸν λόχον Ἀργείων
> καὶ Δαρδανίας ἄταν θεᾷ δώσων,   535
> χάριν ἄζυγος ἀμβροτοπώλου.²⁵

The tenor of the context points to the objective meaning for ἄτη in this instance.²⁶ The synonyms for "evil," which are customary with ἄτη used in its objective sense, are implicit in the entire stasimon's recounting of the total devastation which befell Troy through the deception of the wooden horse, and which now results in the servitude of Hecuba and the other Trojan women. And as he does at *Andromache* 104, Euripides expands the meaning of ἄτη through the use of metonymy. Thus, the gift becomes ruinous, and therefore fateful, for the Trojans.

Shortly before the end of the play, the following lyrical exchange between Hecuba and the chorus takes place:

> Εκ.   ἰώ.
> Πρίαμε Πρίαμε, σὺ μὲν ὀλόμενος
> ἄταφος ἄφιλος
> ἄτας ἐμᾶς ἄιστος εἶ.
> Χο.   μέλας γὰρ ὄσσε κατεκάλυψε   1315
> θάνατος ὅσιος ἀνοσίαις σφαγαῖσιν.²⁷

The ἄτη Hecuba refers to is the "ruin," "disaster," "calamity" which has come upon her, her children and husband, and all of Troy, as a result of the Greek victory. Each of the disasters she details — her impending slavery in 1310, the death of her children in 1303–1304, the death of Priam referred to in the ὀλόμενος of 1312, and the destruction of Troy lamented at the start of the antistrophe beginning in 1317 — is a specification of the κακά envisioned in the ἄτη of 1314.

Finally, the alliteration of this passage, as well as the association of ἄτη with οἶδα, just as ἄτη had been associated with γιγνώσκω at

Hecuba 688, are worthy of note. Indeed, it is possible to see a preposterous conceit in this passage, inasmuch as Hecuba laments Priam's lack of knowledge about her own calamity, while simultaneously addressing him as "graveless," as disastrous a calamity as could happen according to ancient religious beliefs.

ELECTRA

ἄτη occurs only once in the *Electra,* but it is a very significant occurrence. Shortly after the *deus ex machina* appearance of the Dioscouroi in the exodos, the following exchange takes place with Electra:

Δι. μοῖρά τ' ἀνάγκης ἦγ' ᾗ τὸ χρεών,
    Φοίβου τ' ἄσοφοι γλώσσης ἐνοπαί.
Ηλ. τίς δ' ἔμ' Ἀπόλλων, ποῖοι χρησμοὶ
    φονίαν ἔδοσαν μητρὶ γενέσθαι;
Δι. κοιναὶ πράξεις, κοινοὶ δὲ πότμοι,   1305
    μία δ' ἀμφοτέρους
    ἄτη πατέρων διέκναισεν.[28]

Investigation reveals the novelty of this passage and its significance, for the synonym of κακά which appears with ἄτη in the immediate context is πότμοι in line 1305. But allusion to πότμοι leads to a recognition of the highly colored moral terminology in the surrounding context; ἄτη is used in the same context as μοῖρα and ἀνάγκης . . . τὸ χρεών in line 1301, and χρησμοὶ in line 1303, as well as with the πότμοι of line 1305. The clear contextual indications are, therefore, that ἄτη in line 1307 is used for the first time in extant Greek literature to mean "fate."[29]

This significant shift in the concept of ἄτη, important though it obviously is, should not prove too surprising. Its roots are to be found in the Euripidean use of metonymy with ἄτη at *Andromache* 104 and *Trojan Women* 530 and 535.[30] Similarly, in the present passage, it is possible to understand Euripides as indicating the metonymous expansion of the "calamity" which befell Orestes and Electra to something which proves "fateful" for them.

ION

As in the *Electra*, there is only one occurrence of ἄτη in the *Ion*. In the fourth, and final, stasimon the chorus sing:

τίνα φυγὰν πτερόεσσαν ἢ
χθονὸς ὑπὸ σκοτίων μυχῶν πορευθῶ,
θανάτου λεύσιμον ἄταν   1240
ἀποφεύγουσα, τεθρίππων
ὠκιστᾶν χαλᾶν ἐπιβᾶσ᾽,
ἢ πρύμνας ἐπὶ ναῶν;[31]

This is another instance of the use of ἄτη in its objective connotation; the context specifies the synonym for ἄτη in this sense: the θάνατος mentioned in line 1240.

IPHIGENIA IN TAURIS

When the chorus enter in the *Iphigenia in Tauris*, they come at the bidding of Iphigenia, and their parodos takes the form of a kommos with her. Twice in the course of this exchange Iphigenia employs ἄτη while telling the chorus of her dream about the death of Orestes and her subsequent lamentations.

The first of these occurrences comes in her answer to the choral question as to why they had been summoned:

αἲ μοι συμβαίνουσ᾽ ἆται,
σύγγονον ἀμὸν κατακλαιομένα
ζωᾶς, οἵαν <οἵαν> ἰδόμαν   150
ὄψιν ὀνείρων
νυκτός, τᾶς ἐξῆλθ᾽ ὄρφνα.

The objective connotation of "calamity" is secured here by the context, which makes it clear that this is the death of Orestes as revealed in her dream. This "disaster" is the subject of her lament in this kommos. The use of the plural, referring to the various "calamities" implied in the death of her brother — namely, the ruin of her house and family — corroborates this interpretation.

As the parodos continues and the chorus join her in her lament for the dead Orestes, Iphigenia widens the scope of her sorrow to include a review of her own sad life. In the course of this, she sings:

αἱμόρραντον δυσφόρμιγγα   225
ξείνων †αἱμάσσουσ᾽ ἄταν βωμούς,†
οἰκτράν τ᾽ αἰαζόντων αὐδὰν
οἰκτρόν τ᾽ ἐκβαλλόντων δάκρυον.[32]

The ἄτη in line 226 is again used objectively; the "evils" synonymous with it in that sense are expressed in the αἱμάσσουσ᾽ ... βωμούς in the same line.

In the second stasimon, the chorus itself employs ἄτη as they, not unlike Iphigenia in the passage just cited, bemoan their fate:

ζαχρύσου δὲ δι᾽ ἐμπολᾶς
    νόστον βάρβαρον ἦλθον,
ἔνθα τᾶς ἐλαφοκτόνου
θεᾶς ἀμφίπολον κόραν
παῖδ᾽ Ἀγαμεμνονίαν λατρεύ-   1115
ω βωμούς τ᾽ οὐ μηλοθύτας,
    ζηλοῦσ᾽ ἄταν διὰ παν-
τὸς δυσδαίμον᾽·

The depth of the chorus' depression in this passage matches the depth of depression which Iphigenia's sad laments embodied in the previous passage. The choral "jealousy" is a far cry from an Homeric simile, yet their point is that they yearn to be like the afflicted individuals of whom they are jealous, and would trade places with anyone in the whole world who is constantly afflicted with ἄτη. Consequently, the ἄτη here is to be understood in its objective sense. The individuals affected by such a "disaster" would be anyone and everyone among the permanently downtrodden with whom the chorus would gladly change places. Such a permanent state of woe is, of course, controlled by the gods, as the δυσδαίμον᾽ in line 1118 indicates. And the synonymous counterparts of such a state of depression are expressed well in such notions as ἐν ἀνάγκαις in lines 1118–1119, δυσδαιμονία in line 1120, and κακοῦσθαι in lines 1121–1122. Though, given such considerations, it might seem best to construe ἄτη in this passage as "ruin," "disaster," or "calamity," the context might also indicate that here too, as at *Electra* 1307, ἄτη approaches the meaning of "fate."

PHOENICIAN MAIDENS

The first of the two occurrences of ἄτη in the *Phoenician Maidens* takes place in the first epeisodion, during Jocasta's lyrical welcome of Polyneices. Toward the end of this greeting, she sings:

σὲ δ᾽, ὦ τέκνον, [καὶ] γάμοισι δὴ
κλύω ζυγέντα παιδοποιὸν ἁδονὰν
    ξένοισιν ἐν δόμοις ἔχειν
    ξένον τε κῆδος ἀμφέπειν,   340
    ἄλαστα ματρὶ τᾷδε Λα-
    ίῳ τε τῷ παλαιγενεῖ,
        γάμων ἐπακτὸν ἄταν.

The ἄτη mentioned here carries the objective connotation, as the contextual synonym ἄλαστα in line 341 confirms.

The gods figure prominently in the other occurrence of ἄτη in the
Phoenician Maidens. At the end of the third stasimon, the chorus in-
voke Athena:

γενοίμεθ' ὧδε ματέρες   1060
γενοίμεθ' εὔτεκνοι, φίλα
Παλλάς, ἃ δράκοντος αἷμα
λιθόβολον κατειργάσω,
Καδμείαν μέριμναν
ὁρμήσασ' ἐπ' ἔργον,
ὅθεν ἐπέσυτο τάνδε γαῖαν   1065
ἁρπαγαῖσι δαιμόνων τις ἄτα.[33]

The objective connotation for ἄτη in this passage is clearly confirmed
by the synonym for it so understood, ἁρπαγαῖσι in line 1066.

In both passages in the *Phoenician Maidens*, it is interesting to note,
not only does Euripides employ ἄτη in lyric passages, but the word
occurs at the end of the line.

ORESTES

There are two passages in the *Orestes* in which ἄτη also appears at the
end of the line. In the third epeisodion the messenger appears to tell
Electra that the vote has gone against her and against Orestes and that
they are to die. At this Electra sings a θρῆνος which contains ἄτη
twice. The first instance occurs toward the beginning:

στρ.   κατάρχομαι στεναγμόν, ὦ Πελασγία,
       τιθεῖσα λευκὸν ὄνυχα διὰ παρηίδων,   961
              αἱματηρὸν ἄταν,
       κτύπον τε κρατός, ὃν ἔλαχ' ἁ κατὰ χθονὸς
       νερτέρων   Περσέφασσα καλλίπαις θεά.[34]

The two phrases λευκὸν ὄνυχα (line 961) and κτύπον τε κρατός (line
963) are synonymous expressions of "evil" consonant with ἄτη in its
objective sense.

As her lament continues, Electra becomes ever more emotionally
distraught and, thinking of her family lineage, expresses a wish, in the
course of which she narrates:

ὃς ἔτεκεν ἔτεκε γενέτορας ἐμέθεν δόμων,
  οἳ κατεῖδον ἄτας,
ποτανὸν μὲν δίωγμα πώλων
τεθριπποβάμονι στόλῳ Πέλοψ ὅτε
πελάγεσι διεδίφρευσε, Μυρτίλου φόνον   990
  δικὼν ἐς οἶδμα πόντου,
  λευκοκύμοσιν
  πρὸς Γεραιστίαις
  ποντίων σάλων
  ᾐόσιν ἁρματεύσας.[35]

The key to the understanding of ἄτη is to be found in the phrases ποτανὸν μὲν δίωγμα πώλων in line 988 and Μυρτίλου φόνον in line 990. The first of these refers to the death of Oenomaus in the famous chariot race which Pelops won with the connivance of Myrtilus; the second, of course, to Pelops' subsequent perfidious drowning of Myrtilus. Once these are understood, it is obvious that the connotation of ἄτη in this passage is the objective one, for the two phrases make it quite clear that Electra is thinking of two murder victims.

IPHIGENIA IN AULIS

It is almost poetic justice that the last occurrence of ἄτη should focus, probably in the year 406 B.C., on the person of Agamemnon, the king of the Greek troops at Troy about whom the Homeric poets, the first pieces of evidence concerning ἄτη, have so much to say. In the prologue of *Iphigenia in Aulis* the following exchange takes place between Agamemnon and an old retainer whom he is dispatching with the order countermanding Iphigenia's appearance in Aulis:

Πρ. δεινά γ' ἐτόλμας, Ἀγάμεμνον ἄναξ,
  ὃς τῷ τῆς θεᾶς σὴν παῖδ' ἄλοχον
  φατίσας ἦγες σφάγιον Δαναοῖς.   135
Αγ. οἴμοι, γνώμας ἐξέσταν,
  αἰαῖ, πίπτω δ' εἰς ἄταν.
  ἀλλ' ἴθ' ἐρέσσων σὸν πόδα, γήρᾳ
  μηδὲν ὑπείκων.[36]

The Euripidean usage of ἄτη is consistent right to the last of his extant passages in the two respects which have been noted so often: the appearance of ἄτη in a lyric passage and at the end of a line.

The objective meaning of "ruin," "calamity," or "disaster," as also so often, is corroborated by the dramatic context of this passage. Agamemnon is conscious of running the risk of committing a calamity in sacrificing Iphigenia and is desperately trying to avoid it. Thus his message, and thus his cry of anguish at line 137.

CONCLUSION

This review of the Euripidean ἄτη passages prompts some interesting conclusions. The most obvious is that in his use of ἄτη, as in so many other respects, Euripides is more like Aeschylus than Sophocles. Of the thirty-one appearances, ἄτη occurs in its objective connotation in twenty-six.[37] In only four instances — at *Hippolytus* 241 and 276 and twice at *Hercules Furens* 917 — does he adopt the Sophoclean ambivalence with respect to ἄτη, employing it simultaneously in both its objective and subjective meanings. On one occasion, at *Electra* 1307, Euripides breaks new ground, employing ἄτη to mean "fate." But nowhere in the extant Euripidean dramas does ἄτη appear univocally in its subjective meaning.

Thus, in several respects Euripides is a part of the Greek poetic tradition as far as his use of ἄτη is concerned, yet he changes that tradition in other respects. The former will be discussed first, since they are chiefly formal similarities and seemingly less important. First, as was true in both his dramatic predecessors, ἄτη appears much more often in lyric than in non-lyric passages. There are twenty-three such appearances in the extant Euripidean plays, as opposed to only eight texts in which ἄτη appears in non-lyric poetry.[38] Secondly, Euripides uses ἄτη in the singular much more often than in the plural. In his surviving dramas ἄτη appears twenty-six times in the singular, and only five times in the plural.[39] The entire corpus of poetry from Homer to Euripides displays the same preference. Finally, in Euripidean poetry the use of traditional poetic devices in connection with ἄτη is relatively slight. Most prevalent is the appearance of a metaphor drawn from the sea, which occurs in four passages.[40] At *Alcestis* 91 Euripides imitates the Sophoclean use of sound-words in connection with ἄτη,[41] and echoes Aeschylean use at *Andromache* 103 where the image of a lioncub appears with ἄτη.[42] Alliteration finds a place at *Trojan Women* 1314.

The changes which Euripides introduces with respect to ἄτη are quite significant. Chief among these, as indicated perhaps by his reversion to a predominantly Aeschylean meaning, is his view of ἄτη as an archaism, a fossil of tragic and epic language. This would appear to be true for the following reasons. First, no moral argument, no elaborated ethical principle, is constructed on ἄτη; neither a character nor the chorus ever discuss any moral issue taking ἄτη as a central notion. Nor is ἄτη ever connected with such terms as ὄλβος, κόρος, ὕβρις, and the like. The one exception is *Medea* 127ff., but this is a traditional γνώμη. Even such notions as justice and injustice, so critical in Euripides, are developed without reference to ἄτη. And the question of human responsibility, likewise of great importance to Euripides, is not elaborated in relation to ἄτη.

Euripidean usage also manifests a change with regard to ἄτη. Thus, it usually appears in such frozen phrases as "to fall into, to meet, to obtain, to receive, to escape disaster, ruin, or calamity": πίπτω, *Hippolytus* 241, *Phoenician Maidens* 1066, and *Iphigenia in Aulis* 137; ἐξοκέλλω, *Trojan Women* 137; ἔχω, *Hippolytus* 1289, *Hercules Furens* 1284, and *Trojan Women* 530; ὑπό, *Hippolytus* 276; ἄγω, *Andromache* 104; συμβαίνω, *Iphigenia in Tauris* 148; δέχομαι, *Medea* 979; δίδωμι, *Medea* 129 and *Trojan Women* 535; φεύγω, *Medea* 988 and *Ion* 1241; and ἔκβασις, *Medea* 279. The frequent appearance of ἄτη both in lyric passages and at the end of iambic lines is perhaps best explained by the fact that in his drama Euripides shifts discussion of moral topics from the choral portions to the dialogue, in keeping with his de-emphasis of the role of the chorus.

Euripides' use of ἄτη with noetic and ethical vocabulary, favored by the Sophists and adumbrated in the Sophoclean use of sight/sound vocabulary and ethical concepts with ἄτη, marks yet another change. Thus, ἄτη appears in connection with γιγνώσκω at *Hecuba* 688, and with γνώμη at *Iphigenia in Aulis* 137 and οἶδα at *Trojan Women* 1314. Though his use of τύχη with ἄτη at *Hercules Furens* 917 is much the same as Sophocles', his association of ἄτη with αἰσχύνη at *Hippolytus* 241 and with αἰσχυνθείς at *Hippolytus* 1289 represents a very real development from the Homeric poems and their insistence on τιμή.

But, of course, the most startling advance in the use of ἄτη in all of Euripides' extant poetry is at *Electra* 1307. Here, ἄτη appears for the first time in extant Greek literature as a synonym for μοῖρα, or αἶσσα, or any of the other terms used through the centuries to signify human destiny. Euripides has broken new ground with this usage, and it is not difficult to see in it the foreshadowing of the philosophical and dialectical preoccupations which will dominate the fourth century as the Greek poetic tradition goes into decline.

Those preoccupations are already evident in the Euripidean avoidance of the use of ἄτη in its subjective meaning as "blindness," "infatuation," or "folly." He has other words to express these "psychological" phenomena, and in keeping with his general view of ἄτη as a relic of epic and tragic vocabulary, does not need ἄτη to express them. His work frequently uses concepts like νόσος, μωρία, and μανία. The original meaning of ἄτη has become much more nuanced, and thus other concepts move to the forefront of Greek thought.

¹ In addition to the Murray text, the following editions have been consulted: *Euripidis Tragoediae*, ed. August Nauck, 3 vols. (Leipzig: Teubner, 1902–1905); and *Euripides: Alcestis*, ed. A. M. Dale (Oxford: Clarendon, 1954). Miss Dale, ibid., pp. 58–59, discusses the unusual character of the half-choruses, and remarks, on p. 60, on the scholiasts' interpretations of the rare word μεταχύμιος, but there are no *textual* difficulties with this passage.

On the possible influence of satyr plays on the semi-choral form here, see T. B. L. Webster, *The Tragedies of Euripides* (London: Methuen, 1967), p. 49. On the larger question of the *Alcestis* as a "pro-satyr" play, see D. J. Conacher, *Euripidean Drama: Myth, Theme, and Structure* (Toronto: University of Toronto Press, 1967), pp. 333–39.

² Although it is true that at *Prometheus* 886 Aeschylus also associated a sea metaphor with ἄτη in its *subjective* sense, the appearance of φρήν in that passage makes the subjective interpretation of ἄτη incontrovertible. Neither φρήν nor θυμός, needless to say, appears in this Euripidean passage.

See *Euripides: Alcestis*, ed. Dale, ad loc. Wesley D. Smith, in his stimulating article "The Ironic Structure in *Alcestis*," *The Phoenix*, 14 (1960), 127–45, points out, pp. 139–40, the centrality of the "voyage of death" imagery in the *Alcestis*. À propos of our passage, he remarks: "The river Styx is the counterpart of the 'sea of life' (91, 112, 124, 213, 252, 263, 610). Death is a journey, and has its counterpart in the mystical journey of resurrection, of which the prototype is Orpheus' journey to retrieve Eurydice."

³ This passage is treated by Johannes Kaiser in "Bemerkungen zu Euripides' *Medea*," *Gymnasium*, 66 (1959), 502–505. See also the remarks of Gerhard Müller, "Interpolationen in der *Medea* des Euripides," SIFC, 25 (1951), 80.

⁴ See *Euripides: Medea*, ed. Denys L. Page (Oxford: Clarendon, 1938), ad loc. For a different view, see Kaiser, "Bemerkungen zu Euripides' *Medea*," 502–503, and Otto Regenbogen, "Randbemerkungen zur *Medea* des Euripides," *Eranos*, 48 (1950), 24.

⁵ *Euripidean Drama*, p. 189. There may well be a second level of irony at work in this scene, if one accepts the remark of Edouard Delebecque, *Euripide et la guerre du*

Péloponnèse (Paris: Klincksieck, 1951), p. 64, who maintains that: "Le comportement de Créon envers la malheureuse Médée semble être moins encore celui du tyran que celui du Corinthien qui habite en lui (*cf.* 271–6); et l'aversion que le spectateur éprouve à l'endroit du souverain rejaillit sur tout son peuple."

6 For the sinister implications of the metaphor in line 278, see *Euripides: Medea*, ed. Page, ad loc., and E. M. Blaicklock, "The Nautical Imagery of Euripides' *Medea*," CPh, 50, No. 4 (October 1955), 233–37.

7 See above, p. 74, for a discussion of the *Suppliants* passage. See, too, the remarks of Shirley A. Barlow, *The Imagery of Euripides: A Study in the Dramatic Use of Pictorial Language* (London: Methuen, 1971), p. 97.

8 In line 983 Murray has emended to χρυσέων τευκτὸν from the χρυσεοτευκτὸν of the codd. (χρυσοτευκτὸν fortasse Σ): πέπλον χρυσοτευκτόν <τε> Elmsley post Reiskium: ἀμβροσίους τ' αὐγὰς πέπλων χρυσότευκτον <τε> Arnim. Nauck and Kamerbeek both follow Elmsley. For a similar use of ἄτη with ἀποφεύγουσα, see *Ion* 1241.

9 See above, pp. 101–102, for the discussion of the passage from the *Trachinian Women*.

10 This point is worth bearing in mind in the light of the Conacher-Kitto debate over Medea as a "more individually tragic heroine" (Conacher) or as a "tragic victim" (Kitto). For appropriate arguments and references, see Conacher, *Euripidean Drama*, pp. 183–84, 187, and 194–95. For a slightly different focus, see Hermann Rohdich, *Die Euripideische Tragödie: Untersuchungen zu ihrer Tragik* (Heidelberg: Winter, 1968), pp. 44–55.

11 For a discussion of the reasons for dating this play between the *Medea* and the *Hippolytus*, see Conacher, *Euripidean Drama*, pp. 120–24. See, too, the interesting remarks on the theme of voluntary self-sacrifice in Euripides in J. W. Fitton's "The *Suppliant Women* and the *Herakleidai* of Euripides," *Hermes*, 89 (1961), 452–54.

12 This interpretation is considerably strengthened by the following remarks of Bernard Knox in "The *Hippolytus* of Euripides," YCIS, 13 (1952), 6–7, on μανία and ἐμάνην in 241: "The Nurse calls her [Phaedra's] outburst madness (μανία, 214), that is, meaningless speech, and Phaedra, when she comes to her senses, calls it madness too (ἐμάνην, 241), but in a different sense, passion. She has revealed nothing, but she has for the first time put her desire into words, and broken her long silence. Her passion (ἐμάνην) has overcome her judgement (γνώμη, 240); in her case the choice between silence and speech is also a choice between judgement and passion. In the next few lines she defines her dilemma, poses the alternatives, and sees a third course open to her. . . . To be right in judgement (ὀρθοῦσθαι γνώμαν), that is, in her case, to remain silent, is agony (ὀδυνᾷ); passion (τό μαινόμενον), in her case, speech, is evil (κακόν). Better (ἀλλὰ κρατεῖ) to make no choice and perish (μὴ γιγνώσκοντ' ἀπολέσθαι) — to perish unconscious of the alternatives, to abandon judgement and choice, to surrender free will. This is what she comes to in the end, but she has not yet reached such desperate straits. She is still in the no man's land between the alternatives of speech and silence, for her delirious outburst has not revealed her secret to the Nurse. But it has brought her a momentary relief and thus weakened her determination. She is now less able to withstand the final assault on her silence which the Nurse, at the request of the chorus, proceeds to make."

Similarly, see the remarks on αἰδούμεθα (line 244) in *Euripides: Hippolytos*, ed. Barrett.

Conacher, *Euripidean Drama*, p. 34, disagrees, interpreting ἄτη here in its objective sense of "ruin": "Phaedra herself, as she returns to sanity, feels it to have been a more than human force: 'I was raving, overwhelmed by god-sent ruin.' (241)." See also the incisive observations of Charles Segal, "Shame and Purity in Euripides' *Hippolytus*," *Hermes*, 98 (1970), 278–99.

13 Barrett's remarks, in *Euripides: Hippolytos*, on the ἄτη in line 241 are quoted above, in their entirety, on pp. 4–5.

14 À propos of his adopted reading of οὐκ οἶδα in line 277, Barrett remarks, in ibid., ad loc.: "οὐκ οἶδα: the θανεῖν of the mss. would mean '(it is in an attempt) to die (that she is eating nothing)', with ἀσιτεῖ κτλ. 'she is eating nothing *in order to* end her life' (εἰς of the purpose). This is impossible: the Nurse can give no such answer, for she is just as ignorant as the Chorus themselves. (A further objection is to the complete tautology between the two parts of the line.) The corruption must be due to deliberate change: someone took εἰς of Ph.'s purpose, and since that made the Nurse profess to know the answer, he changed οὐκ οἶδα out of hand to θανεῖν. — Musgrave, who first saw the impossibility of θανεῖν, suggested ἄδηλ(α) (sc. ἐστιν); Wilamowitz replaced this by οὐκ οἶδα. In repairing a deliberate alteration such as this the letters are no help, and our only guides are sense and metre; but for 'I don't know' with the scansion ⏑ – the odds on οὐκ οἶδ(α) are heavy." For a defense of θανεῖν, see C. W. Willink, "Some Problems of Text and Interpretation in the *Hippolytus*," CQ, 18 N.S. (1968), 39.

For the possibility that lines 274ff. evoke the terrors of the Athenian plague, see Delebecque, *Euripide et la guerre du Péloponnèse*, p. 98.

15 In this regard, see the excellent remarks of Knox, "The *Hippolytus* of Euripides," on free will throughout the play. Barrett agrees; see his remarks, in *Euripides: Hippolytos*, on line 276. For the dramatic interdependence of mental and physical illness here, see Barlow, *Imagery of Euripides*, p. 82.

16 For a detailed study of the epithet συζύγιαι, see Eugene W. Bushala, "Συζύγιαι χάριτες, *Hippolytus* 1147," TAPA, 100 (1969), 23–29.

17 For the imagery in the passage, see the remarks of Charles P. Segal, "The Tragedy of the *Hippolytus*: The Waters of Ocean and the Untouched Meadow," HSPh, 70 (1965), 150.

18 It is interesting to note the verbal similarities in Poly*x*ena and Poly*d*orus, analogous to the word echoes contained in this passage: δύστηνος (683) and δύστηνε (688); τέκνον τέκνον (684); all of lines 689 and 690; and δείν', δεινὰ (693). For further insight into the completeness of Hecuba's bereavement, see the remarks of Conacher, *Euripidean Drama*, p. 160.

19 See chaps. 1 and 2 passim. See also the excellent article of Arthur W. H. Adkins, "Basic Greek Values in Euripides' *Hecuba* and *Hercules Furens*," CQ, 16 N.S. (1966), 193–219.

20 For the unique character of this lament, see D. L. Page, "The Elegiacs in Euripides' *Andromache*," in *Greek Poetry and Life: Essays Presented to Gilbert Murray*, edd. Cyril Bailey, E. A. Barber, C. M. Bowra, J. D. Denniston, and D. L. Page (Oxford: Clarendon, 1936), pp. 206–30.

21 *Euripides: Andromache*, ed. P. T. Stevens (Oxford: Clarendon, 1971), p. 71.

22 See above, p. 83.

23 See above, pp. 110–111; and Dawe, "Some Reflections on Ate and Hamartia," 121.

[24] For a proposed reading for 119, see Felix Scheidweiler, "Zu den *Troerinnen* des Euripides," *Hermes*, 82 (1964), 250. On the persistent nautical imagery throughout this ode, see Barlow, *Imagery of Euripides*, pp. 50–52.

[25] For ἄτη in line 530, see Long, *Language and Thought in Sophocles*, p. 121n29.

[26] On the descriptive imagery's becoming dramatic imagery in this stasimon, see the excellent remarks of Barlow, *Imagery of Euripides*, pp. 28–30.

[27] For the connection of this scene with the beginning of the trilogy, see Webster, *Tragedies of Euripides*, p. 177.

[28] For a detailed discussion of the text here, see Franz Stoessel, "Die *Elektra* des Euripides," RhM, 99 (1956), 83–85; and *Euripides: Electra*, ed. J. D. Denniston (Oxford: Clarendon, 1939), ad loc.

[29] Conacher, *Euripidean Drama*, p. 210, substantiates this: "At v. 1302, Apollo is again rebuked for his advice and at vv. 1301, 1305–7, it is further suggested that 'fate' and the ancestral doom, i.e., from Tantalus, Pelops, and Atreus, share this responsibility with Apollo."
This use of ἄτη is a development already presaged by Euripides' association of the word in its *objective* sense with μοῖρα at *Medea* 987, discussed above, p. 125.

[30] See above, pp. 128–129 and 132.

[31] The following slight variant occurs for line 1242 — ὠκίσταν χαλὰν — found in L and P, and read by Nauck (in *Euripidis Tragoediae*, ad loc.). For a defense of Murray's reading, see *Euripides: Ion*, ed. A. S. Owen (Oxford: Clarendon, 1939), p. 153. Delebecque, who dates this play to 418, sees a possible reference in lines 1241–1243 to the conditions of the peace of Nicias which allowed access to Delphi (*Euripide et la guerre du Péloponnèse*, pp. 238–39). The use of ἀποφεύγουσα here recalls the appearance of ὑπεκφεύξεται with ἄτη at *Medea* 988.

[32] Although Nauck (*Euripidis Tragoediae*, ad loc.) prints the same text as Murray for this passage, he does not obelize line 226. It should be noted that the MSS problems here are with αἱμάσσουσ' and βωμούς (see Murray's apparatus) and that neither textual difficulty involves ἄταν. Paul Hanschke, "Textkritisches zu den griechischen Tragikern: Euripides," RhM, 90 (1941), 214–15, suggests ἐκμάσσουσ' for αἱμάσσουσ'. But Maurice Platnauer, *Euripides: Iphigenia in Tauris* (Oxford: Clarendon, 1938), ad loc., says that "the easiest emendation of this nonsensical and unmetrical line is Matthiae's rejections of βωμούς as a gloss."

[33] Conacher, *Euripidean Drama*, p. 247, discusses the tone and the significance of this entire stasimon. For a discussion of the recurrent imagery involving the sphinx, see Anthony J. Podlecki, "Some Themes in Euripides' *Phoenissae*," TAPA, 93 (1962), 364.

[34] Although there is a MS discrepancy with respect to the ἄτη in line 962 — M reads ἄτα and M² has ἄταν — Murray, Nauck (*Euripidis Tragodiae*, ad loc.), and Vincenzo di Benedetto (*Euripides: Orestes* [Florence: La Nuova Italia Bibliografica, 1965], ad loc.) accept ἄταν.

[35] By the liberal use of square brackets in lines 983–985, Nauck (*Euripidis Tragoediae*, ad loc.) shows that he is aware of the difficulties indicated in Murray's apparatus, but *de facto* Nauck prints the same text as Murray for this passage — as does di Benedetto (*Euripides: Orestes*, ad loc.), with two minor exceptions: in 985 he accepts πατέρι of A, B, V, and in 988 he accepts the τὸ πτανὸν rather than Porson's emendation to

ποτανόν. For the aptness of the metaphor here, see Barlow, *Imagery of Euripides*, p. 112.

³⁶ For πίπτω with ἄτη, see *Hippolytus* 241 and *Phoenician Maidens* 1066.

³⁷ Aeschylus used ἄτη in this sense in thirty-one of the forty-eight pertinent passages; Sophocles, on only sixteen of forty occasions. See the table in Appendix A.

³⁸ See the table in Appendix A.

³⁹ See the table in Appendix A.

⁴⁰ The passages are *Alcestis* 91, *Medea* 279, and *Trojan Women* 137 and 163.

⁴¹ See chap. 6, passim, for this Sophoclean usage.

⁴² See above, note 22.

CONCLUSION

THE CORPUS OF EXTANT GREEK POETRY from Homer to Euripides contains ἄτη one hundred and sixty-nine times.[1] The word appears fifty-five times in its subjective meaning of "blindness," "infatuation," or "folly."[2] On eighty-four occasions it is used by the poets in its objective meaning of "ruin," "calamity," or "disaster."[3] In twenty-five texts it is used in *both* its subjective and objective meanings.[4] There are five texts in which ἄτη is used with special meanings which are neither of the above. Thus "loss" is the sense at Hesiod, *Works and Days* 352 and 413, Theognis 133, and Aeschylus, *Suppliants* 444; finally, Euripides, at *Electra* 1307, uses ἄτη in a startling meaning: "fate." With the relatively few exceptions noted, therefore, during the three and one-half centuries covered by this survey, ἄτη retains its two basic meanings, and it appears roughly half the time in each sense.

The subjective meaning of ἄτη is the one favored by Homer.[5] In addition to general contextual considerations, there exist three other observable phenomena which appear, alone or in various combinations, with ἄτη in this sense. These are that ἄτη (*a*) is said to affect some human faculty, (*b*) is used in an erotic context, and (*c*) is attributed to some daemonic agency.

By far the most prevalent concomitant of ἄτη in its subjective meaning is its effect on some human faculty. This is true, from Homer through Aeschylus, in twenty-one of the fifty-five passages in which ἄτη appears in its subjective connotation.

There are four, and only four, such faculties associated with ἄτη in this sense. They are φρήν, θυμός, νόος, and λῆμα. Of these, φρήν is the most important since it appears in thirteen of the texts.[6] θυμός is affected by ἄτη on five occasions;[7] νόος, twice;[8] and λῆμα, once — at *Pythian* 3.24. Thus, the concept of ἄτη as "blindness," "infatuation," or "folly" appears consistently from Homer to Aeschylus as something which is interior to, subject to, man insofar as it affects one of his faculties. This seems to be the most comprehensive note associated with ἄτη in this sense, and the terminology favored by Homer perdures well into the fifth century.

With Sophocles there is a shift in usage. For Sophocles associates φρήν, θυμός, and νόος with ἄτη in its ambivalent subjective and objective meaning on five occasions,[9] and in its objective meaning once — at *Antigone* 1097. This usage probably reflects the Sophistic influences prevalent in the latter part of the fifth century, and is indicative, as well, of the involvement of ἄτη in the development of Greek thought concerning human freedom and responsibility.

ἄτη as "infatuation," a particular kind of mental "blindness" or "folly," appears in particular contexts in the Greek poetry under discussion. The contexts are generically described as erotic; hence, this special meaning of ἄτη is most suitable for them. Such is the case in fourteen passages.[10] Homer employs ἄτη in this manner on five occasions, and in each of these *loci* it is considered a cause of suffering — a notion which is echoed only once in post-Homeric poetry, at *Agamemnon* 1192.

But the most significant concomitant of ἄτη in its subjective connotation is the final one mentioned above: the attribution of ἄτη in this sense to some daemonic agency. Of significance, first of all, are the gods who supposedly cause ἄτη in the sense of "blindness," "infatuation," or "folly" for human beings. They are only five: Zeus, Aphrodite, Apollo, an indefinite θεός, and an Erinys. Thus Zeus inflicts ἄτη in its subjective sense in ten Homeric passages,[11] and in three passages in Hesiod and the lyric poets.[12] Twice Homer attributes ἄτη in its subjective connotation to the intervention of Aphrodite,[13] once to Apollo,[14] once to an indefinite θεός,[15] and twice to an Erinys.[16] But of even greater significance are the facts that the preponderance of such attributions of ἄτη in its subjective meaning occurs in Homer and that, with a sole exception,[17] no such attribution appears at all after Theognis. Furthermore, even in the lyric poets the tragedians' usage on this point is adumbrated inasmuch as Hesiod, at *Works and Days* 231, Alcaeus in D12.12, Ibycus at 1.8, and Pindar at *Olympian* 1.57 all attribute ἄτη in its *objective* meaning to daemonic activity. In Homer this happens uniquely at *Odyssey* 12.372, but in the tragedians, with the exception of the ambivalent meaning of ἄτη at *Hippolytus* 241 and *Hercules Furens* 917, this is the only way in which daemonic agency is associated with ἄτη. That is to say, it is in this respect that one of the most important developments takes place in the use and meaning of ἄτη in Greek thought. The implications of this change for the relationship of the concept of ἄτη to the questions of human freedom and responsibility are profound, but they are best left until the discussion of ἄτη in its objective connotation. Suffice it to note here that, with the few exceptions indicated, it is fair to say that in Homer and the few lyric passages mentioned, ἄτη in its subjective meaning is regularly attributed to daemonic activity, whereas in the even more numerous lyric passages listed and, most importantly, all but universally in the tragedians this is never the case; when the latter do associate ἄτη and daemonic activity, it is the objective concept of ἄτη, something outside himself which afflicts man and something independent of his control, which is meant.

Homeric *stylistic* precedents — namely, the association of ἄτη in its subjective connotation with the faculties of φρήν and θυμός, and its use in an erotic context — prove to be normative for his poetic successors. But with respect to *conceptual* precedents — i.e., the impingement of daemonic activity on human affairs connected with ἄτη — Homer's successors break radically with him, as their concept of man's relationship to the gods changed significantly from his.[18]

The objective concept of ἄτη, which occurs only once in Homer,[19] appears both absolutely and proportionately much more frequently in his successors. In Hesiod and the lyric poets, ἄτη signifies "ruin," "calamity," or "disaster" in nine of the extant twenty-four pertinent passages.[20] But it is in the tragedians, and particularly in Aeschylus and Euripides, that ἄτη in this sense appears most often. Aeschylus is responsible for the major shift from the preponderance of the subjective connotation to a majority of objective ἄτη passages; in his seven extant tragedies, ἄτη appears in its objective connotation thirty times in a total of forty-eight appearances of the word.[21] Euripides employs ἄτη in its objective sense in twenty-six of the thirty-one appearances which it makes in his extant poetry.[22] Though Sophocles does not reject the objective use of ἄτη, he shows a preference for the ambivalent connotation of the word, and thus employs ἄτη in its objective meaning on only sixteen of the forty times in which it appears in his seven surviving plays.[23] Hence, after Homer, and especially in the tragedians, there is a definite shift to an increased use of the objective connotation of ἄτη.[24]

This change and its relevance to our consideration of the use and meaning of ἄτη in Greek poetry can best be seen in terms of the questions of human responsibility and freedom. The first element in understanding this change is recognition of the fact that in each of the three tragedians, with minor exceptions,[25] daemonic activity is associated with ἄτη *only* in its objective connotation.

With that fact in mind, let us ask the question: What do the Homeric poems have to say about ἄτη and human guilt or man's responsibility for his actions? As soon as the question is raised, several aspects of the answer become obvious from our study of the ἄτη passages in Homer. First, the odds are extremely high that no matter what, if anything, Homer has to say about "guilt" in connection with ἄτη, he will cast his statement in terms of human "blindness," "infatuation," or "folly," since that is the meaning of the word in all but one of the Homeric passages in which it appears.[26] Secondly, it is consistent Homeric practice to attribute such ἄτη, not to any human activity, much less to "failure" or "guilt," but rather to daemonic activity.[27] Thirdly, there are seventeen Homeric texts in which ἄτη means "blindness," and in five of those it is connected with τιμή or κύδος, but — what is important for present considerations — never with "guilt."[28] And, of course, each of these generic aspects of Homer's use of ἄτη vis-à-vis the question of human responsibility receives confirmation in the two Homeric ἄτη passages in which the questions of blame and guilt are raised. Thus, at *Iliad* 19.86–87 Agamemnon specifically states that he is not guilty because Zeus, μοῖρα, and an ἐρίνυς afflicted him with ἄτη.[29] And at *Iliad* 9.523ff. Phoenix exonerates Achilles from any blame for the same reason.[30] In other words, in the Homeric poems ἄτη is not conceived as a concept pertinent to the questions of human responsibility and freedom.

There are two slight indications of a change in this attitude in the lyric poets. Solon, at 13.68, seems to make man more responsible than Zeus for the ἄτη.[31] And Theognis, at 206 and 631, associates ἄτη with ἀμπλακία, "error" or "fault." These are indications that the relationship of man to the gods and the questions of man's responsibility for his actions are becoming a bit more nuanced than they were in Homer's day. But they are only indications.

As in so many other respects where ἄτη is concerned, it is with Aeschylus that the term becomes extremely important in the matter of freedom and responsibility. First of all, Aeschylus makes the startling shift, already noticed, from associating daemonic activity with ἄτη in its subjective meaning to such an association with ἄτη in its objective meaning. The result of this is, of course, to leave human "blindness," "infatuation," or "folly" outside the divine–human relationship in which questions of "guilt" occur. Having anchored the daemonic activity à propos of ἄτη clearly on the side of objective ἄτη, "ruin," "calamity," or "disaster," Aeschylus then proceeds to show in two ways who is responsible for these disasters, who is "guilty" enough to have had them befall. First, he links the occurrence of "ruin," "calamity," or "disaster" to the central fact of human choice.[32] He is extremely aware of the importance of human choice, and eminently conscious that a bad choice can, and often does, bring "ruin," "calamity," or "disaster" on human beings through the imposition of that ἄτη by some daemonic power. But he never once says that this is unjust on the part of the gods. And that is the second way in which he indicates that it is men themselves who are responsible for being inflicted with ἄτη in its objective sense: he frequently links this type of ἄτη with the entire question of man's relationship to the gods.[33]

Very differently from Homer, therefore, Aeschylus shows that he is extremely interested not only in the problems of human responsibility and freedom, but also in the connection of the concept of ἄτη with these problems. His cast of the fundamental human concerns involved is, to be sure, not that of the philosopher, for he was, first and foremost, a poet. It is certainly not that of modern man. Indeed, it is not even that of his successors in Greek tragic poetry, who lived later in the fifth century when philosophical, or at least Sophistic, agitation of these problems was becoming a fact of Athenian life. But his concept of man, of man's relationship to the gods, and of the interplay of ἄτη in that relationship, indicate that in Aeschylus there is a definite shift from the Homeric view of these questions, and that in some real sense man's freedom to choose makes him liable, if guilty of a bad choice, to be visited by divinely sent "ruin," "calamity," or "disaster."

Sophoclean tragedy manifests a different type of focus on the interrelationship of ἄτη and the questions of human freedom and responsibility. To be sure, Sophocles continues the Aeschylean insight of usually associating daemonic activity with ἄτη in its objective meaning. But rather than focusing on the bigger issues of human choice and man's relationship to the gods in the question of ἄτη, as Aeschylus does, Sophocles shows his interest more in the vocabulary he employs with ἄτη. It is the vocabulary used by the Sophists and the philosophers when addressing themselves to the fundamental human problems of freedom and responsibility. Thus, in connection with ἄτη in its ambivalent connotation of both "blindness," "infatuation," or "folly" and "ruin," "calamity," or "disaster," Sophocles uses μόρος (*Ajax* 848), ὄνειδος (*Ajax* 1189), μοῖρα (*Trachinian Women* 850), οἶτος, πότμος, δυσμόρος (all at *Antigone* 864), ἁμάρτων (*Antigone* 1260), and ἀέκων (*Oedipus at Colonus* 526 and 532). Clearly he sees this type of ἄτη as in some sense connected with man's μόρος, ὄνειδος, μοῖρα, οἶτος, πότμος, or ἁμαρτία. The subjective, interior, mental dispositions of a man, Sophocles seems to be implying, have a bearing on his guilt or innocence, on his fate or destiny. In some sense man is in control. And Sophocles gives his clearest indication that this is his concept in the two passages in the *Oedipus at Colonus* (526 and 532) which employ ἄτη in conjunction with ἀέκων; this particular ἄτη afflicts a human being against his will, i.e., in a situation in which he is not in control. Such a situation would be much more understandable to Sophocles if it were cast in terms of τύχη, those random happenings of life which are completely outside man's control. And he manifests this by associating ἄτη in its *objective* sense — i.e., something which comes to man from outside himself and his control — with the word for chance: namely, τύχη (*Electra* 936, 1002, and 1298).

This Sophoclean positioning of the problem of the relationship of ἄτη to the questions of human freedom and responsibility is much more philosophical than the Aeschylean view of the problem. But of course it would be, since Sophocles lived in an era when terms like μοῖρα, πότμος, and τύχη, terms which had been in the language for centuries, were being used precisely in connection with such large philosophical issues as freedom and responsibility. What his poetry (poetry, not philosophy!) manifests is an awareness of such issues, and a vision that ἄτη in both its traditional senses is also connected with such concerns.[34]

In Euripides the connection between ἄτη and the questions of human freedom and responsibility develops even further. Like Sophocles, he employs ἄτη in connection with vocabulary which was becoming more and more current in the evolution of Sophistic and philosophical thought concerning human freedom and responsibility. Thus, with ἄτη in its ambivalent connotation of both "blindness" and "ruin," we find Euripides using αἰσχύνα (*Hippolytus* 241). With ἄτη in its objective connotation, Euripides also uses vocabulary from the contemporary milieu of concern with fundamental human values and problems. Thus, with ἄτη in this sense, Euripidean tragedy also manifests καιρός (*Medea* 129), μοῖρα (*Medea* 987), πότμος and δυστυχία (*Hippolytus* 1149), αἰσχύνθεις (*Hippolytus* 1289), and ἀνάγκη (*Iphi-*

genia in Tauris 1117). Finally, ἄτη in its ambivalent sense is used with
τύχη (*Hercules Furens* 917 bis).[35]

The specifically Euripidean development in the connection of ἄτη
and the problems of human freedom and responsibility is his recognition of the epistemological concerns which are a part of those problems,[36] manifested through his use of ἄτη with a noetic vocabulary.
With ἄτη in its objective connotation of "ruin," "calamity," or "disaster," he employs γνώμη at *Iphigenia in Aulis* 137, γιγνώσκω at *Hecuba*
688, and οἶδα at *Trojan Women* 1314. Somehow for Euripides, therefore, as evidenced by the very terminology employed, ἄτη no longer
is an irrational, emotional phenomenon (something affecting merely
man's φρήν or θυμός); it pertains to man's intellect and is susceptible of
understanding. Once ἄτη is used in this manner, it obviously is in the
realm of human responsibility and involves man's free choice.[37]

The final facet of the Euripidean use of ἄτη displays even more
strikingly how the concept has evolved from the time of Homer.
For Euripides is not content merely to shift the association of ἄτη from
the visceral, emotional human faculties to man's intellectual capacity;
he also breaks new ground in the very meaning of the term itself as
it affects man's human destiny. At *Electra* 1307, for the first time in all
of extant Greek literature, ἄτη is employed, not *in connection with*
human fate, but as *meaning* that fate itself. Euripides introduces this
new meaning for ἄτη in a context which contains five other contemporary expressions frequently employed in discussions of human destiny: μοῖρα, ἀνάγκη, τὸ χρεών, χρησμοί, πότμοι. It is difficult to imagine how Euripides could indicate more clearly the importance he
attached to ἄτη. It means, in this context, not something which results
subjectively in human "foolishness" or objectively in human "disaster."
It is something much more important, something much more connected with man's human capacity: it is man's very destiny, his fate.
The problems of human freedom and responsibility are certainly germane to this, and the fifth-century realization of the complexity of
man's destiny has moved far, far away from the Homeric notion of
man's relationship to the gods. And the relatively simple Homeric concept of ἄτη has also changed, and, Euripides indicates
unmistakably in this passage, is now conceived as pertaining to the
very essence of man's destiny. ἄτη is no longer only the subjective
state of foolishness, for which man may or may not seem responsible
at a given moment in Greek thought. ἄτη is no longer merely the

vagaries of misfortune which come independently of man's control into all human lives simply because they are human. ἄτη is now seen to be part of the human condition itself. ἄτη is said by Euripides, at *Electra* 1307, to *be* man's fate.

There had been similar fundamental shifts in the meaning before: Homer's first use of ἄτη in its objective meaning at *Odyssey* 12.372, after consistently employing the subjective meaning in the *Iliad* and earlier in the *Odyssey*; Hesiod's use of ἄτη at *Works and Days* 352 and 413 to mean "losses" in an economic sense; and Sophocles' use of ἄτη at *Ajax* 123, and frequently thereafter, in both its objective and subjective meanings. But in each of those cases, it is possible to trace the development of such new nuances in the subsequent poetic tradition and to study the usages which surround them.

Now, with Euripides' new meaning of "fate," the area of concern with such matters is changing from the dramatic stage to the agora, the academy, and the βῆμα. The genres employed there are no longer poetry, but the rapidly advancing prose forms of philosophical and oratorical discourse. It becomes impossible to trace the development of the use of this new meaning of ἄτη without embracing all the new matrices such an investigation would demand. The task becomes properly philosophical and ceases to concern poetry. The use and meaning of ἄτη from Homer to Euripides is an instructive study of the Greek poetic tradition through the end of the fifth century. After that the task begins afresh.

NOTES

[1] These one hundred and sixty-nine appearances are distributed as follows: Homer, twenty-six; Hesiod and the lyric poets, twenty-four; Aeschylus, forty-eight; Sophocles, forty; and Euripides, thirty-one. Throughout this chapter ready reference should be made to the table in Appendix A for more detailed information on any given point.

[2] This meaning for ἄτη occurs as follows in the various poets: Homer, twenty-five; Hesiod and the lyric poets, eleven; Aeschylus, seventeen; Sophocles, two.

[3] This meaning for ἄτη appears distributed as follows in the various poets: Homer, one; Hesiod and the lyric poets, ten; Aeschylus, thirty; Sophocles, sixteen; Euripides, twenty-six.

⁴ This usage occurs twenty-two times in Sophocles and four times in Euripides.

⁵ The subjective connotation occurs is twenty-five of the twenty-six ἄτη passages in Homer; the sole exception is *Odyssey* 12.372.

⁶ These are: *Iliad* 6.356, 16.805, 19.88, 126, 129, 136; *Odyssey* 15.233; Hesiod, *Shield* 93; Aeschylus, *Persians* 112; *Suppliants* 110, 850; *Libation-Bearers* 597; and *Prometheus* 886.

⁷ These are: *Iliad* 19.270; *Odyssey* 21.302, 23.223; Theognis 631; and Aeschylus, *Seven Against Thebes* 687.

⁸ These are: *Iliad* 9.115 and 10.391.

⁹ These are: *Ajax* 123; *Antigone* 624; *Electra* 215; *Philoctetes* 706; and *Oedipus at Colonus* 202.

¹⁰ These are: *Iliad* 3.100, 6.356, 24.28; *Odyssey* 4.261, 23.223; *Pythian* 2.28, 3.24; *Agamemnon* 1192; Sophocles, in the ambivalent passages at *Trachinian Women* 1001, 1082, 1104, *Antigone* 864, and *Oedipus at Colonus* 526 and 532.

¹¹ These are: *Iliad* 2.111, 6.356, 8.237, 9.18, 504, 505, 512, 19.88, 136, 270.

¹² These are: *Shield* 93; Solon 13.75; and Theognis 231.

¹³ *Iliad* 24.28, and *Odyssey* 4.261.

¹⁴ *Iliad* 16.805.

¹⁵ *Odyssey* 23.223.

¹⁶ *Iliad* 19.88, and *Odyssey* 15.233.

¹⁷ At *Hippolytus* 241, Euripides employs δαίμων in connection with ἄτη in its subjective meaning. But it may well be that not even this is an exception, since it is possible that all Euripides means in speaking of a δαίμων is to say that love is something special in human life.

¹⁸ Before we leave the consideration of the subjective concept of ἄτη one subordinate point must be noted. First, the distinction between "blindness," "infatuation," and "folly," relatively sharp and somewhat easy to determine in the Homeric poems (see chap. 1), begins to break down with the lyric poets, and by the time of Sophocles the three meanings are used interchangeably in the large majority of passages.

¹⁹ *Odyssey* 12.372.

²⁰ These are: Hesiod, *Works and Days* 231; Solon 13.68; Alcaeus D12.12; Ibycus 1.8; Theognis 103, 206; Pindar, *Olympian* 1.57, 10.37, and *Nemean* 9.21.

²¹ These are: *Persians* 1007, 1037; *Seven* 315; *Suppliants* 470, 530; *Agamemnon* 361, 643, 730, 735, 770, 819, 1124, 1230, 1433, 1523, 1566; *Libation-Bearers* 68, 272, 339, 383, 403, 404, 467, 825, 830, 836; *Eumenides* 376, 982; *Prometheus* 1072, 1078.

²² These are: *Alcestis* 91; *Medea* 129, 279, 979, 987; *Heraclidae* 607; *Hippolytus* 1149, 1289; *Hecuba* 688; *Andromache* 103; *Hercules Furens* 1284; *Trojan Women* 121, 137, 163, 530, 535, 1314; *Ion* 1240; *Iphigenia in Tauris* 148, 226, 1117; *Phoenician Maidens* 343, 1066; *Orestes* 962, 987; *Iphigenia in Aulis* 137.

²³ These are: *Ajax* 976; *Trachinian Women* 1274; *Antigone* 4, 185, 533, 584, 614, 625; *Oedipus Tyrannos* 165, 1205, 1284; *Electra* 936, 1002, 1298; *Oedipus at Colonus* 93, 1244.

²⁴ Of the total one hundred and forty-three times ἄτη appears in post-Homeric poetry, it is used in its objective connotation eighty-two times. This is a dramatic change from the single Homeric use of ἄτη in its objective sense (at *Odyssey* 12.372) in a total of twenty-six appearances of the word.

²⁵ *Antigone* 584, *Hippolytus* 241, and *Hercules Furens* 917.

26 The exception is *Odyssey* 12.372.

27 For the passages, see notes 11, 13–16 above.

28 Thus, ἄτη means "blindness" at *Iliad* 1.412, 2.111, 8.237, 9.18, 504, 505, 512, 16.274, 805, 19.88, 91, 126, 129, 136, 270, and *Odyssey* 15.233 and 21.302.

29 In addition to the discussion of this passage in chap. 1, see Bremer, *Hamartia*, pp. 107–109.

30 In this same regard, see *Iliad* 1.412, 2.111, 9.18, and 16.274.

31 See chap. 2, pp. 26–27.

32 See chap. 5, pp. 73–81, for the detailed discussion of the fourteen pertinent Aeschylean passages.

33 See chap. 5, pp. 82–87, for the detailed discussion of the twelve pertinent Aeschylean passages.

34 See chap. 6 for the detailed discussion of the pertinent Sophoclean passages.

35 The difficulty of the problem, and its unsettled state at the time of Sophocles and Euripides, can be seen in connection with three terms each employed with ἄτη. πότμος is the first such term, and the two poets disagree on how to use it: it is used in conjunction with ἄτη in its ambiguous meaning by Sophocles at *Antigone* 864 and with ἄτη in its objective meaning by Euripides at *Hippolytus* 1149. μοῖρα is the next such term, and the two poets again disagree about its usage: Sophocles associates it with ἄτη in its ambivalent connotation at *Trachinian Women* 850, while Euripides employs it with ἄτη in its objective meaning at *Medea* 987. τύχη is the third such term. In various forms of the same root (δυστυχής, εὐτυχεῖ, and εὐτυχή-σωμεν) Sophocles employs it with ἄτη in its objective meaning at *Electra* 936, 1002, and 1298. Euripides agrees with this usage when he employs δυστυχία, with ἄτη in its objective meaning at *Hippolytus* 1149. But then he reverses himself and uses πλήμονη τύχη with ἄτη in its ambivalent sense at *Hercules Furens* 917. This phenomenon should not prove alarming. It probably is due as much to the unsettled state of the problem as to the fact that our two authors are poets and not philosophers from whom one might expect a certain consistency of terminology in considerations of this nature.

36 This is perhaps yet another example of the greater influence which the contemporary thinking of the Sophists had on Euripides' thought than on that of Sophocles.

37 How far this concept of ἄτη also is from the supposedly ineluctable process of ὄλβος, κόρος, ὕβρις, and ἄτη should also be noted. Far from pertaining to some supposedly blind, quasi-spontaneous process, ἄτη by its very association with γνώμη and γιγνώσκω is under the control of man's higher faculties. See chap. 3, passim, for the reasons for rejecting the supposed ὄλβος, κόρος, ὕβρις, ἄτη tetralogy.

APPENDICES

A

᾿ATH FROM HOMER TO EURIPIDES

The following table shows the chronological development of the concept of ἄτη from Homer to Euripides. Four entries seem useful: the basic meaning of the word; whether it occurs in the singular or plural; where applicable, whether it appears in a lyric or non-lyric passage; and any points of particular interest in the passage.

Author	Work		Meaning	Number	Lyric or Non-Lyric	Notanda
Homer	*Iliad*	1.412	Blindness	S		
		2.111	Blindness	S		Zeus
		3.100*	Infatuation	S		Erotic context
		6.356	Infatuation	S		φρήν; Zeus; erotic context
		8.237	Blindness	S		Zeus
		9.18	Blindness	S		Zeus
		115	Follies	P		νόος
		504	Blindness	S		Zeus; allegory
		505	Blindness	S		Zeus; allegory
		512	Blindness	S		Zeus; allegory
		10.391	Follies	P		νόος; Hector
		16.274	Blindness	S		
		805	Blindness	S		φρήν; Apollo
		19.88	Blindness	S		φρήν; Zeus, Moira, Erinys; allegory
		19.91	Blindness	S		Allegory
		126	Blindness	S		φρήν; allegory
		129	Blindness	S		φρήν; allegory
		136	Blindness	S		φρήν; Zeus; allegory
		270	Blindness	P		θυμός; Zeus
		24.28	Infatuation	S		Aphrodite; erotic context

Author	Work	Meaning	Number	Lyric or Non-Lyric	Notanda
	480	Folly	S		
	Odyssey 4.261	Infatuation	S		Aphrodite; erotic context
	12.372	Ruin	S		Group; Zeus & others
	15.233	Blindness	S		φρήν; Erinys
	21.302	Blindness	S		θυμός
	23.223	Infatuation	S		θυμός; θεός; erotic context
Hesiod	Works and Days 216	Follies, false hopes	P		ἐσθλός, ὕβρις, ἄτη
	231	Ruin, destruction	S		Group; Zeus
	352	Losses	P		
	413	Losses	P		Wrestling metaphor
	Theogony 230	Blindness, infatuation, folly	S		Erinys; personification
	Shield 93	Blindness	S		φρήν; Zeus
Solon	4.35	Folly	S		Ἐυνομίη; growth metaphor; κόρος, ὕβρις, ἄτη
	13.13	Folly	S		πλοῦτος, ὕβρις, ἄτη
	13.68	Ruin, calamity, disaster	S		
	13.75	Blindness	S		πλοῦτος, κορέννυμι, ἄτη; Zeus; metaphor
Alcaeus	D12.12	Ruin	S		Group; τις Ὀλυμπίων
Ibycus	1.8	Ruin	S		Group; Aphrodite
Theognis	103	Ruin	S		
	119	Infatuation	S		
	133	Loss	S		θεοί
	206	Ruin	S		Group; νόος; ἀμπλακία
	231	Blindness	S		Zeus; metaphor; πλοῦτος, κορέννυμι, ἄτη
	588	Ruin	S		
	631	Follies	P		θυμός and νόος; ἀμπλακία
Pindar	Olympian 1.57	Calamity	S		Zeus; ὄλβος, κόρος, ἄτη
	10.37	Ruin	S		Group; sea metaphor

Author	Work		Meaning	Number	Lyric or Non–Lyric	Notanda
	Pythian	2.28	Infatuation	S		Erotic context; φϱήν; ὄλβος, ὕβϱις, ἄτη;
		3.24	Infatuation	S		λῆμα; erotic context
	Nemean	9.21	Ruin	S		Group
Aeschylus	Persians	112	Blindness	S	L	φιλόφϱων and φϱήν; net metaphor
		653	Follies	P	L	
		822	Blindness, infatuation, folly	S	NL	ὄλβος, ὕβϱις, ἄτη; φϱονεῖν; growth metaphor
		1007	Ruin, calamity	S	L	Group; δαίμονες; κακόν
		1037	Disasters, ruin	P	L	Group; πῆμα and κακόν; first plural as "ruin"
	Seven	315	Ruin, destruction	S	L	Group; θεοί; ἀνδϱολέτειϱα
		601	Blindness	S	NL	Growth metaphor
		687	Blindness, infatuation	S	L	θυμοπληθής
		956	Blindness, folly	S	L	Metaphor of trophy
		1001	Blindness, folly	S	L	
	Suppliants	110	Infatuation	S	L	φϱήν; growth metaphor
		444	Loss	S	NL	
		470	Ruin, disaster	S	NL	Group; κακά; wrestling and sea metaphor
		530	Ruin, disaster	S	L	
		850	Folly	S	L	φϱήν
	Agamemnon	361	Ruin, calamity	S	L	Group; Zeus; δουλεία; net metaphor
		386	Blindness, infatuation, folly	S	L	πλοῦτος, κόϱος, ἄτη; growth metaphor
		643	Ruin, destruction	S	NL	Group; Ares; πήματα and ἕλκος
		730	Disasters, ruins	P	L	Group; θεός; αῖμα; pastoral metaphor
		735	Ruin, disaster	S	L	Group; θεός; ἄλγος and σίνος; growth metaphor

Author	Work		Meaning	Number	Lyric or Non-Lyric	Notanda
		770	Ruin, destruction, calamity	S	L	ὄλβος, ὕβρις, ἄτη; group; ὕβρις and θράσος; growth metaphor
		819	Destruction	S	NL	Group; θεοί; σποδός
		1124	Ruin, destruction	S	L	Group; Erinys; κροκοβαφὴς σταγών
		1192	Infatuation	S	NL	Erotic context and cause of suffering
		1230	Ruin, destruction	S	NL	Group; κακὴ τύχη
		1268	Blindness, folly	S	NL	
		1283	Follies	P	NL	Growth and building metaphor
		1433	Ruin, destruction	S	NL	δίκη and Erinys; ἔσφαξ'
		1523	Ruin, destruction	S	L	Group; μόρος
		1566	Ruin, destruction, calamity	S	L	Group; Zeus; ἀραῖον; growth metaphor
	Libation-Bearers	68	Ruin, calamity, disaster	S	L	φόνος
		272	Calamities, disasters	P	NL	
		339	Ruin, calamity	S	L	Group; κακά; wrestling metaphor
		383	Ruin, destruction	S	L	Group; Zeus; ποινή
		403	Ruin, destruction	S	L	Group; Erinys; αἷμα and λοιγός
		404	Ruin, destruction	S	L	Group; Erinys; αἷμα and λοιγός
		467	Ruin, destruction	S	L	Group; θεοὶ κατὰ γᾶς; πόνος; κήδη; ἄλγος
		597	Follies	P	L	φρήν and φρόνημα
		825	Ruin, destruction	S	L	Group; Perseus; μόρος
		830	Ruin, destruction	S	L	Group; Perseus; μόρος

Author	Work		Meaning	Number	Lyric or Non-Lyric	Notanda
		836	Ruin, destruction	S	L	Group; Perseus; μόρος
		968	Follies	P	L	
		1076	Blindness, folly	S	L	
	Eumenides	376	Calamity	S	L	Group; Furies; σφαλερὰ . . . κῶλα
		982	Ruin, calamities	P	L	Group; Eumenides; αἷμα
	Prometheus	886	Blindness, insanity, delusion, delirium	S	L	φρήν; sea metaphor
		1072	Ruin, calamity, disaster	S	L	Group; Zeus; πῆμα; net metaphor
		1078	Ruin, calamity, disaster	S	L	Group; Zeus; πῆμα; net metaphor
Sophocles	Ajax	123	Both	S	NL	Physical sight and blindness; προνούστερος
		195	Both	S	L	Medical metaphor
		307	Both	S	NL	διοπτεύει and ’θώνξεν
		363	Both	S	L	Physical blindness; medical metaphor
		364	Both	S	L	Physical blindness; medical metaphor
		848	Both	P	NL	μόρος
		909	Folly	S	L	Physical blindness; medical metaphor
		976	Ruin, calamity, disaster	S	NL	Group: βοῶντος and ἐπίσκοπον
		1189	Both	S	L	ὄνειδος
	Trachinian Women	850	Both	S	L	μοῖρα
		1001	Both	S	L	Medical metaphor; erotic context
		1082	Both	S	NL	Medical metaphor; erotic context
		1104	Both	S	NL	Medical metaphor; erotic context

Author	Work		Meaning	Number	Lyric or Non-Lyric	Notanda
		1274	Ruin, calamity, disaster	S	L	ἀφορᾷ
	Antigone	4	Ruin, calamity, disaster	S	NL	Group; Zeus; κακά; ὄπωπ'
		185	Ruin, calamity, disaster	S	NL	Group; Zeus; ἀντὶ τῆς σωτηρίας; ὁρῶ and σιωπήσαιμι
		533	Ruin, calamity, disaster	Dual	NL	Group; ἐμάνθανον; metonymy
		584	Ruin, calamity, disaster	S	L	Group; θεόθεν; ἂν σευσθῇ ... δόμος; ὁρῶμαι
		614	Ruin, calamity, disaster	S	L	
		624	Blindness, infatuation, folly	S	L	φρήν
		625	Ruin calamity disaster	S	L	
		864	Both	P	L	Erotic context; with οἶτος, πότμος, δυσμόρος
		1097	Both	S	NL	φρήν and θυμός
		1260	Both	S	L	ἁμαρτών
	Oedipus Tyrannos	164	Ruin, calamity, disaster	S	L	Group; Athena, Artemis, Apollo; φλόγα πήματος; κεκλομένος and ἰώ
		1205	Ruins, calamities, disasters	P	L	Erotic context
		1284	Ruin, calamity, disaster	S	NL	Group; κακά; ὀνόμα
	Electra	215	Both	P	L	δύσθυμος
		224	Both	P	L	
		235 bis	Both	S&P	L	
		936	Ruin, calamity, disaster	S	NL	Group; δυστυχής; ἄλλα ... κακά; εἰδυῖ

Author	Work		Meaning	Number	Lyric or Non-Lyric	Notanda
		1002	Ruin, calamity, disaster	S	NL	Group; δαίμων; κακά; εἰσορᾷς; εὐτυχεῖ; wrestling metaphor
		1298	Ruin, calamity, disaster	S	NL	Group; τις θεῶν; death of Orestes; στέναζ' and λελεγμένη; εὐτυχήσωμεν
	Philoctetes	706	Both	S	L	δακέθυμος; medical metaphor
	Oedipus at Colonus	93	Ruin, calamity, disaster	S	NL	Group; Apollo; siege of Thebes; κάμψειν; κέρδη
		202	Both	S	L	Physical blindness δύσφρων; medical metaphor
		526	Both	S	L	Group; ἤνεγκ' and ἀέκων; κακότατ'; erotic context
		532	Both	Dual	L	Group; ἤνεγκ' and ἀέκων; κακότατ'; erotic context
		1244	Ruins, disasters	P	L	Group; δειναί; κλονέουσιν; simile from nature
Euripides	Alcestis	91	Ruin, calamity, disaster	S	L	Group; Apollo; στεναγμόν, χειρῶν κτύπον, and γόον; sound words; sea metaphor
	Medea	129	Ruins, calamities, disasters	P	NL	Group; δαίμων; ὀργισθῇ; καιρός
		279	Ruin, calamity, disaster	S	NL	Group; ἀπόλλυμαι, l. 278, and κακῶς πάσχουσ'; sea metaphor
		979	Ruin, calamity, disaster	S	L	Group; Hades; φόνον
		987	Ruin, disaster	S	L	Group; Hades; ἕρκος, μοῖρα
	Heraclidae	607	Ruin, calamity, disaster	S	NL	Group; Oracle; οἰχόμεθα, λύπη, and τούτοις...πεπραγμένοις

Author	Work		Meaning	Number	Lyric or Non-Lyric	Notanda
	Hippolytus	241	Both	S	NL	δαίμων; αἰσχύνα
		276	Both	S	NL	
		1149	Ruin, calamity, disaster	S	L	πότμος, μανίω, συ-ζύγιαι, and δυστυχία
		1289	Ruin, calamity, disaster	S	NL	αἰσχυνθείς
	Hecuba	688	Ruin, calamity, disaster	S	NL	Group; ἀλάστωρ; κα-κά; used with γιγνώ-σκω
	Andromache	103	Ruin, calamity, disaster	S	L	Group; Ares; δορὶ καὶ πυρὶ; two-level echo of lioncub in *Agamemnon*; metonymy
	Hercules Furens	917 bis	Both	S	L	Group; θεόθεν; κακά and τλήμονας τύχας
		1284	Ruins, calamities, disasters	P	NL	
	Trojan Women	121	Ruins, calamities, disasters	P	L	Group; μοῦσα; κα-κά in ll. 122–133; sea metaphor
		137	Ruin, calamity, disaster	S	L	Group: μοῦσα; κακά in ll. 122–133; sea metaphor
		163	Ruin, calamity, disaster	S	L	Group; κακά in ll. 161–162; sea metaphor
		530	Ruin, calamity, disaster	S	L	Group; Athena; fall of Troy; metonymy
		535	Ruin, calamity, disaster	S	L	Group; Athena; fall of Troy; metonymy
		1314	Ruin, calamity, disaster	S	L	Group; μέλας; θάνατος ὅσιος; κακά of fall of Troy; used with οἶδα; alliteration

Author	Work		Meaning	Number	Lyric or Non-Lyric	Notanda
	Electra	1307	Fate	S	L	First time in this meaning; μοῖρα, ἀνάγκης, τὸ χρέων, χρησμοί, and ἱποτμός; metonymy
	Ion	1240	Ruin, calamity, disaster	S	L	Group; θεός; θάνατος
	Iphigenia in Tauris	148	Ruins, calamities, disasters	P	L	
		226	Ruin, calamity, disaster	S	L	Group; Artemis; αἱμάσσουσ' ... βώμους
		1117	Ruin, calamity, disaster	S	L	Group; δυσδαίμον'; ἐν ἀνάγκαις, δυσδαιμονία, and κακοῦσθαι
	Phoenician Maidens	343	Ruin, calamity, disaster	S	L	Group; ἄλαστα
		1066	Ruin, calamity, disaster	S	L	Group; δαιμόνων; ἁρπαγαῖσι
	Orestes	962	Ruin, calamity, disaster	S	L	Group; Persephone; λευκὸν ὄνυχα and κτύπον τε κράτος
		987	Ruins, calamities, disasters	P	L	Group; φόνος
	Iphigenia in Aulis	137	Ruin, calamity, disaster	S	L	Used with γνώμη

B

PERSIANS 107–114

On p. 49 above, Broadhead's proposed text for *Persians* 107–114 is presented. Since there are significant differences between it and the MSS for this passage, the discrepancies must be accounted for. In the MSS the lines appear as follows:

δολόμητιν δ' ἀπάταν θεοῦ
τίς ἀνὴρ θνατὸς ἀλύξει;
τίς ὁ κραιπνῷ ποδὶ πηδή-
ματος εὐπετέος ἀνάσσων;
φιλόφρων γὰρ σαίνου-
σα τὸ πρῶτον παράγει
βροτὸν εἰς ἀρκύστατα
τόθεν οὐκ ἔστιν ὑπὲρ θνα-
τον ἀλύξαντα φυγεῖν.

The initial difficulty with this passage is its position in the parados. In the MSS it appears immediately after line 92. O. Müller was the first to transpose it, making it follow line 114, and his transposition has been followed by most subsequent editors — namely, Wilamowitz, Smyth, Murray, and Broadhead. The basic justification for this arrangement (which Broadhead ably defends on pp. 53–54 of his edition) is that the meaning of the parados as a whole becomes much clearer.

The textual differences between the MSS and Broadhead's version are: (*a*) the substitution of δηλήματος for πηδήματος in lines 109–110; (*b*) the substitution of εὐπιθοῦς ἀπάσσων for εὐπετέος ἀνάσσων in line 110; (*c*) the adoption of Seidler's emendation παρασαίνει for σαίνουσα in line 111; (*d*) the deletion of line 111a; (*e*) the adoption of Hermann's ἄρκυας ἄτα for ἀρκύστατα in line 112; (*f*) the recasting of lines 113–114 to read

τόθεν οὐκ ἔστιν ἀλύξαν-
τα φυγεῖν ὕπερθ' ἄνατον

instead of

τόθεν οὐκ ἔστιν ὑπὲρ θνα-
τον ἀλύζαντα φυγεῖν.

These are extensive changes, to be sure, yet Broadhead argues so cogently for them that they merit careful consideration.

Broadhead's first consideration is metrical. He writes: "Since even a tentative restoration of this passage cannot be attempted until we have reached a conclusion about the metre, it is essential to consider the clues given by the traditional text" (p. 255). He then notes that not only are the six preceding strophes and antistrophes of the parodos all Ionic *a minore*, they are all regular except for two variations: syncopation (in lines 70–72, 77–80, 94, 100, 101, and 106) and anaclasis (in lines 86, 93, 99 and 106). Consequently, he argues, "Since the 'mesode' [i.e., the text under consideration] also is obviously written in the same Ionic metre, there is at least a reasonable presumption that any variations will be of the same kind as those in the preceding stanzas" (p. 255).

Lines 107–109 offer no difficulty, since they are regular Ionics. Line 110, according to the MSS reading, does afford some difficulty, since it is susceptible of two possible scansions: (*a*) two Ionics, the first of which contains a resolved long (εὐπε̆τ̆εος); or (*b*) "broken" Ionic with εὐπέτεος taken as a cretic (εὐπ̆ετ̄εο̄ς). Broadhead prefers the second scansion because it corresponds with lines 86, 92, 99, and 106 in the employment of anaclasis, and because the "resolution of the long syllable of the ionic *a minore* is in general rare, and certainly unique in Aesch[ylus]" (p. 256).

Line 111, according to the MSS reading, offers a serious metrical problem, and various proposals have been made to remedy it. Hermann and Murray would emend to <ποτι>σαίνουσα. Wellauer and Wilamowitz read <παρα>σαίνουσα. Dindorf and Wecklein, choosing not to emend, read the metrically impossible σαίνουσα of the MSS. Smyth, Broadhead, and S. M. Adams ("Salamis Symphony: The *Persae* of Aeschylus," in *Studies in Honour of Gilbert Norwood*, ed. Mary E. White [Toronto: University of Toronto Press, 1952], p. 54*n*3) follow Seidler and prefer παρασαίνει. The fact that this reading restores line 111 to regular Ionics is clear enough, but the reasons for preferring it to the metrically equally valid <ποτι>σαίνουσα and <παρα>σαίνουσα are excellent. First, if παρασαίνει is taken to be the genuine reading, it makes the present MSS reading, σαίνουσα τὸ πρῶτον παράγει, readily intelligible as a gloss which has crept into the text. Secondly, the recognition of σαίνουσα τὸ πρῶτον παράγει as a gloss allows its elimination, the consequent reduction of the number of lines to eight, and the possibility of dividing them into strophe and antistrophe in keeping with the rest of the ode instead of having to consider them as an awkward "mesode." (For these arguments, see pp. 59–60 and 256 of Broadhead's edition.)

No metrical difficulties are posed by lines 112 and 113 if, as with most editors (that is, Wilamowitz, Smyth, Murray, and Broadhead), one accepts Hermann's correction to ἄρκυας ἄτα in line 112. Such an emendation is required to restore line 112 to an Ionic line in keeping with all the others. (Wecklein, Hartung, and Adams would read ἄτας. Though metrically this is no different from ἄτα, it does differ grammatically and contextually, and will be examined below. Only Dindorf and Paley retain the metrically impossible ἄρκύστατα of the MSS.)

Line 114, however, does present metrical difficulties. In itself the line is a catalectic Ionic, which would be acceptable. What causes suspicion about it is that as such it differs from the concluding lines of the preceding six stanzas which, if not pure Ionics, are Ionics with anaclasis (with or without syncopation). Perhaps most to the point is the fact that line 114 should respond to line 110 but cannot in its present catalectic state.

Starting from this metrical discrepancy, Broadhead considers various possibilities for the line. The first is Seidler's (ἀλύξαντ)α φυγεῖν ὕπερθε θνατόν, which meets the metrical difficulty, retains the MSS reading in different order, and requires only the slight change of ὕπὲρ to ὕπερθε. Yet Broadhead rejects this arrangement of the line because he "cannot . . . believe that the clausula ended with θνατόν, which merely echoes βροτόν of the preceding clause and is equivalent to an unemphatic pronoun (e.g. αὐτόν)" (p. 60). In place of the weak θνατόν, he would use Wecklein's suggestion of ἄνατον, and points out the palaeographical similarity between ΥΠΕΡΘΝΑΤΟΝ and ΥΠΕΡΘΑΝΑΤΟΝ. Nor should the contextual appositeness of ἄνατον — that is, "not stricken by ἄτη" — be overlooked. Consequently, in its final form, Broadhead would read (ἀλύξαντ)α φυγεῖν ὕπερθ' ἄνατον in lines 113–114.

As to this suggestion of Broadhead's, a certain amount of caution seems advisable. Metrically 114 responds to 110. The change from ὕπὲρ to ὕπερθ' is not too great. Broadhead may well be correct with regard to the ineptness of θνατόν echoing βροτὸν, although this is not a strong point. And ἄνατον makes good sense in the context. Nonetheless, it is very difficult to explain palaeographically the radical displacement involved in the change from

τόθεν οὐκ ἐστιν ὑπὲρ θνα-
τὸν ἀλύξαντα φυγεῖν.

to

τόθεν οὐκ ἔστιν ἀλύξαν-
τα φυγεῖν ὕπερθ' ἄνατον.

In sum, Broadhead's suggestions for lines 113–114 may be adopted tentatively, since they resolve more of the difficulties than any of the other readings yet proposed, but there is room for reservation on palaeographical grounds.

Thus far the investigation has been primarily metrical. Yet there are other discrepancies, involving sense, context, and interpretation, between the MSS reading given at the start of this appendix and the proposed version given on p. 49 which must be justified.

First there is the substitution of δηλήματος for πηδήματος in lines 109–110. Broadhead bases this substitution, correctly it would seem, on the contention that "there is nothing in lines 107–10 to justify the conception of overleaping a net: this conception is reserved for the end of the passage" (p. 58). He then offers two other considerations which made him suspect πηδήματος. The first is that "κραιπνῷ ποδί means not 'with nimble (agile) foot' — this rendering is an accommodation to the idea of 'leaping' — but 'with fleet foot' (as in Homer's phrase ποσὶ κραιπνοῖσι), so that one would expect the action described in 109–10 to be flight (from the onset of Ate): 'What man is so fleet of foot as to . . .'" (pp. 58–59). The second is the scholiast's remark, ἡ γὰρ ἐκ θεοῦ . . . ἀμαύρωσις καὶ δόλωσις ἄφυκτός ἐστιν. ἅμα γὰρ δολοῖ καὶ προσαίνει καὶ κακοποιεῖ, and his allusion to Iliad 9.505ff. (this text is treated on pp. 9–12 in chap. I). Broadhead observes that the κακοποιεῖ of the scholiast himself, as well as the Homeric βλάπτουσ' in the passage which he quotes, together with the οὐλομένη in the corresponding passage in Iliad 19.91ff. (given on pp. 8–9 in chap. I), and a correct interpretation of κραιπνῷ ποδί conspire to indicate the question: "'What mortal is so fleet of foot as to be able to escape from this bane?'" Hence, he proposes δηλήματος for πηδήματος.

The adjective modifying δηλήματος is the next discrepancy between the proposed text and the MSS. Once again, there is no metrical difficulty involved, for the proposed εὐπιθοῦς scans in exactly the same way as the preferred cretic, trisyllabic scansion of the MSS εὐπε-τέος discussed above. There are two reasons for advocating εὐπιθοῦς.

First, with the adoption of δηλήματος, the retention of the MSS εὐπε-
τέος would result in "fortunate bane," an oxymoron which, even for
Aeschylus, approaches an outright contradiction. Secondly, as Broadhead notes, "'persuasive bane' is a forcible and quite Aeschylean description of the sinister power that infatuates men and drives them on to
ruin" (p. 59).

Another non-metrical difference between the MSS and the proposed
reading involves the participle in line 110. The MSS read ἀνάσσων
("being lord, master"). Most editors have agreed with Sidgwick, who
called this "grotesque" (quoted by Broadhead, p. 58), and have emended
to ἀνᾴσσων ("starting up"). This is the reading of Brunck, Dindorf,
Wecklein, Wilamowitz, and Smyth. But there are two objections
to this emendation. The first is that in so doing these editors must twist
the meaning of ἀναΐσσω from "start up, get up in a hurry" to the in-
valid "jump, leap." This distortion was noticed by Page (as quoted in
Broadhead, p. 256); and its error is confirmed by the citations given in
LSJ *sub voce*. The second objection is that if ἀνᾴσσων is adopted, the
genitive (whether πηδήματος or δηλήματος is adopted is a matter of
indifference here) becomes unintelligible. Hence, it seems better to
follow Stahl and Broadhead, who read ἀπᾴσσων ("springing, darting
away"), thereby avoiding both difficulties.

The final non-metrical emendation involves ἄτα in line 112. Two
questions are raised: one, grammatical; the other, interpretative.

To begin with the grammatical point: Wecklein, Hartung, and
Adams would read ἄτας instead of ἄτα. To Adams it is self-evident
that "the subject of παρασαίνει is clearly ἀπάτη" ("Salamis Symphony,"
p. 54n3). Perhaps a case might be made for this view if line 111a were
retained, but with line 111a already rejected as a gloss, there are several
good reasons for rejecting Adams' view as well. First, when the noun
ἀπάταν occurs in line 107, it occurs, not as a subject of anything, but
as the object of ἀλύξει. To understand it as a subject some four lines
later might be possible, but not necessarily probable. Secondly, between
the occurrence of ἀπάταν and the verb παρασαίνει there is an intervening subject (τίς, 109) together with its verb (ἀπᾴσσων, 110). To
maintain that the force of ἀπάταν, changed now from an object to a
subject, would be felt after this intervening subject and predicate is to
imply that Aeschylus' Greek is somewhat more difficult than is or-
dinarily thought. There is also a contextual reason for rejecting this
interpretation: namely, the implicit rejection of the strophic–anti-

strophic structure, and their consequent distinction from one another.

The interpretative question pertinent to ἄτα is whether or not it should be capitalized and, consequently, considered as personified. Editorial opinion is evenly divided. Paley, Smyth, and Murray capitalize it; Wecklein, Wilamowitz, and Broadhead do not. But Broadhead does consider it to be personified, as his expressions "the personified Ate" (p. 59) and "the personified ἄτα" (p. 61n1) make clear.

Discerning a reason for the personification is difficult here. First of all, such a use of ἄτη is very rare in pre-Aeschylean literature, occurring only once (Hesiod's *Theogony* 230). Nor is there any question of personifying ἄτη in the parallel *Suppliants* passage, at line 110, where it is used in conjunction with ἀπάτα. And if the scholiast's reference to *Iliad* 9.505ff. has any weight, the absence of personification there may well be a further argument for a similar absence in the current passage. Finally, it is difficult to accept Broadhead's statement that "This ἄτη is objectified into an external power that with a show of friendliness lures her victim into her net" (p. 58). This tendency to turn a perfectly good, and quite valid, *poetic* metaphor into a theological–philosophical statement is a critical failing which confounds the two types of literature.

Despite some reservations, then, there are good grounds for accepting the reading proposed by Broadhead, with the reading ἄτα considered quite probable.

C

SUPPLIANTS 443-445

The passage at *Suppliants* 443-445 is quite difficult textually. At this point M reads:

καὶ χρήμασι μὲν ἐκ πορθουμένων
ἄτην γε μείζω μεγ' ἐμπλήσας γόμου   444
γένοιτ' ἂν ἄλλα κτησίου Διὸς χάριν.

There are several connected, but subsidiary, textual problems. The first affects line 443. M reads χρήμασι and πορθουμένων, and χρημάτων is written in the margin. Varying combinations of these readings, or of emendations, have been adopted by the various editors. Thus χρήμασιν is read by Dindorf, Paley, Murray, Rose, and Page; χρημάτων, by Wecklein, Tucker, Wilamowitz, and Smyth; πορθυμένων, by Dindorf, Wecklein, Paley, Wilamowitz, and Smyth; πορθουμένοις, by Scholefield, Murray, Rose, and Page; and προειμένων, by Tucker. But regardless of the combination adopted, the sense is substantially the same, whether the construction is a dative with γένοιτ' ἂν or a genitive absolute.

Similarly, there is variance in the arrangement of lines 444-445. The MS order has been followed by Dindorf, Wecklein, Wilamowitz, and Smyth. But the lines have been inverted by Scholefield, Paley, Tucker, Murray, and Page. Perhaps Rose has the most pertinent comment: "it makes the whole construction clearer if, with Scholefield . . . , we transpose 444 and 445, but it is not absolutely necessary" (*Commentary on the Surviving Plays of Aeschylus*, p. 46, ad loc.).

However, the major textual problem here involves ἄτην in line 444. In the accusative this simply will not construe. This much is implicitly admitted by Smyth, who, in his text, obelizes the reading of M, and in his translation simply omits line 444. Dindorf, Wilamowitz, and Page likewise obelize the line.

ἄτην is retained by Wecklein, whose line reads: ἄτην γεμίζων καὶ μεγ' ἐμπλήσας γόμου. His emendation of γεμίζων for γε μείζω is clearly attributable to the scholion, which reads τοῦ Διὸς ἐπιπλῶντος καὶ γεμίζοντος ἄτη τὸν γόμον. Presumably Wecklein would have to be translated somewhat as follows: "And when goods have been plundered from houses, there may be others, thanks to Zeus Ktesios, loading a doom and filling completely full of cargo." To say the least, this is strained. It would also appear to be unnecessary, as will be shown in what follows.

Some editors (notably Dindorf, Scaliger, Paley, Murray, and Rose), taking their cue from the scholiast, have emended ἄτην to ἄτης. For the sake of thoroughness, the complete line read by each of these editors will be given (it should be noted that the other emendations, if any, affect the sense very little and that either the aorist infinitive or the aorist optative will construe):

> Scaliger: ἄτης γε μείζω καὶ μέγ᾿ ἐμπλήσας γόμον.
> Dindorf: ἄτης γε μείζω, καὶ μέγ᾿ ἐμπλησας γόμον.
> Paley: ἄτης τε μείζω καὶ μέγ᾿ ἐμπλήσαι γέμος.
> Murray: ἄτης γε μείζω, καὶ μετεμπλήσαι γόμον.
> Rose: ἄτης γε μείζω καὶ μετεμπλῆσαι γόμον (v).

Since this emendation retains the root ἄτη, which is the reading in M, it seems preferable to other proposed emendations which substitute completely different words for the impossible ἄτην. Droysen, for example, reads ἀκάτην γεμίζων καὶ μετεμπλήσας γόμον; Oberdick emends to σκάφην γεμίζειν καὶ μέγ᾿ ἐμπλῆσαι γόμον; and Tucker, most radical of all because of his introduction of ναῦν, has ἄλλην τε μείζω ναῦν μετεμπλῆσαι γόμου.

Since the genitive of comparison, ἄτης, satisfies the grammatical consideration, the question of the meaning of ἄτης in this context presents itself. The meaning proposed by Rose is "loss," as, presumably, is that proposed by Paley. (I say "presumably" because Paley's own edition does not contain an explanation, but he is quoted by Tucker ['Supplices' of Aeschylus, p. 95] as having translated: "'cum opes a domo rapiuntur, fieri potest ut aliae Iovis gratia accedant, et damno maiores et sufficientes ad navis alveum magno onere implendum....'" Unfortunately, Tucker does not indicate where Paley wrote this translation.) Among the established meanings of ἄτη, this is the only one which could apply. Though Rose cites only one parallel for this sense of ἄτη, Herodotus 1.32.6 (W. W. How and J. Wells, A Commentary on Herodotus [Oxford: Clarendon, 1912; repr. 1961] is silent on this point; J. E. Powell, A Lexicon to Herodotus [Cambridge: Cambridge University Press, 1938; repr. Hildesheim: Olms, 1960] gives the meaning as "disaster"), the pre-Aeschylean tradition contains several parallels: *Works and Days* 352 and 413, Theognis 103 and 133 (see chap. 2, pp. 24, 28, and 29); Aeschylus himself uses ἄτη in this sense, it will be recalled, at *Libation-Bearers* 825 (see chap. 5, pp. 78–80).

In the passage under discussion, "financial loss" suits the context somewhat better than the finality connoted by "bane," "ruin," or "doom." Since the passage is quite controverted, this may seem a narrow basis on which to establish a firm meaning; still the precedents, other Aeschylean usage, and the context seem to indicate that it be accepted here.

LIBATION-BEARERS 819-837

In *Libation-Bearers* 819–837, the following readings differ from Page's text for the reasons given:

828. Following ἐπαύσας the MSS have πατρὸς ἔργωι, which is retained by Wecklein and Dindorf. All other editors suspect ἔργωι as a scribe's erroneous repetition of ἔργων from the preceding line. The method of rectifying the mistake takes two forms. Seidler's deletion of the phrase πατρὸς ἔργωι seems too radical, for, although it is conceded that ἔργωι is suspect, there is no reason to doubt πατρὸς. Consequently, a group of editors — Auratus, Paley, Smyth, and Thomson — suggests the reading adopted above, πατρὸς αὐδάν, thereby providing the noun for πατρὸς to modify. This seems justifiable, for it furnishes a direct object for ἐπαύσας, and αὐδάν can be supplied from the MSS themselves, which read it in line 829.

    The other departure from Page's text in line 828 involves the correct spelling of the participle of the verb θροέω. The MSS reading, retained by Wecklein, Dindorf, Wilamowitz, Paley, and Smyth, is adopted as preferable to Schneider's correction to θροεούσαι, which Page follows. Two of the passages (*Persians* 64 and *Prometheus* 542) cited to justify his spelling have nothing to do with the case, and a third, *Persians* 542, involves, not θροέω, but ποθέω.

829. Page has followed Schwenk in deleting the MS πρὸς σὲ. There seems to be no reason for this, except the other transpositions already made.

832. The MSS read the metrically deficient καρδίαν σχεθών. The reading above is Grotefend's, which is also accepted by Smyth. It is adopted here not only because it supplies the missing syllables necessary for responsion but also because it is easier to accept on palaeographical grounds than any of the other proposed

emendations, supposing, as it does, a conflation of -αν ανα- into -αν, a fairly common type of scribal error.

834. πρόπρασσε, Hermann's reading, is also read by Smyth; χάριν is Emperius' emendation, which is also adopted by Smyth. This reading is preferable to the προπράσσων χάριτος of the MSS, which contains an extra syllable for responsion. It must be admitted, however, that Hartung's προφράσσ᾽ ὧν χάρις, which Page adopts, is also possible.

835. Wecklein and Dindorf follow M in reading ὀργᾶς λυπρᾶς, and the reading seems perfectly sound. λυπρᾶς is a good Aeschylean word (cf. *Persians* 1034 and *Eumenides* 174); hence it seems unnecessary to emend it to λυγρᾶς.

837. Heimsoeth, followed by Smyth, proposed ἐξαπολλύων, and this is acceptable in responsion. Both the ἐξαπολλὺς of M and the ἐξαπόλλυ᾽ of Murray, which Page follows, lack a syllable for responsion purposes. μόρον of M, G, Aldine, and Robortelli seems preferable to Turnèbe's μόρου, for ἐξαπόλλυμι in the active governs an accusative (cf. Sophocles' *Electra* 588 and Euripides' *Heraclidae* 950). Murray's εἰσορῶν, adopted by Page, seems impossible to explain.

On balance, however, Smyth's general warning, given on p. 78 above, and Murray's note — "827–837 lectio incertissima" — must always be kept in mind.

BIBLIOGRAPHY

Adams, S. M. "Salamis Symphony: The *Persae* of Aeschylus." In *Studies in Honour of Gilbert Norwood*. Ed. Mary E. Whyte. Toronto: University of Toronto Press, 1952. Pp. 46–54.

——. *Sophocles the Playwright*. Toronto: University of Toronto Press, 1957.

Adkins, Arthur W. H. "Basic Greek Values in Euripides' *Hecuba* and *Hercules Furens*." CQ, 16 N.S. (1966), 193–219.

——. *Merit and Responsibility*. Oxford: Clarendon, 1960.

Aeschylus. *Aeschylus*. Trans. Herbert Weir Smyth. 2 vols. London: Heinemann; Cambridge: Harvard University Press, 1933, 1938.

——. *Eschyle*. Ed. Paul Mazon. 2 vols. Paris: "Les Belles Lettres," 1955.

——. *Fabulae*. Ed. N. Wecklein. 2 vols. in 3. Berlin: Calvary, 1885.

——. *Septem quae supersunt tragoediae*. Ed. Gilbert Murray. 2nd ed. 3 vols. Oxford: Clarendon, 1955.

——. *Septem quae supersunt tragoediae*. Ed. Denys L. Page. Oxford: Clarendon, 1972.

——. *Tragoediae*. Ed. Ulrich von Wilamowitz-Moellendorf. Berlin: Weidmann, 1914.

——. *Tragoediae superstites et deperditarum fragmenta*. Ed. Wilhelm Dindorf. 2 vols. Oxford: Clarendon, 1832, 1841.

——. *The Tragedies of Aeschylus*. Ed. F. A. Paley. London: Whittaker, 1855.

——. *The Oresteia of Aeschylus*. Ed. George Thomson, Rev. and enl. ed. Amsterdam: Hakkert; Prague, Academia, 1966.

——. *Agamemnon*. Edd. J. D. Denniston and Denys L. Page. Oxford: Clarendon, 1957.

——. *Agamemnon*. Ed. Eduard Fraenkel. 3 vols. Oxford: Clarendon, 1950. Repr. 1962.

——. *The Persae of Aeschylus*. Ed. H. D. Broadhead. Cambridge: Cambridge University Press, 1960.

——. *Prometheus*. Ed. Joseph Edward Harry. New York & Cincinnati: American Book Co., 1905.

——. *The Prometheus Bound*. Ed. George Thomson. Cambridge: Cambridge University Press, 1932.

——. *The Seven Against Thebes of Aeschylus*. Ed. T. G. Tucker. Cambridge: Cambridge University Press, 1908.

——. *Zeven tegen Thebe*. Ed. Pieter Groeneboom. Groningen: Wolter, 1938.

——. *Zeven tegen Thebe*. Ed. Gabriel Italie. Leiden: Brill, 1950.

——. *The 'Supplices' of Aeschylus*. Ed. T. G. Tucker. London & New York: Macmillan, 1889.

——. *Scholia Graeca in Aeschylum quae extant omnia. I. Scholia in Agamemnon, Choephoros, Eumenides, Supplices continens*. Ed. Ole Langwitz Smith. Leipzig: Teubner, 1976.

Allen, James Turney, and Italie, Gabriel. *A Concordance to Euripides*. Berkeley & Los Angeles: University of California Press; London: Cambridge University Press, 1954. Repr. Groningen: Bourna, 1970.

Ameis, Karl Friedrich, and Hentze, Karl. *Anhang zu Homers Iliad*. 2 vols. Leipzig: Teubner, 1879.

Anthologia lyrica Graeca. Ed. Ernst Diehl. 3rd ed. 4 vols. Leipzig: Teubner, 1949.

Aristotle. *Minor Works*. Trans. W. S. Hett. Cambridge: Harvard University Press; London: Heinemann, 1936.

Barlow, Shirley A. *The Imagery of Euripides: A Study in the Dramatic Use of Pictorial Language*. London: Methuen, 1971.

Bates, William Nickerson. *Sophocles: Poet and Dramatist*. Philadelphia: University of Pennsylvania Press; London: Oxford University Press, 1940.

Blaiklock, E. M. "The Nautical Imagery of Euripides' *Medea*." CPh, 50, No. 4 (October 1955), 233–37.

Böhme, Robert. *Bühnenbearbeitung Äschyleischer Tragödien*. Basel & Stuttgart: Schwabe, 1956.

Boisacq, Emile. *Dictionnaire étymologique de la langue grecque*. 4th ed. Heidelberg: Winter, 1950.

Booth, N. B. "The Run of the Sense in Aeschylus, *Choephoroi* 22–83." CPh, 54 (1969), 111–13.

Bowra, C. M. *Early Greek Elegists*. Cambridge: Harvard University Press, 1938.

——. *Greek Lyric Poetry from Alcman to Simonides*. 2nd rev. ed. Oxford: Clarendon, 1961.

——. *Sophoclean Tragedy*. Oxford: Clarendon, 1944. Repr. 1965.

——. "Theognis." In *The Oxford Classical Dictionary*. Edd. N. G. L. Hammond and H. H. Scullard. 2nd ed. Oxford: Clarendon, 1970. P. 1057.

Bremer, J. M. *Hamartia: Tragic Error in the Poetics of Aristotle and in Greek Tragedy*. Amsterdam: Hakkert, 1969.

Burton, R. W. B. *Pindar's Pythian Odes: Essays in Interpretation*. London: Oxford University Press, 1962.

Bushala, Eugene W. "Συζύγιαι χαρίτες, *Hippolytus* 1147." TAPA, 100 (1969), 23–29.

Campbell, A. Y. "Aeschylea." *Hermes*, 84 (1956), 117–21.

——. "Aeschylus, *Agamemnon* 1227–30." CQ, 26, No. 1 (January 1932), 45–51.

——. "Aeschylus, *Agamemnon*, 1223–38 and Treacherous Monsters." CQ, No. 1 (January 1935), 25–36.

——. "The Fall of Paris: Aeschylus, *Agamemnon* 373–398." AAL, 28 (1948), 64–82.

Chantraine, Pierre. *Dictionnaire étymologique de la langue grecque*. 4 vols. Paris: Klincksieck, 1968–1980.

Conacher, D. J. *Euripidean Drama: Myth, Theme, and Structure*. Toronto: University of Toronto Press, 1967.

Coulon, V. "Note sur Sophocle, *Oed. R.* 1204-1206 et 696." REG, 69 (1956), 446–48.

——. "Observations critiques et exégétiques sur divers passages controversés de Sophocle." REG, 52 (1939), 1–18.

Coxon, A. H. "The μέλος ἀπὸ σκηνῆς in Sophocles' *Trachiniae* (ll. 1004–1043)." CR, 61, No. 3 (December 1947), 69–72.

Daube, Benjamin. *Zu den Rechtsproblemen in Aischylos' Agamemnon.* Zurich: Niehans, 1939.

Dawe, R. D. *The Collation and Investigation of Manuscripts of Aeschylus.* Cambridge: Cambridge University Press, 1964.

——. "Some Reflections on *Ate* and *Hamartia*." HSPh, 72 (1967), 89–123.

Delebecque, Edouard. *Euripide et la guerre du Péloponnèse.* Paris: Klincksieck, 1951.

Dodds, E. R. *The Greeks and the Irrational.* Sather Classical Lectures 25. Berkeley: University of California Press, 1951. Repr. 1963.

Dumortier, Jean. *Les Images dans la poésie d'Eschyle.* Paris: "Les Belles Lettres," 1935.

Earp, F. R. *The Style of Aeschylus.* Cambridge: Cambridge University Press, 1948. Repr. New York: Russell & Russell, 1970.

——. *The Style of Sophocles.* Cambridge: Cambridge University Press, 1944.

Edwards, W. M. "*Agamemnon* 767f." CR, 56 (1942), 71.

Errandonea, Ignacio, s.j. "Le chœur dans l'*Electre* de Sophocle." LEC, 23, No. 4 (October 1955), 369–70.

——. "Les quatre monologues d'*Ajax* et leur signification dramatique." LEC, 26, No. 1 (January 1958), 21–40.

Euripides. *Fabulae.* Ed. Gilbert Murray. 3 vols. Oxford: Clarendon, 1901–1913.

——. *Tragoediae.* Ed. August Nauck. 3 vols. Leipzig: Teubner, 1902–1905.

——. *Alcestis.* Ed. A. M. Dale. Oxford: Clarendon, 1954.

——. *Andromache.* Ed. P. T. Stevens. Oxford: Clarendon, 1971.

——. *Electra.* Ed. J. D. Denniston. Oxford: Clarendon, 1939.

——. *Hippolytos.* Ed. W. S. Barrett. Oxford: Clarendon, 1964.

——. *Ion.* Ed. A. S. Owen. Oxford: Clarendon, 1939.

——. *Iphigenia in Tauris.* Ed. Maurice Platnauer. Oxford: Clarendon, 1938.

——. *Medea.* Ed. J. C. Kamerbeek. Leiden: Brill, 1962.

——. *Medea.* Ed. Denys L. Page. Oxford: Clarendon, 1938.

——. *Orestes.* Ed. Vincenzo di Benedetto. Florence: La Nuova Italia Bibliografica, 1965.

Fitton, J. W. "The *Suppliant Women* and the *Herakleidai* of Euripides." Hermes, 89 (1961), 430–61.

Fletcher, F. *Notes to the Agamemnon of Aeschylus.* Oxford: Blackwell, 1949.

Flickinger, Roy C. *The Greek Theatre and Its Drama.* 4th ed. Chicago: The University of Chicago Press, 1936.

Fragmente der Vorsokratiker. Ed. Hermann Diels. 6th ed. 3 vols. Berlin: Weidmann, 1952.

Frisk, Hjalmar. *Griechisches etymologisches Wörterbuch.* 2 vols. Heidelberg: Winter, 1960, 1970.

Goheen, R. F. "Aspects of Dramatic Symbolism." AJP, 76 (1955), 113–37.

———. *The Imagery of Sophocles' Antigone: A Study of Poetic Language and Stucture.* Princeton: Princeton University Press, 1951.

A Greek-English Lexicon. Edd. H. G. Liddell and Robert Scott. Rev. ed. H. S. Jones and Roderick McKenzie. 9th ed. Oxford: Clarendon, 1940.

Greene, William Chase. "Dramatic and Ethical Motives in the *Agamemnon*." HSPh, 54 (1943), 25–31.

Hanschke, Paul. "Textkritisches zu den griechischen Tragikern: Euripides." RhM, 90 (1941), 212–16.

Hesiod. *Carmina.* Ed. Alois Rzach. Leipzig: Teubner, 1902.

———. *The Epics of Hesiod.* Ed. F. A. Paley. London: Whittaker, 1861.

———. *Scholia vetera in Hesiodi Opera et dies.* Ed. Agostino Pertusi. Milan: Vita e pensiero, 1955.

Homer. *Iliad.* Edd. D. B. Munro and T. W. Allen. 3rd ed. 2 vols. Oxford: Clarendon, 1920.

———. *The Iliad.* Ed. Walter Leaf. 2nd ed. 2 vols. London & New York: Macmillan, 1900, 1902.

———. *Odyssey.* Ed. T. W. Allen. 2nd ed. 2 vols. Oxford: Clarendon, 1917, 1919.

———. *Index Homericus.* Ed. August Gehring. Leipzig: Teubner, 1891.

———. *Lexicon Homericum.* Ed. Heinrich Ebeling. 2 vols. Leipzig: Teubner, 1885.

———. *Scholia Graeca in Homeri Iliadem.* Ed. Wilhelm Dindorf. 6 vols. Oxford: Clarendon, 1865–1888.

Hoffmann, Otto. *Geschichte der griechischen Sprache.* Leipzig: Göschen, 1911.

How, W. W., and Wells, J. *A Commentary on Herodotus.* 2 vols. Oxford: Clarendon, 1928.

Iambi et elegi Graeci. Ed. M. L. West. 2 vols. Oxford: Clarendon, 1971.

Italie, Gabriel. *Index Aeschyleus.* Leiden: Brill, 1955.

Jaeger, Werner. *Paideia: The Ideals of Greek Culture.* Trans. Gilbert Highet. 2 vols. New York: Oxford University Press, 1945.

———. "Solons Eunomie." *Sitzungsberichte der Preussischen Akademie der Wissenschaften* (1926), 69–85.

Kaiser, Johannes. "Bemerkungen zu Euripides' *Medea*." *Gymnasium*, 66 (1959), 502–505.

Kamerbeek, J. C. "Aeschylea." *Mnemosyne*, 13, 3rd ser. (1947), 79–80.

———. *The Plays of Sophocles: Commentaries.* 6 vols. Leiden: Brill, 1953–1980.

———. "Sophoclea IV: Notes, Critical and Exegetical, on the *Trachiniae*." *Mnemosyne*, 10, 4th ser. (1957), 117–27.

———. "Sophoclea V." *Mnemosyne*, 14, 4th ser. (1962), 24–30.

Kaufman-Bühler, D. *Begriff und Funktion der Dike in den Tragödien des Aischylos.* Heidelberg: Winter, 1951.

Kirkwood, G. M. *A Study of Sophoclean Drama.* Cornell Studies in Classical Philology 31. Ithaca, N.Y.: Cornell University Press, 1958.

Kitto, H. D. F. *Poiesis: Structure and Thought.* Sather Classical Lectures 36. Berkeley: University of California Press, 1966.

Knox, B. M. W. "The Date of the *Oedipus Tyrannus* of Sophocles." AJP, 77 (1956), 133–47.

———. *The Heroic Temper: Studies in Sophoclean Tragedy.* Sather Classical Lectures 35. Berkeley: University of California Press, 1964.

———. "The *Hippolytus* of Euripides." YClS, 13 (1952), 1–31.

———. "The Lion in the House (*Agamemnon* 717–36)." CPh, 47 (1952), 17–25.

———. "Why is Oedipus Called Tyrannos?" CJ, 50 (1954), 97–102.

Korzeniewski, Dietmar. "Interpretationen zu Sophokleischen Chorliedern." RhM, 104 N.S. (1961), 193–201.

Kranz, W. "Zwei Leider des 'Agamemnon'." Hermes, 54 (1919), 301–20.

Lawson, J. C. "Aeschylus, *Agamemnon*, 1227–32." CQ, 27, No. 2 (April 1933), 112–14.

Leaf, Walter. *A Companion to the Iliad.* London & New York: Macmillan, 1892.

Lesky, Alvin. "Decision and Responsibility in the Tragedy of Aeschylus." JHS, 86 (1966), 78–85.

———. *Greek Tragedy.* Trans. H. A. Frankfort. 2nd ed. London: Benn; New York: Barnes & Noble, 1967.

Lexikon des frühgriechischen Epos. Ed. Bruno Snell. Göttingen: Vandenhoek & Ruprecht, 1955.

Linforth, Ivan M. *Solon the Athenian.* Berkeley: University of California Press, 1919.

———. *Three Scenes in Sophocles' "Ajax."* Berkeley: University of California Press, 1954.

Livingstone, R. "The Problem of the *Eumenides* of Aeschylus." JHS, 45 (1925), 120–31.

Lloyd-Jones, Hugh. "The End of the *Seven Against Thebes*." CQ, 9 N.S. (1959), 80–114.

———. "The Guilt of Agamemnon." CQ, 12 N.S. (1962), 187–99.

———. *The Justice of Zeus.* Sather Classical Lectures 41. Berkeley: University of California Press, 1971.

Long, A. A. *Language and Thought in Sophocles.* University of London Classical Studies 6. London: Athlone, 1968.

Luppino, A. "*Antigone* 4; 82; 99." RFIC, 35 (1957), 167–70.

Mazon, Paul. "Notes sur Sophocle." RPh, 24 (1951), 7–17.

Mazzarino, A. "Note filologiche." Maia, 2 (1949), 282.

Meerwaldt, J. D. "Ad Antigones Exordium." Mnemosyne, 1, 4th ser. (1948), 284–93.

Mellert-Hoffmann, Gudrun. *Untersuchungen zur Iphigenie in Aulis des Euripides.* Heidelberg: Winter, 1969.

Müller, Gerhard. "Interpolationen in der *Medea* des Euripides." SIFC, 25 (1951), 65–82.

Murray, Gilbert. *Aeschylus, the Creator of Tragedy.* Oxford: Clarendon, 1962.

Musurillo, Herbert. *The Light and the Darkness: Studies in the Dramatic Poetry of Sophocles.* Leiden: Brill, 1967.

Nestle, Walter. *Menschliche Existenz und politische Erziehung in der Tragödie des Aischylos.* Stuttgart & Berlin: Kohlhammer, 1934.

Owen, E. T. *The Harmony of Aeschylus.* Toronto: Clarke, Irwin, 1952.

The Oxford Classical Dictionary. Edd. N. G. L. Hammond and H. H. Scullard. 2nd ed. Oxford: Clarendon, 1970.

Page, Denys L. "The Elegiacs in Euripides' *Andromache*." In *Greek Poetry and Life: Essays Presented to Gilbert Murray*. Edd. Cyril Bailey, E. A. Barber, C. M. Bowra, J. F. Denniston, and D. L. Page. Oxford: Clarendon, 1936, Pp. 206–30.

——. *History and the Homeric Iliad*. Sather Classical Lectures 31. Berkeley: University of California Press, 1959. Repr. 1963.

——. *Sappho and Alcaeus: An Introduction to the Study of Ancient Lesbian Poetry*. Oxford: Clarendon, 1955.

Payne, Robert. *Hubris: A Study of Pride*. Rev. ed. New York: Harper & Row, 1960.

Pindar. *Carmina*. Ed. C. M. Bowra. Oxford: Clarendon, 1951.

——. *Carmina cum fragmentis*. I. *Epinicia*. Edd. Bruno Snell and Herwig Moehler. Leipzig: Teubner, 1971.

——. *The Olympian and Pythian Odes*. Ed. Basil Gildersleeve. New York: Harper & Brothers, 1885. Repr. New York: Arno, 1979.

Podlecki, Anthony J. *The Political Background of Aeschylean Tragedy*. Ann Arbor: The University of Michigan Press, 1966.

——. "Some Themes in Euripides' *Phoenissae*." TAPA, 93 (1962), 355–73.

Poetae melici Graeci. Ed. Denys L. Page. Oxford: Clarendon, 1962.

Poetae minores Graeci. Ed. Thomas Gaisford. 4 vols. Oxford: Clarendon, 1814–1820.

Poetarum Lesbiorum fragmenta. Edd. Edgar Lobel and Denys Page. Oxford: Clarendon, 1955.

Porzig, Walter. *Die attische Tragödie*. Leipzig: Wiegandt, 1926.

Powell, J. Enoch. *A Lexicon to Herodotus*. Cambridge: Cambridge University Press, 1938.

Regenbogen, Otto. "Randbemerkungen zur *Medea* des Euripides." *Eranos*, 48 (1950), 21–56.

Reinhardt, Karl. *Aischylos als Regisseur und Theologe*. Bern: Francke, 1949.

Rohdich, Hermann. *Die Euripideische Tragödie: Untersuchungen zu ihrer Tragik*. Heidelberg: Winter, 1968.

Romilly, Jacqueline de. *La Crainte et l'angoisse dans le théâtre d'Eschyle*. Paris: "Les Belles Lettres," 1958.

Rose, H. J. *A Commentary on the Surviving Plays of Aeschylus*. 2 vols. in 1. Amsterdam: Noord-Holland, 1957.

——. "On an Epic Idiom in Aeschylos." *Eranos*, 45 (1947), 88–99.

Schadewaldt, W. "Der Kommos in Aischylos' *Choephoren*." *Hermes*, 67 (1932), 312–54.

Scheidweiler, Felix. "Zu den *Troerinnen* des Euripides." *Hermes*, 82 (1964), 250–51.

Segal, Charles P. "Shame and Purity in Euripides' *Hippolytus*." *Hermes*, 98 (1970), 278–99.

——. "The Tragedy of the *Hippolytus*: The Waters of Ocean and the Untouched Meadow." HSPh, 70 (1965), 117–69.

Silk, M. S. *Interaction in Poetic Imagery.* London & New York: Cambridge University Press, 1974.
Smith, Wesley D. "The Ironic Structure in *Alcestis.*" *The Phoenix,* 14 (1960), 127–45.
Solmsen, Friedrich. "The Erinys in Aischylos' *Septem.*" TAPA, 68 (1937), 197–211.
———. *Hesiod and Aeschylus.* Ithaca, N.Y.: Cornell University Press, 1949.
Sophocles. *Fabulae.* Ed. A. C. Pearson. Oxford: Clarendon, 1923.
———. *The Plays and the Fragments.* Ed. R. C. Jebb. 7 vols. Cambridge: Cambridge University Press, 1900-1928. Repr. Amsterdam: Hakkert, 1962–1965.
———. *Sophocle.* Ed. Alphonse Dain. Trans. Paul Mazon. 3 vols. in 1. Paris: "Les Belles Lettres," 1955–1960.
———. *Sophocle.* Ed. Paul Masqueray. 2 vols. Paris: "Les Belles Lettres," 1922, 1924.
———. *Sophocles.* Ed. F. H. M. Blaydes. 2 vols. London: Bell, 1859.
———. *Sophocles.* Ed. Lewis Campbell. 2 vols. Oxford: Clarendon, 1879, 1881.
———. *Tragoediae septem.* Ed. R. F. P. Brunck. Oxford: Bliss, 1808.
———. *Tragoediae septem.* Ed. Gottfried Hermann. 2 vols. London: Black, Young & Young, 1825.
———. *Tragoediae superstites.* Ed. Wilhelm Dindorf. 2 vols. Leipzig: Teubner, 1863.
———. *Lexicon Sophocleum.* Ed. Friedrich Theodor Ellendt. 2nd rev. ed. Hermann Franz Genthe. Berlin: Barntraeger, 1872. Repr. Hildesheim: Olms, 1958.
———. *Scholia in Sophoclis tragoedias.* Ed. Petros N. Papageorgios. Leipzig: Teubner, 1888.
Stevens, P. T. "Colloquial Expressions in Aeschylus and Sophocles." CQ, 39 (1945), 95–105.
Stoessel, Franz. "Die *Elektra* des Euripides." RhM, 99 (1956), 83–85.
Thomson, George. "Mystical Allusions in the *Oresteia.*" JHS, 55 (1935), 25–37.
———. "Notes on the *Oresteia.*" CQ, 28, No. 2 (April 1934), 72–78.
Todd, O. J. *Index Aristophaneus.* Cambridge: Harvard University Press, 1932.
Triclinius, Demetrius. *In Aeschyli Persas scholia.* Ed. Lydia Massa Positano. Naples: Libreria Scientifica Editrice, 1948.
Turyn, Aleksander. *The Manuscript Tradition of the Tragedies of Aeschylus.* New York: Polish Institute of Arts and Sciences in America, 1943. Repr. Hildesheim: Olms, 1967.
Webster, T. B. L. *An Introduction to Sophocles.* Oxford: Clarendon, 1936.
———. *The Tragedies of Euripides.* London: Methuen, 1967.
Wecklein, N. *Studien zu Aeschylus.* 2 vols. Berlin: Calvary, 1872.
West, M. L. "Hesiod." In *The Oxford Classical Dictionary.* Edd. N. G. L. Hammond and H. H. Scullard. 2nd ed. Oxford: Clarendon, 1970. P. 511.

Whitman, Cedric H. *Sophocles: A Study of Heroic Humanism*. Cambridge: Harvard University Press, 1951.

Wilamowitz-Moellendorf, Ulrich von. *Aischylos: Interpretationen*. Berlin: Weidmann, 1914.

Willink, C. W. "Some Problems of Text and Interpretation in the *Hippolytus*." CQ, 18, N.S. (1968), 11–43.

Winnington-Ingram, R. P. "Euripides, *Electra* 1292–1307." CR, 51, No. 2 (May 1937), 51–52.

Wyatt, William F. Jr. "Homeric ἄτη." AJP, 103 (1982), 247–76.

INDEX LOCORUM

<small>AESCHYLUS</small>

Agamemnon	355–361	82–83
	381–388	43–44
	638–643	86
	727–736	83
	750–771	39–41, 75
	819–820	86
	1119–1124	76
	1188–1193	59
	1188–1193	59
	1227–1230	76
	1264–1268	60
	1279–1283	60
	1431–1436	76–77
	1521–1526	77
	1560–1566	83–84
Eumenides	372–376	80, 85
	976–983	80, 85
Libation-Bearers	66–69	86
	269–274	77–78
	336–339	87
	382–385	84
	400–404	84–85
	466–470	85
	594–598	61
	819–837	78–80, 177–79
	965–968	61
	1073–1076	62–63
Persians	107–114	49–50, 167–72
	653–656	50–51
	821–826	38–39
	1002–1007	73
	1035–1037	73
Prometheus	877–886	63–64
	1071–1079	81
Seven	312–317	82
	597–608	51–52
	686–688	52

HESIOD
  Works and
  Days   213–218   36
              228–231   23–24
              352   24
              410–413   24

  Shield   89–93   26

  Theogony 226–232   25

HOMER
  Iliad   1.410–412   12–13
              2.110–115   13
              3.97–100   15
              6.354–358   15
              8.236–239   13–14
              9.17–22   13
              115–116   17
              496–523   9–12
              10.391–393   16–17
              16.271–274   12–13
              805–806   7–8
              19.85–89   8
              90–92   8–9
              125–138   8–9
              270–274   13–14
              24.25–30   14–15
              480–483   17

  Odyssey   4.259–262   14
              12.371–373   18
              15.231–234   12
              21.297–302   8
              23.218–224   15–16

IBYCUS   1.1–9   27–28

PINDAR
  Nemean   9.21–22   31

  Olympian 1.54–59   42
              10.34–38   31

  Pythian   2.25–31   37–38
              3.21–25   31–32

SOLON   4.30–35   44
              13.9–16   37
              67–70   26–27
              71–76   41–42

SOPHOCLES

Ajax	121–123	97
	192–195	97–98
	305–308	98
	356–363	98–99
	641–645	99–100
	845–849	100
	909–912	100
	974–976	100
	1185–1191	101
Antigone	1–6	103–104
	184–186	104
	531–535	104
	583–625	104–106
	863–866	106–107
	1095–1097	107–108
	1257–1260	108
Electra	213–235	110–11
	934–937	111
	1001–1004	111
	1296–1300	111–12
Oedipus at Colonus	84–93	114
	199–204	114–15
	521–532	115
	1242–1248	115–16
Oedipus Tyrannos	163–167	109
	1204–1206	109
	1282–1285	109–10
Philoctetes	701–706	113
Trachinian Women	849–850	101–102
	1000–1002	102–103
	1082–1084	102–103
	1103–1106	102–103
	1270–1274	103
THEOGNIS	1.101–104	28
	117–120	28–29
	133–136	29
	203–206	30
	227–232	42
	587–590	30
	631–632	29